D1592783

Miziker's Complete Event Planner's Handbook

Miziker's Complete Event Planner's Handbook

Tips, Terminology, and Techniques for Success

Ron Miziker

UNIVERSITY OF NEW MEXICO PRESS · ALBUQUERQUE

LIBRARY OF CONGRESS CATALOGING-IN-PUBLICATION DATA

Miziker, Ron, 1941–
Miziker's complete event planner's handbook : tips, terminology, and techniques
for success / Ron Miziker.
pages cm
Includes bibliographical references and index.
ISBN 978-0-8263-5551-5 (paperback) — ISBN 978-0-8263-5552-2 (electronic)
1. Special events—Planning—Handbooks, manuals, etc. 2. Special events—
Management—Handbooks, manuals, etc. 3. Meetings—Planning—Handbooks,
manuals, etc. I. Title. II. Title: Complete event planner's handbook.
GT3405.M59 2015
394.2—dc23
2014031701

Cover illustration and book design by Lila Sanchez
Illustrations by Jenessa Warren
Composed in Sabon and Frutiger

To my patient and understanding wife,
Susan, always the "hostess with the mostess."

I would like to acknowledge my sons *Robert* and *Ryan*, who have added their skills and talents to make many of our event projects a reality, and also *Frank* for his unwavering support. I would also like to thank our many wonderful clients over the years, who placed their trust in us to make their events special.

Contents

Introduction

You can make a lot out of nothing if you use too much of it.

This guide is designed as a fast reference and quick aid to assist those in the turmoil and heat of battle of making an event come together on time, within budget, and in a manner that excites, educates, or entertains those attending. Events can be very different, yet they have one overriding purpose—to bring people together. An event can be a wedding, festival, business dinner, fair, benefit, seminar, performance, meeting, exhibition, casual gathering at home, or a host of other things. It can be intimate or world-class with an audience of millions. But if no one attends, it is not an event. Every event requires planning, notification, execution, show elements, and expenditures. And as the expression goes, *there is never enough time or money.*

The lyrics of the old song say "there's no business like show business," and if there is only one point one takes away from the many in this guide, it must be . . . *think show.* All events are shows in their basic nature. Therefore those planning and executing an event must not think of it simply as a business meeting, a party, or a benefit. Instead, think of every event as a show, with you as the maestro, the one who will make it different, entertaining, and a special time for your audience.

As an event organizer, you are a "jack of all trades." Every event is made up of a combination of many, many elements, such as food, entertainment, and publicity to name just a few of the broad categories that you must know many details about, understand, and manage in order to make a whole event. Once you have the basics accomplished, then you need to make the event *special.*

It has been my experience that those who take on the making of an event, either professionally or as a volunteer, are the hardest working and most innovative, ambitious, and talented people on earth. That is why you need helpful, concise information quickly and in a form that is both portable and easy to use. Thus, this handbook.

Tips on Using This Book

The terminology entries are arranged alphabetically and are defined as they relate to event planners rather than with their strict dictionary definitions. The purpose is to provide a helpful guide indexed alphabetically for quick accessibility. All terms selected are words or subjects that an event maker may encounter at some time in planning some particular event. Words *italicized* within the definition are key words that cross-reference more information related to the subject. For example, the term **table** may have the italicized word *napkin* in its description. This indicates that *napkin* is a related term, and its entry will provide additional information. If a word (or words) within the term's definition is in bold, it indicates it is either another word for the same term or is a variation of the term. For example, **ballyhoo** is often referred to as a **bally**. **Auction** may be a **celebrity auction** or a **silent auction**. All term entries are in lower case except where capitals are required, such as for proper names. Occasionally I add a related personal experience, which is in a box and italicized.

Many definitions are followed by helpful tips or other resources indicated as follows:

🖉 The pencil symbol indicates a tip or tips to "make note of." They are suggestions for consideration.

✓ The check mark symbol indicates tip suggestions to spur the imagination. Often the simplest event can be improved by thinking outside the box and adding something special or unexpected. These suggestions will help you do that. Or, they may help you do something normal in a better way.

All tips and suggestions are based on my years of experience with creating and executing events. While there are many different ways to do the same thing, these suggestions have worked well for me and will aid you in creating a successful event.

📋 The clipboard symbol under a term's definition indicates that further pertinent information relating to the subject is in the "Tables and Techniques" section. There you will find specific tables, techniques, charts, and other supplemental information. To make this easy, the page number in "Tables and Techniques" is also indicated.

This clipboard also appears in "Tables and Techniques," indicating pages in the terminology section that will provide more information relating to the table, chart, or diagram.

All information in "Tables and Techniques" is grouped by subject, and the groups are arranged alphabetically.

One last word of wisdom: It is never possible to do too much planning. The more you plan the details of the event, the better the event—guaranteed.

Now, as is said in show business . . . *Go break a leg!*

Thirty Keys to a Great Event

Ron Miziker's Best Pieces of Advice
for Event Planners

1. "One of the best ways to persuade others is with your ears . . . by listening to them."—Dean Rusk

2. Simple things make a big difference, such as straightening chandeliers, pressing linens, and hiding extension cords. When people notice you "fussed," they appreciate everything more.

3. Carry out the theme.

4. Too much rehearsal robs the final presentation of its greatest assets: spontaneity, nervous excitement, challenging thought in process, and enthusiasm.

5. Question every detail.

6. Eliminate the unnecessary details.

7. Give credit where credit is due.

8. Work out your ideas with others.

9. No one person ever ran a successful event.

10. Keep your sense of humor.

11. Don't create emergencies. They typically result from not properly anticipating potential problems.

12. If you think people don't want to work anymore, perhaps it is because you haven't motivated them.

13. Volunteers are easily discouraged if you have nothing of importance for them to do.

14. "If you do things merely because you think some other fool expects you to do them because he thinks you expect him to expect you to do them, it will end in everybody doing what nobody wants to do, which is in my opinion a silly state of things."—George Bernard Shaw

15. Never ignore a complaint. Listen thoroughly and intently to it. Express concern, whether you think it is right or wrong, and write the complaint down. Smile when you say you will see what can be done to correct the situation. And say thanks for bringing it to your attention.

16. Take pride in your work.

17. Stay cool. No matter what tension you are experiencing inside, never look harried or tense and worried.

18. Adaptability is essential.

19. You can bet that everything will not go according to plan.

20. Be creative—throughout every step.

21. Be a showman. Showmanship is that dash of excitement that makes the difference between an event that is just routine and an event that is truly special.

22. "It is kind of fun to do the impossible."—Walt Disney

23. Lead . . . don't manage.

24. "Simplify . . . simplify . . . simplify!"—Napoleon

25. Involve the right people at the right time.

26. Avoid committees. They don't accomplish much.

27. Choose "workers," not "friends."

28. A committee is a group of people who individually can do nothing, but as a group decide that nothing can be done.

29. To get something done, a committee should consist of no more than three people, two of whom are absent.

30. Meetings are indispensable when you don't want to do anything.

Terms and Tips

Make no little plans; they have no magic to stir men's blood.

—Daniel Burnham (1846–1912),
American architect and urban planner who directed the 1893 World's Fair in
Chicago, and whose designs and plans have had great influence nationwide

a-board A sign or display structure of which the side view forms an "A" with two sloping sides for the message that meet at the top. Made to be lightweight and fold flat.

abstract An idea, plan, script, or scenic setting that can be interpreted in many different ways. Not representational, duplicate, or ordinary, but suggestive.

AC See *alternating current.*

accordion display A structure that is hinged so that it folds up like an accordion. With this zigzag hinging of the panels it can be stretched wide or kept close depending on the space available.

acoustics The science that deals with the study of sound. As it relates to events, it is most often referred to as the quality of sound within a

A

given space such as a concert hall. Everything within a performance hall—the surface materials, balcony design, angles of the walls, and even the audience—affects the quality of the sound as it travels throughout the space, bouncing off some elements while being absorbed by others. Background noise, such as falling water, machinery, or the sound from an adjoining room may affect the acoustics of the space. The acoustics of every venue should be reviewed and considered for the type of presentation planned, be it speech or music, to ensure clarity, quality, and understandability of the intended sound free of any random noise.

acoustic shell The hard curved background of a performance stage or bandstand designed to reflect the sound waves created by the musicians or speakers out toward the audience to increase the volume of the natural sound. Utilizing audio and computer technology, these shells can be shaped to accentuate certain frequencies to enhance the quality and definition of the sound.

act call The signal in the foyers, lobbies, lounges, etc., of a theater announcing that the performance, or an act, is about to begin. It is made by the stage manager, generally two minutes before the rise of the curtain, and is also given to the actors backstage.

act curtain The *main curtain* or the front curtain. This is the curtain directly behind the proscenium that conceals the stage area from the audience before the performance and opens to reveal the stage. It is known as either a fly curtain, which is drawn up and lowered vertically; or as a *traveler curtain*, which is parted in the center, with each half being drawn apart and back together horizontally.

acting area Any space, be it on the stage, in the aisles, or elsewhere, that is used by actors during a performance.

A/D Analog to digital conversion. The process of converting analog voltage into a digital signal for electronic processing.

A

ADA The Americans with Disabilities Act, which outlines the state and federal laws governing the equal treatment of people with disabilities. For the event maker, these laws codify federal requirements for such concerns as ramps for wheelchair access, seating for the disabled at shows and events, restrooms, stage access, etc. It is important to be familiar with the requirements of this act. Substantial fines can be levied for ignoring the rules.

I produced the week-long International Festival for Very Special Arts, an organization celebrating disabled artists, both performing and visual. It was at this event, held in Washington, D.C., with over two thousand disabled artists from around the world, that I became very acquainted with ADA regulations because the event had to be a model for those rules. Meeting the requirements necessitates careful planning and additional costs.

addendum A list of extra items added to the contract for a hotel, equipment rental, catering company, or other services or goods. Typically it is used to address something that was overlooked in an agreement after the contract is already in place. Troublesome addenda can be avoided by negotiating one good solid contract that covers all terms, thus reducing confusion and potential conflict.

addressable A lighting fixture or other piece of theatrical equipment that can be controlled by means of an electronic signal.

ad lib Impromptu remarks by actors or speakers that are not part of the script. These remarks may result from a lapse of memory or a reaction to an incident or remark. They can be used to cover an incident on the stage, such as a late entrance, or simply because the speaker's style is impromptu.

adventurous Presenting event elements that are new, different, and "out there." Being unusual, not typical. Being adventurous brings rewards.

advertising Promotion of an event through the media such as newspapers, radio, television, or the Internet. Most often this promotion is paid for at the rates charged by the media. These rates vary depending on the size of the audience reached and are typically calculated as "cost per thousands" of the potential audience, or the cost divided by one thousand viewers.

advertising agency A company that, for a fee, develops a strategy for reaching the largest potential audience for the budget, and then designs a creative campaign and produces the graphics, commercials, or other materials required. The agency then places the ads with the media at the standard rates minus a discount, which the agency typically keeps as a placement fee. Also see *publicity*.

AEA The abbreviation for a labor union that represents stage actors and stage managers, the Actors Equity Association.

AFM The abbreviation for the American Federation of Musicians labor union representing musicians, bands, and orchestras, as well as music conductors, arrangers, and copyists.

afternoon tea or **low tea** A popular afternoon social occasion. A light meal typically eaten between 3:00 p.m. and 5:00 p.m. The meal consists of brewed tea traditionally accompanied with biscuits and scones. A fancier affair will have small sandwiches (usually cucumber, egg, fish paste, or salmon), scones (with clotted cream and jam), and cakes and pastries (fruitcake or sponge). It is eaten at a low table, not a dining table, thus the name. Also see *high tea*.

AFTRA The abbreviation for the labor union that represents actors and performers on radio and television, the American Federation of Television and Radio Artists.

agate line A unit of measurement used by newspapers in determining the size of an advertisement.

agent A person, or company, who represents another person, such as a performing artist, in business matters. In the entertainment industry, most known performers are represented by an agent who negotiates with the buyer the fees, availability, and conditions of employment and then prepares the contract. Most often (and by law in some states) the agent receives a 10 percent commission for this service. This commission is often included in the quoted price, but not always, so it is important to ask when inquiring about costs. Sometimes an agent is also the talent's manager, but in some states the law does not permit anyone to be both. Also see *talent manager* and *rider.*

AGVA The abbreviation for the American Guild of Variety Artists labor union representing performers of many different types, including magicians and nightclub entertainers.

air shipment The shipping of exhibit or show materials by scheduled or nonscheduled airlines and air forwarders. This is the fastest way to relocate these materials. The time-reducing capabilities of airfreight combined with the ancillary services that carriers offer provides an efficient, but costly, means of transportation. Air shipments are typically required for international transportation, particularly when shipping via slow-moving ocean vessels is the only other option.

aisle cloth The fabric, typically white, rolled onto the aisle prior to the bride's entrance. While popular with many brides, it can be a problem in that someone can trip on the cloth. Because of the liability, some venues will not permit the cloth. Also, if the floor is stone or wood, the cloth can slip unless taped down. If it is not pre-installed, someone must be designated to roll it out.

aisle space The passageway between tables, seats, displays, or structures. For *banquets* and event situations, this space is determined and enforced by local fire code regulations to ensure safe audience egress in case of an emergency.

alarum A warning or **alarm**. In theater it typically refers to a call to arms as with trumpeting soldiers or jungle drums.

allowances Additional funds included in estimates to cover the cost of known but undefined miscellaneous expenses and requirements for an individual activity or account.

alternate A request from the client for the cost of adding or deleting an item or work element for the basic bid. An increase is an **additive alternate** while a deletion is a **deductive alternate**. Also, a substitute cast member of a show. If the regular cast member plays a leading role, an announcement stating the substitution must be made prior to the start of the show.

alternating current or **AC** A form of electrical current that is typically found in homes, offices, and most appliances. In this type of current the electric charge reverses direction 120 times, or 60 cycles, per second. The AC system, with advancements by Nicola Tesla and marketing by George Westinghouse, was selected over Edison's DC system for ease in building electric generators, motors, and power distribution systems. Also see *direct current*.

ambrosia A fruit salad or dessert of chilled fruit mixed with coconut. The name comes from Greek mythology, where it was the food of the gods.

amenity Something that contributes to mental or physical comfort. At resorts it is typically a beach, golf course, spa, or stables, or special services such as turning the bed down at night, leaving a chocolate on the pillow, providing in-room Wi-Fi, or various social courtesies of the staff. Often the amenities offered are key to the selection of hotels and other *venues* for meetings, conferences, and other events.

amperage or **amps** In an electrical circuit the number of electrons, or volume, that pass a given point in the wire in one second is measured in amperes. If it were water in a hose, it would be the amount of water flowing. A typical wall outlet in the United States is 15 amps (divided by two plugs). A typical 100-watt light bulb uses .83 amps, a laptop about 1.5. Therefore, about eighteen 100-watt bulbs or ten laptops can be placed on one wall outlet before the circuit breaker stops the flow. Amps are determined by watts divided by *volts* (for example, 2000 watts ÷ 120 volts = 16.6 amps).

amphitheater An open-air venue used for performances, entertainment, and sports able to accommodate a large number of spectators. Amphitheaters were first built by the ancient Greeks in a semicircle with tiered seating above the performance area. Ancient Romans built amphitheaters in both circular and oval shapes, such as the Coliseum. Modern amphitheaters are typically designed for concerts.

amplifier An electronic device that increases the volume of sound systems. Also referred to as an **amp**. Most sound systems require an amplifier to enable the system to work. The quality of the amplifier has a great effect on the quality, as well as the volume, of the sound. Systems with excellent amplifiers and other components can be played at higher volume levels without sounding light; the sound produced is loud, enabling a broader and more even coverage over the audience area.

analog or **analogue** A control that is not an on/off type but allows for a smooth and continuous control over the speed of an action and the amount of time it takes to execute it. In literature, a literary work that shares characters and events with other literature but is not directly derived from it. In catering, a food substitute.

analogue recording A method used to store audio signals as a continual wave in or on the medium, such as recording tape. Different from *digital* recording, which converts audio signals into discrete numbers.

anchor To fasten to the floor, wall, or other substantial structure.

angel Someone who invests financially in a theatrical production, film, or event.

angle of view Projection screens, either front or rear projection, must be viewed within limited angles. When the angle of view is beyond 40° from the centerline of the screen, the perspective is foreshortened, distorting the image. Also, a large amount of the projected light is not visible, making the image dark and difficult to see. The audience should be positioned within the screen's viewing limits.

aniline dyes Dyes used for painting scenery that requires transparency, such as the detail of stained glass windows or transparent skies, water, clouds, or areas where lights and special effects are used behind scenic drops.

animated prop A *prop* that simulates movement in what would normally be an inanimate object, such as a book that opens itself, or a chair that collapses on *cue*.

anniversary A date observed on an annual basis that commemorates or celebrates an important event. Typical anniversary dates are for weddings, deaths, historical happenings of all kinds, and birthdates of companies, cities, organizations, and individuals.

   📖 For a list of anniversary names and traditional gifts see "Tables and Techniques" (page 357).

announcement A written notice such as a card or newspaper article giving news of a wedding, birth, retirement, death, or other family event. This notification is typically sent out by family or close friends and contains all pertinent information about who, what, why, when, and where. A **marriage announcement** often also contains information about the parents, the bride's and groom's professions, the minister, and where the couple will reside. Also see *press release*.

antagonist In a story, a character or group of characters, institution, or force, in conflict with the main character, typically the hero. The villain or adversary of the hero. Simply, the bad guy. Also see *protagonist*.

antipasto An Italian term that refers to food served "before the meal," such as *hors d'oeuvre*. A typical antipasti assortment includes olives, fish, and cheese.

anti-pros Lighting instruments that are hung in front of, or on the audience side of, the *proscenium*.

antique The technique of **aging** furniture and props to make them appear older or worn by utilizing paints and stains. This same technique is used to soften the brightness of white objects on stage or screen.

aperitif or **apéritif** Any light alcohol beverage served before lunch or dinner. While there are many different aperitifs available, the most popular are *champagne*, *sherry*, *Dubonnet*, and *kir*.

app Application software designed as a tool to allow mobile device users access via the Internet to many different types of information. Apps have become a great aid to those producing, managing, and attending events. Event apps can provide specific information to attendees such as the event *schedule*, exhibitor list and *floor plan* updates, and breaking news, or the ability to download speaker handouts and rate conference sessions, plus much more. For an event maker, apps can be invaluable, providing quick ticketing, *guest list* management, marketing, *checklists*, sponsorship opportunities, and an ever-growing host of other aids and functions. Apps have become an event producer's best friend.

apron The stage area in front, or downstage, of the *proscenium*. It can be of different sizes and proportions and actually extend out into the audience area in a variety of different configurations. Also see *passerelle*.

arena An outdoor or indoor area surrounded by spectator seating where shows or sporting events take place. Originally the center, or floor area, of a Roman amphitheater where gladiator contests and various other forms of entertainment were staged. Typically arenas are large enough to accommodate a wide variety of different performances, sport competitions, and other events.

arena theater The style of theater with the acting area in the center of the *auditorium*, with the audience seated around on all sides.

arm A short pipe or *batten* extending at an angle, usually perpendicular, from the main supports or curtains onstage from which curtains or *legs* are hung. Typically it is used to form a blind for actor's entrances.

arms Guns, swords, and other weapons used onstage.

arranger A musical person who converts a written musical composition into the many written parts required for the various instruments of an orchestra. Since the size, instrumentation, and style of orchestras vary, the arranger must decide how to best combine or divide the various musical parts to achieve the tonal qualities and impact conceived by the *composer.* Also see *score* and *instrumentation.*

art director The person responsible for the artistic look of the stage setting, decorations, scenic elements, or other visual aspects of a presentation. Also see *designer.*

asbestos curtain The term for a fireproof curtain made of asbestos located immediately in front of the *main curtain*, but behind the *proscenium*, to prevent a fire from spreading between the *stage house* and the audience area. Now out-of-date, it was designed to be raised just before the start of a performance, and everyone onstage was required to know where the knife was located to cut the supporting line in case of a fire. Fire prevention laws in some areas still require this type of curtain, which is no longer made of asbestos, or some other system to separate the *stage house* from the audience in an emergency.

aside A dramatic device whereby the character onstage speaks directly to the audience while the other characters supposedly do not hear.

aspect ratio The relationship of an image height to its width expressed by two numbers with a colon between them. The two most common aspect ratios are 4:3, the standard video image size, and 16:9, the picture size of high-definition video and DVD screens. In still photography, the most common standards have been 4:3 and 3:2. Motion pictures are typically projected in theaters at either 1.85:1 or 2.39:1. With all these different aspect rations, it is easy to see how going from one format to another can be difficult. Add to this the different computer monitor screens, which are based on pixel counts. When preparing visual material for presentation, it is critical to know how it will be ultimately presented to the audience.

See aspect ratio chart in "Tables and Techniques" (page 360).

ASTM Abbreviation for American Society for Testing Materials. An organization that through testing establishes voluntary consensus standards internationally. For example, they rate and certify a fabric's flammability and establish what degree is acceptable to fire departments. *Flameproofing* methods typically must meet their established standards.

asymmetric design Design and design elements that lack symmetry. It is an imbalance of design elements or a predefined pattern and is an effective tool to create interest in and impact to the overall design. An example of asymmetry is a tree and its branches. While each is different, together they form an interesting whole. Also see *symmetry*.

ATF Bureau of Alcohol, Tobacco, Firearms and Explosives. This federal law enforcement agency is responsible for monitoring illegal use of liquor and monitoring explosives including *fireworks*.

at home card Mailed with the invitation, traditionally it informs the recipient of the bridal couple's new address after the wedding. However, today they also tell the recipient how they want to be known after the wedding, such as, Jonathan Doe and Candice Smith-Doe.

at liberty A term used for a performer given free rein over the material and method of the performance.

atmosphere The general mood or "feeling" created by the show, presentation, or décor of an event. This mood may be formal, wild and crazy, exciting, or just pleasant. The goal of any event is to not create a boring atmosphere. There are many tools that can be used to enhance the atmosphere, including music, lighting, décor, venue, color, layout, and even smell. The atmosphere can be planned to change during periods of the event. It could start very formal and then change at the moment the honoree is awarded in a gala celebration. That would certainly break up the evening!

auction Many events, especially fund-raisers, utilize auctions of different types as a key part of the event. **Celebrity auctions** utilize the draw and skill of celebrity auctioneers (national, local, or a member of the appropriate business or group) to host and actually conduct the auction, with the result often being higher receipts for the goods and services offered. Depending on the skill of the celebrity, this type of auction can be very entertaining and the highlight of the event. In **silent auctions**, the items being offered, accompanied by bid sheets, are placed on tables and guests circulate to view and bid, providing excellent interactive involvement before the event or during a cocktail reception. Many auctions, such as a show-horse sale, are the reason for the entire event.

🖊 Tips for auctions:

✓ Small items need to be well secured during the viewing period—even at black-tie events.

✓ Ensure that a celebrity auctioneer has the experience and skill to conduct the auction. If not it could be disastrous and costly.

✓ Not everyone raising his or her hand will pay if awarded the bid. Avoid this by issuing bid numbers secured by credit cards.

✓ Auction items may have more than just street value. Perhaps an item was used by a celebrity, or signed by one, or has another interesting heritage or trait. It is purported that actress Sharon Stone kissed two $100 bills and then auctioned the lipstick-marked bills for $5,000 each.

audarena The style of event building that functions both as an *auditorium* and an *arena*. This type of facility is the result of designing structures to accommodate a very wide range of events, from sporting events to exhibitions to concerts and many other types of functions.

audience A group of people watching a performance or presentation or experiencing an event.

audience involvement At a presentation, the participation of the members of the audience in some way that enhances both the presentation and the audience's experience. The simplest example is during a church service when the congregation is asked to stand and shake hands, hug, or speak a phrase to members seated or standing near them. Participation makes the audience feel emotionally involved and aids in their retention of the presentation's message. Find ways to involve your audience.

✎ **Tips for audience involvement:**

✓ Whenever possible, turn your audience into participants.

✓ Something as simple as asking attendees to wear a costume to a theme party allows the attendees to participate on a higher level. Add to this by bringing the best onstage to be awarded for their effort.

✓ *Team-building activities* are used to bring participants into the spirit of the message being presented.

A

✓ Utilize audience members in a comedy skit or simple song.

✓ A question-and-answer session encourages audience involvement by permitting the audience to voice their interests and opinions.

✓ Challenge yourself to find a unique way to get your audience involved in your event.

audience left   The reference for the side of the stage that is on the left-hand side as the audience views the stage. Audience left is also referred to as *stage right*.

audience right   The reference for the side of the stage that is on the right-hand side as the audience views the stage. Audience right is also referred to as *stage left*.

audio system   See *sound system*.

audiovisual (AV)   The general term for all sight and sound elements of a presentation, including both the equipment, such as *projectors* and *sound system*, as well as the graphic or recorded materials being presented. Equipment includes film screens, video screens, projectors, audio equipment, computers, and pads. Materials include PowerPoint presentations, slides, films, videos, and charts.

audition   A performance given before a *producer*, *director*, client, or others for the purpose of obtaining a position in a production. Auditions can evaluate acting, speaking, singing, dancing, or any number of other skills. Also called *tryouts*.

auditorium   A large building for artistic performances. Also it often refers to the section of the theater where the audience sits versus the stage and other areas of the theater. This area is also called the *house*.

auditorium lights   See *house lights*.

Austrian or **Austrian curtain**   Another name for a *contour curtain*. Also see *main curtain*.

award show Any staged presentation whose main purpose is to grant recognition for outstanding achievement by an individual, company, or organization. A typical *format* is the presentation of one award after another, each presented by a noteworthy individual or group of individuals, sometimes alternating with music and/or entertainment. There are a variety of different formats that effectively break this clichéd style, such as *table hosts* presenting the award from a position at their table to the recipient at the same table. New styles of presentation eliminate predictability and add interest to the event.

baby spot A small spotlight used to cover special small areas on the stage.

back bar Tables behind a bar used to hold glasses, liquor bottles, and other accouterments essential to running the bar efficiently.

backdrop The upstage most scenic piece that forms a background for the entire stage scene. Most often it is either a large painted canvas with scenes, such as sky, woodland, company logo, etc.; a projection screen; or a large fabric curtain, perhaps with twinkle lights or other effects. Large scenic backdrops are also effective to decorate or set the theme for parties and other events. They quickly transform a dull-looking banquet room into a complete atmosphere. Many sources exist for renting backdrops of different themes and sizes. Also see *cyclorama* and *backing*.

background (BG) The visual area behind a subject in a photograph or video. The background should not be obtrusive, detract from the prime subject, or suggest something to the viewer other than the message intended. A background is also the visual behind a *dais*, a speaker, or other performances. Also see *backdrop*.

B

background music (BGM)   Music at an event can create an air of excitement, charm, patriotism, or fun, for example, or inspire a variety of emotions depending on the music selected. The musical choice should be appropriate for the type of event to effectively enhance the theme, level of formality, and mood. Background music can be effective before, during, or after the event. The correct volume level is imperative. Too loud and it destroys easy conversation; too low and it has no effect. As more people enter an event, such as a cocktail party, where a lot of talking takes place, the BGM volume level needs to increase to be heard (but not so high that it destroys conversation). Background music also refers to music used under a speech or visual presentation. Also see *soundscaping.*

backing   Another term for *backdrop.* A drop, or flat, used behind a scene on a stage or behind an opening in the set such as a door, arch, or window. Sometimes it is very elaborate, as in the case of a fully painted scene behind, for example, a forest scene onstage or gardens behind a set of French doors; or it may be simple, such as a painted neutral color behind a door that an actor opens. Large painted backings can be used effectively in many types of events. For example, large backings of a forest scene hung to cover one or two walls of a banquet room instantly change the atmosphere of the space into an outdoor setting. Backings with many different images can be rented for special events.

backing light   Lights used to illuminate or give a visual effect to a *backing.*

backlight   Lights used behind a performer or speaker to highlight their backs and make them visually stand out from the *backdrop.* It is typically better to backlight a speaker with two lights off the shoulder at 45° so the speaker's shadow does not fall directly onto the script or other prompting materials placed on the lectern surface. Also, backlights are lights used behind sets or pieces of *scenery* to illuminate the set piece or highlight it in a special way.

back of house A service area not open to the audience, visitors, or the public, such as offices or storage rooms.

back of the house The area behind the last seats in a theater or auditorium often used to stand overflow audience. Also see *S.R.O.*

backstage Any area around the stage not seen by the audience. This can be the area on the right or left of the stage performance area, or the area behind the stage or behind drops onstage, or the area of dressing rooms, the *green room*, scenic storage, etc.

backstory Generally the history of the characters or other elements, including the story line, that underlies the situation existing at the start of the main narrative. For example, in a theatrical production, if the character is evil, the backstory, revealed through flashback or description, is what happened to make the character evil. It can also be the background of a speaker presented to qualify the speaker's experience, or the underlying reason for the event.

back wall The backside of a trade-show booth. Most commonly these are fabric supported by aluminum pipe. Also the wall in back of a stage area behind the *scenery.*

badge A device to display information on a person. While there are all types of badges such as military, police, and political promotion, events deal primarily with name badges, which often double as admission tickets, VIP identifiers, and membership-status indicators, among other things. Considerable attention needs to be paid to the information placed on badges to ensure it meets the needs of the event.

✐ **General tips on badges:**

✓ Always encourage wearing them on the right side of a wearer's upper body. This is the easiest location for reading as people shake hands with their right hand.

✓ Many badges have become very large and are worn by a cord

around a person's neck. While organizers seem to like these, many wearers consider this personal signage awkward, bothersome, and too much. Certainly it is not appropriate at a formal affair.

✓ Companies and some organizations prefer to have the word "host" or "guest" above the individual's name.

✓ Keep the names simple. Only professional titles need to be included, such as "Dr.," "Senator," or "Judge."

✓ If spouses or significant others are unknown, or their last name is different from their spouse, it is helpful to also have the associated spouse's name on the badge distinguished by color, parenthesis, or type style.

✓ Many *VIPs* and *celebrities* find it an affront to wear a name badge. This can be overcome by having previously identified and trained escorts for such individuals.

balcony or booth spotlight Large spotlights placed in front of the balcony or in the projection booth, or special platforms that project intense light onto the performing areas or performers. Often these lights utilize operators during the performance to aim and color the light.

balloon Wonderful inflatable and flexible bags that can be used in many applications to add color and decoration to most events. Common uses are helium-filled balloon arches, walls, ceiling treatments, and centerpieces. Air-filled balloons are typically used on floors, suspended from lines, and attached in multiple ways. The balloons can be screened with logos, come in many shapes, and be made with different materials, including Mylar and biodegradable latex.

 Warning: Some municipalities and venues require all helium-filled balloons to be tethered in a manner that makes it impossible for them to get away.

For a new product presentation, I put small pyro charges inside each balloon that was hung to create a balloon wall. On cue, the charges were popped, creating a vibrant flash, and instantly the wall of balloons was gone, revealing the product behind.

B

balloon release The release of hundreds or thousands of colorful helium-filled balloons at a key or climactic moment in the presentation can fill the sky with color. This term also refers to the cascade of air-filled balloons from the high ceilings of a venue as they drop onto the audience. Releasing a large number of balloons outdoors became an environmental problem until a recent innovation developed balloons made of 100 percent biodegradable latex.

🖋 **Tips for a successful release, be it a cascade or aerial:**

✓ Be sure to fully fill the balloons with air or helium at the last possible moment. The content escapes the balloons rather quickly, reducing their size. If it is a helium aerial release, the balloons need maximum lift to "jump" out of the containment device, which will not happen if the balloons were filled too early.

✓ Ensure that the release mechanism holding the balloons works effectively for an instant release. Rehearse it ahead of time.

✓ Rather than tying the filled balloons closed, use specially made clips. It is faster and easier.

✓ Know which way the wind will be blowing so that the balloons will go in the direction that makes the biggest impact on the audience.

✓ For a cascade, keep the balloons in their bags hidden from the audience as much as possible to prevent giving away the surprise element.

✓ If aerial releases are permitted, be sure to follow the governing body regulations, which sometimes include notifying local airports.

🖋 **Warning:** Many states now forbid outdoor releases of mylar or foil helium balloons for environmental or safety reasons. Some states forbid balloon releases of any kind. Always check with local airports prior to a balloon release so that they can warn any airplanes in the area at the time of the release.

My team once held the record for the most balloons released. It was fifty thousand balloons on the occasion of the grand opening of Walt Disney World. What made it so spectacular was the instant and simultaneous release of the balloons both from decorated boxes in front of the audience as well as from very large boxes hidden behind the audience. All the balloons combined overhead to virtually fill the sky with color.

ballyhoo To move the spotlights in a fast, random fashion all around the space to add excitement, for example, at the end of a musical performance. Also referred to as a **bally**.

banner A headline in a newspaper announcing or highlighting an element of the event (such as a celebrity attending). In advertising it is a purchased broad strip on a newspaper or web page designed to carry the event's message. Banners are also flags with the organization's logo or symbol as traditionally carried by knights of a king. Often banners are large, thin flags of any color or design placed to add excitement and visual effects to an event. Long pieces of paper or cloth placed at an event bearing a slogan, message, or name are also called banners.

banquet An elaborate, often formal, meal attended by many invited guests, usually for the purpose of honoring or celebrating a person or occasion. In business the occasion can be anything from an award for a long day of meetings to strengthening the bonds between those assembled. Most often a banquet includes some sort of a presentation, if only speeches. A banquet can take place any time of the day. Also see *feast* and *dinner.*

barn doors A device consisting of two or four hinged metal flaps, which is placed in front of a spotlight to reduce the beam spread in one or more directions. See *shutter.*

baroque An extravagant artistic style including paintings, architecture, and furniture popular in the sixteenth through eighteenth centuries. Originally founded in Rome, it spread through Europe and was used extensively in cathedrals and palaces. The style is described as exaggerated motion expressing drama, tension, motion, and grandeur.

barricade or barrier Devices used to restrict pedestrian movement for the purpose of safety, security, or general crowd flow or control. These devices can be permanent or temporary. Temporary units vary from the traditional wooden board on triangular legs, to portable steel or plastic units, to water-filled oil drums with rope stretched between. In large rock concerts, often very strong and/or tall barricades are used in front of the concert stage (called **front-of-stage barriers**), with space for security and first-aid personnel behind (in an area referred to as the "pit") to separate the performers and audience.

 A curved front-of-stage barrier is recommended for the following reasons:

✓ Dissipates audience surges away from the center of the stage.

✓ Assists means of escape.

✓ Provides a wider front row *sight line.*

✓ Improves performer safety by placing a greater distance between the stage and performer, making it more difficult for the audience to reach the stage.

✓ Provides more space in the pit for security and first aid personnel.

🖉 **The placement of any barricade for crowd control should always be done in coordination with local fire and/or police personnel. An excellent planning guide is the *Life Safety Code* of the National Fire Protection Association.**

barware See *glassware*.

baseline A comparison of the original planned schedule against the actual schedule to track and evaluate the project's progress.

batik Fabric with beautiful patterns and designs of flowers, nature, animals, and folklore, hand-printed using an ancient wax-resistant dying method. Traditionally worn by nobility during ceremonies in Southeast Asia, Egypt, and Nigeria.

batten A steel pipe or wooden bar suspended from the grid, rigging system, or roof structure, from which scenery, curtains, or lights are hung.

battery of lights A large group of lighting instruments mounted together to create great lighting intensity. Used often in extravaganzas, rock concerts, or large outdoor stages.

bead A thin piece of molding used on the inside edge of picture frames, around doors and windows, and wherever additional ornamentation is needed.

beam effects The visuals created by laser beams in space (as opposed to on a screen or building). These effects require high-power lasers and haze or smoke, dim lighting, and other environmental controls. Also see *hazer*.

beer talent A slang phrase for inexpensive entertainers. Often inexpensive talent can be very good, and through proper selection and combinations of different individuals, the overall effect can be better than that of one expensive performing group.

belaying pin A round, steel pin about one inch thick and a foot long used in *pin rails* to tie ropes from the *gridiron*.

benefactor A supporter of the arts, usually one who makes a financial bequest or endowment.

beverage requirements The amount of liquid refreshments anticipated to be required for an event, such as a cocktail party or dinner. Also see *cocktail party*.

🛍️ For a complete guide to both quantities and type, see "Tables and Techniques" (page 308).

bid documents The information made available to bidders to ensure accurate comparison of the costs and performance of the various vendors. These documents typically include a scope of work, drawings, specifications, schedule, etc.

bird's-eye spot A bulb shaped like a mushroom that is silvered on the inside, creating a built-in reflector. It fits into many normal types of light sockets and often substitutes as an inexpensive spotlight.

bird's-eye view A *plan* view looking straight down on the subject, venue, or activity. Also refers to a drawing or photograph made from an imaginary, high vantage point at about 45° up from the horizon that shows perspective in both *elevation* and plan in one image.

birthstone A precious or semiprecious stone that is associated with the month someone is born. Some believe a birthstone brings luck and wealth and therefore present jewelry with the appropriate stone as a gift.

🛍️ See list of birthstones in "Tables and Techniques" (page 358).

B

bistro A style of café that specializes in moderately priced food, small menus, and quick service. The word "bistro" is Russian for "quickly" and entered the French language when the Russians occupied Paris in 1815. Legend has it that the Cossacks were always in a hurry for their food and would constantly yell "bistro!"

bit part A small role in any production or presentation, rarely with more than a couple of lines, if any. Also see *walk-on*.

blacklight Common term for *ultraviolet* (UV) light that is used as a special effect. The light turns certain chemicals, paints, dyes, and even one's teeth into different vibrant colors. Special UV paint is available that when used is invisible until the UV light hits the paint. This allows the painting of one scene on top of another. The scenes switch immediately by changing the light source from normal to UV. **Ultraviolet** light comes in three spectrums: UV-A, UV-B, and UV-C. Commercial blacklight used for entertainment filters out all but the harmless UV-A spectrum.

blackout A lighting cue, typically at the end of a scene, segment, or script line, in which all of the lights are suddenly extinguished. Blackouts are effectively used to dramatize a point, emphasize the end of a musical performance, or indicate the end of a presentation.

blacks The set of curtains, including *borders* and *legs*, used on a stage to black out certain elements not to be seen by the audience, or to visually isolate and accent certain elements placed in front of these curtains.

black tie The reference for a formal event. Often used on invitations, it denotes that the appropriate dress for men is a tuxedo (black coat, not white) and for ladies a formal gown.

blanket-wrapped The technique of wrapping exhibit materials in moving blankets rather than crating. This allows the truck driver (in many locations, except where unions mandate labor to perform this service) to deliver the material directly to the booth, remove the blankets, and return them to the truck. Blanket-wrapping of materials means that they are lighter in weight and require less cubic footage in the van, thereby reducing the costs of transportation. Plastic bubble wrap now often replaces blankets.

bleachers In an indoor *venue*, these are tiered seats or benches that can be expanded or retracted to allow for multiple uses of the floor space. In sports stadiums they are typically the uncovered audience area. Events often utilize bleachers as portable, temporary, and very versatile audience seating. Also see *grandstands*.

blinder See *barn doors*.

block and tackle A system of two or more *pulleys* with a rope going through them designed to achieve a mechanical advantage in lifting or pulling. With two pulleys, 100 pounds (45.3 kg) can be raised with just 25 pounds (11.3 kg) of force. Additional pulleys increase this advantage.

blocking The movement and stationary positions of actors, speakers, or other participants on a stage. Typically the director designates the blocking by placing each person in relative positions, or specifying how and when the movement of each person will occur.

blog A website usually maintained by an individual with commentary, descriptions, and other regular entries. Often blogs represent special interests and therefore can be effective marketing tools for special events. For example, if the event is of special interest to country music fans, the opinion expressed on appropriate blogs about the event and the musicians to be performing may influence attendance at the event. The term "blog" is a contraction of "web log."

blow-up An enlargement (usually made by a photographic or electronic process) of an advertisement, picture, or printed piece.

blue screen photography When actors or *props* are filmed in front of a brightly illuminated blue screen background that can be eliminated, allowing the images of the actors or props to be placed on any background shot separately.

blue-sky list The broadest possible list of initial concepts for a project, derived without consideration for budget, schedule, or other possible limitations. The final details of a project are eventually derived from a blue-sky list.

bobbinet A cloth netting with small hexagonal mesh ideal for see-through effects and transparent drops onstage. Also see *scrim*.

bobeche A wide, flat ring below a candlestick socket designed to catch dripping wax. Some are designed to hold small glass chimneys on candelabras when using *tapers*, allowing them to meet local fire code regulations.

book The manuscript of a production or presentation. It typically contains the words to be spoken, visuals, cues, notations, blocking diagrams, and other necessary information for all concerned.

boom The style of microphone on a pole, or beam, that can extend out close to the speaker or performer while the operator remains out of sight of the audience or camera. News crews often use hand-held booms. A **lighting boom** is vertical pipe for mounting theatrical lighting fixtures.

border A short drop, scenic piece, or curtain at the top of the set that masks the ceiling, *fly loft*, lighting instruments, or other elements above the actors or performers from audience view.

border lights A row of theatrical lighting instruments usually hung from a *batten* over the stage area. Typically these are numbered from downstage to upstage and referred to as first border, second border, etc.

bounce Light that is reflected off the stage floor, walls, or other surfaces. Photographers bounce light off a white card or other surface to light a subject. Bounce is a problem when the light reflects and illuminates something that should not be seen.

bourbon An American-made whiskey distilled from a mash containing a minimum of 51 percent corn. In 1964 it was declared America's national spirit by an act of Congress. Most bourbon is 86 proof and aged for four years with some aged twelve years or longer. Those from Kentucky are considered the best because the distilleries sit on a huge natural limestone shelf through which percolates the spring water, free of iron, that is used in the mash. Also see *whiskey* and *rye*.

box office A place where tickets are sold for shows, events, rides, sports, many other entertainment amusements. Typically the transaction takes place over a counter. The term originates from Shakespearean times when a box was passed through the audience to collect admission fees and when full was placed in an office to be safe from thieves. "Box office" is also used as a term to measure the success of ticket sales for shows, events, and most notably motion pictures.

box set A traditional stage scenic piece or *set* with three solid walls such as, but not limited to, a living room.

brand beverages Beverages that have a name recognized as high in quality, or preferred, and are usually more expensive to purchase. Coca Cola® is a brand cola. A popular spirit, such as vodka, will have brands currently considered better tasting or more popular and therefore will be more costly. Popularity often quickly changes, so it is critical to know what brands are important for the intended audience. Also see *cocktail parties* and *well drinks*.

brayer A small hand roller made of hard rubber to rub down material glued with rubber cement or other adhesive.

break Used in publicity to mean getting a story and/or photos and video out to the media quickly.

break a leg Traditional theatrical wish of good luck before a first performance or on opening night, but now more widely used before any performance. There are many stories as to its origin. A favorite is that originally when stages were sharply *raked* from front to back, actors had to be careful how they walked so they didn't trip, fall, and break a leg. So the original expression is believed to have been, "*Don't* break a leg!"

breakaway A prop, piece of scenery, or costume that quickly changes form in full view of the audience. A typical example is a long gown that is quickly pulled off to reveal a smaller costume underneath.

breakout A session at a *conference* where a small number drawn from a larger group convene to discuss certain subjects or aspects of the broad theme of the main gathering. A **breakout room** is a room designed to comfortably accommodate these small sessions with simple visual devices such as *whiteboards*. Oftentimes these aren't rooms but comfortable spaces alongside the pool, or in a clearing in the woods providing relief from being in a room and aimed to inspire creativity.

bright Describes music that is lively and cheerful in mood. In audio it is used to describe sounds with a crisp and clear quality or that have a high volume. In lighting it describes light that is intense.

bring down To decrease the intensity or volume of the lights or sound. Also see *dim*.

bring up To increase the intensity or volume of the lights or sound. Also see *dim*.

budget An itemized estimate of the costs and income for an event, typically done in a generally accepted accounting format. Most often this is achieved by utilizing an accepted computer financial program.

The challenge to building a budget is to anticipate and estimate *all* possible costs, a difficult feat for many events since they are often first-time or one-time happenings for which there is no history to draw upon.

🖋 **Tips on developing a budget:**

✓ If the event is large and has multiple functions within the overall event, it is simpler to make a separate budget for each of the functions with a summary page for the overall budget.

✓ Don't guess at prices, but take the time to contact vendors and get written estimates.

✓ Be prepared to ask the right questions when calling for estimates to prevent vendors from lowballing and then following with a long list of items not originally discussed.

✓ It's not important to price out every croissant, but be consistent with regard to how and where you break down certain line items. For example: Will your A/V section be one lump sum, or will you have each function detailed with each piece of equipment priced individually?

✓ Don't forget taxes, tips, delivery charges, and all those other little fees that add up so quickly.

✓ Add labor rate, either at cost or at the calculated charge-out rate.

✓ Add a reasonable *contingency* fund for those "forgotten" items.

✓ Add overhead expenses.

📑 **For information about calculating rates, see "Tables and Techniques" (page 324).**

📑 **For a proven and workable budget format, see "Tables and Techniques" (page 328).**

buffet A meal at which guests serve themselves from various dishes set out on a table. Buffets are common for informally serving a large number of people economically. They are the easiest way to serve a large number of guests. There are two distinctly different types of buffets. One is for an event planned as a "stand up" event, such as a *cocktail reception*, when the buffet is never intended to provide a full meal, but rather just *finger food*. The second buffet type is an actual full dinner, planned without waiter table service. Some guests like buffets because, unlike with a set meal, they can pick and choose the foods and portions they like. Others dislike buffets because they are not served and one has to deal with a line, the balancing of plates, the need to move back and forth from an eating table to the food table, and interruption of the rapport with the table group.

Another approach to a buffet is referred to as "scatter bars" or "food islands," in which various serving tables spaced around the room offer different types of food. This technique provides a wider choice of food selections, eliminates the long lines (although some types may be more popular than others), and adds interest to the event.

📖 **For more information about buffets, see "Tables and Techniques" (page 352).**

🖊 **Tips for a successful finger food buffet:**

✓ Avoid plates. The biggest mistake made in this type of buffet is that the food selected and the portions are too messy or too large to be easily handled, particularly by guests holding a drink. Small, manageable morsels are best.

✓ How the guest handles the small portions needs to be considered. Traditionally a cheese cube on a toothpick or a morsel on a small toast triangle have been served. Some better ideas are wasabi cotton candy on an edible stick, shrimp on sugarcane skewers, shot glasses of creamed buffalo wings, small baked cones filled with fruit salad, or thick cucumber slices filled with a mini salad all on a thick cracker. Be clever and stun guests with innovation.

✓ Think beyond the usual presentation of a buffet table with large dishes of food. Good caterers offer all sorts of interesting ways to present the food. Consider the "scatter bar" method described above.

✓ If plates are a must, use those that have a slot to hold a stemmed glass so that everything can be safely held in one hand. Caution, this also requires that all drinks be served in stemware.

🖉 **Tips for a successful full-dinner buffet:**

✓ It is awkward for guests to search for a place to sit at a table after going through a buffet line and having their hands filled with plates of food. Plan the event so that there is an initial presentation and guests first find a place at a table with people they want to be with. Then announce that dinner is served, ensuring that the guests have a defined place to come back to after going through the buffet line.

✓ Always order 50 percent more china to allow for second helpings.

✓ Nothing is worse than long lines for the buffet. This common unpleasantry can be solved in different ways. One is to ensure that there are enough buffet tables, with lines on both sides, to quickly serve the guests. A well-planned buffet setup can serve seventy-five guests in a twenty- to thirty-minute time frame. One line is needed for every fifty to sixty people. Another method to shorten the line is to announce in the opening remarks that a host or hostess will come to each table when it is time for that table to go to the buffet.

B

✓ People take a longer time serving themselves. Having servers speeds the line (and controls portions).

✓ Plan the menu for the buffet with items that are easy for the guests to serve to themselves while holding on to their plates. Avoid hard-to-handle items such as corn on the cob, whole bone-in meats, chicken breasts, and spareribs.

✓ If you are using a serve-it-yourself plan, lay out the serving dishes and decorations on the serving table in a way to allow room for diners to set down their plates along the food line, making it easier for them to serve themselves.

✓ Having separate tables for desserts and beverages solves two problems. One, it speeds up the serving lines. Two, it means fewer dishes for guests to juggle on their way from the serving line to their table. On the other hand, it also increases the number of times the guests must leave their table.

✓ A "scatter" buffet, with different food stations placed around the room, is great for cocktail receptions and parties, but very difficult as a dinner. It takes too long to gather the food selections, and guests are constantly leaving their table to go to another table for a different food or course.

✓ Consider the age of the guests before selecting a buffet. Older people have a much more difficult time with a buffet dinner. The mobility-impaired need assistance. A mother loading children's plates will have a difficult time and will slow the serving line.

✓ Never run out of food. At buffets people tend to load a lot onto their plate, or go back for seconds, or select more of the preferred items, leaving less of these items for those coming later. (Boiled shrimp always goes quickly.) Increase the amount of food available, especially the favored items, or have servers.

📖 See portion planning in "Tables and Techniques" (page 349).

buffet plate See *dinner plate*.

bump To bring up the sound or light level as fast as possible and then down again. For example, at the end of a performer's song, one often bumps the lights to emphasize the last note with a bright visual effect.

bundle The term used for a group of cables, either lighting or sound cables, taped together.

bunting Festive fabric typically in the national colors (in America—red, white, and blue). Use in lieu of the national flag. Since bunting is not a flag its usage does not fall under *flag protocol*. Therefore it can be used to cover the front of a speaker's platform or strung throughout the hall or theater without fear of violating provisions affecting the use of the flag. U.S. flag code does suggest, however, that the bunting used be displayed with the blue above (as in the blue field), white in the middle, and red below. Bunting is made in various shapes from long and wide gathered at the ends (a fan) to tall and narrow (a pull-down). **Bunting swags** are pre-sewn fans with a rosette at each end and sometimes with a short piece of bunting falling from the rosettes. **Rosettes**, of different sizes and shapes, are available for the corners. The use of bunting enhances the feeling of patriotism for any festive occasion and may be used for any general decoration.

📖 See "Tables and Techniques" (page 343).

burlap An inexpensive, heavy, loosely woven textured *background* fabric made of jute or hemp.

busker A street performer. **Busking** is receiving gratuities for performances from the passing crowd in public places. Street performing dates back to antiquity and includes anything that people find entertaining, such as fire eating, singing, magic, card tricks, *pantomime* (see *mime*), living statues, musical performances, and clowning.

butterfly release The instant visual of hundreds of live butterflies fluttering over the audience is both effective and charming. Particularly popular at weddings, it signifies a change in life. Different species of butterflies are used in different areas. Be aware that some environmental sympathizers consider this practice an endangerment.

buy-off The client's written acceptance of a phase of a project, such as the project bid, *schedule*, talent list, *script*, etc.

BYOB or **BYOA** Appreciation for Bring Your Own Bottle (or Booze or Alcohol). Commonly used on informal invitations to tell those invited that alcoholic drinks will not be provided but guests are welcome to bring their own.

C

cable The electrical definition is any flexible wire for conducting electrical current. At an event there are electrical cables for power, for audio signals, and for computer and control signal purposes. A stage definition is steel wire used to hold or hang scenic pieces, lights, and other equipment.

cable box A sturdy wooden box, usually with casters, designed to hold a considerable amount of heavy lighting, power, or audio cables. Once it is emptied and the cables are in place for the presentation, the box requires space to be stored until the *strike* of all equipment.

cable covers or **cable ramps** These durable plastic or wooden devices are used to cover or enclose cable in places of high foot or vehicle traffic as a safety device to avoid tripping over the cables or accidentally catching and pulling a cable. They are also used to protect the cables from breakage and other damage. Cable ramps are required by fire and safety codes in all audience areas.

CAD or **CADD** Abbreviation for Computer Aided Design and Computer Aided Design and Drafting. The use of computer technology for the process of creating design documentation such as *floor plans*, table layouts, scenery, and stage *elevations*.

call This notice to actors, performers, and other participants announces the time of rehearsals and performance. It is also a notice made backstage for the amount of time before the start of the event.

callboard A bulletin board located backstage on which are posted important notices for actors, crew, etc., including *rehearsal* times, performance *schedules*, and house rules.

calligraphy Skillful handwriting. Also called **hands**. A perfected style of writing that is flowing and beautiful, with quirks and flourishes adding to the interest of each letter. All formal invitations must be handwritten, which is to say that they must be written in calligraphy.

 See font styles in "Tables and Techniques" (page 369).

campfire songs Traditional songs that we all know from youth such as "Row, Row, Row Your Boat," "Camptown Races," and "She'll be Coming Round the Mountain." While often sung around a campfire, their larger importance in an event is that their familiarity encourages audience participation and camaraderie.

✐ Familiar music, be it pop standards, contemporary hits, or even certain classics, typically has a much bigger impact on the audience than new or original music because it is known, generally liked, and often conjures up personal memories.

Canadian whisky A style of whiskey made exclusively in Canada, distilled from blends of wheat, corn, rye, and barley. It is considered to have a lighter and smoother taste than other whiskeys. It is aged in casks for a minimum of three years.

canapé Crackers, pastry, or small pieces of bread topped with a wide variety of tasty garnishes from anchovies to zucchini. Typically served with cocktails, or as appetizers before a meal, they can be hot or cold and themed to the event. Also see *hors d'oeuvre*.

cancellation Should it be necessary to cancel or even postpone an event after original commitments are made, terminating contracts can be difficult and expensive. Have an understanding of, and written commitment as to, the terms of the vendor's cancellation policy. Usually the penalties vary depending on how far ahead of the event date the cancellation is made.

candy store A **wish list** of projects, or elements within a project, that may or may not be on the final list to be included, often depending on time or money. Also referred to as a **laundry list** or a **grocery list**.

canopy A small, portable fabric structure, usually 8–10 feet square, widely used for a variety of event functions. Also see *tent*.

canopy ceiling A style of ceiling decoration in which fabric is attached to the sides and gathered into the center point, allowing it to hang in a puffy manner. The center point is then decorated with a hanging fixture such as a chandelier. In some cases fabric does not cover the entire ceiling but is draped in strips to eliminate interference with air conditioning or sprinkler systems. *Garland* is sometimes used to create the same effect.

canton A rectangular area in the top corner of a shield or on a flag next to the staff. In the American flag it is the blue area with stars.

capacity The limit of the number of people that the local fire department code allows in a given space, be it a meeting room, ballroom, exterior tents, etc. The square footage of the area determines the number of people permitted in the area, and it varies depending on the type of event, number of exit doors, and other conditions. Approximate capacity calculation for a stand-up *cocktail party* is usually around

7 square feet (0.65 square meters) per person, versus a banquet, which may be about 12 square feet (1.15 square meters), while a person sitting in a theater-style chair requires 4 square feet (0.37 square meters). By law in most municipalities, the capacity of a public gathering room is posted visibly within the room. Exceeding these capacities can have severe penalties for the owner and event planner.

caption Descriptive material used under a photograph.

carnival An amusement show that travels constantly from place to place and is made up of rides, food and merchandise vendors, games of chance and skill, thrill acts, animal acts, and sideshow curiosities. Often carnivals combine with other events such as a *fair* or *festival*.

Also, **carnival** is the oldest and largest continually celebrated public event. Roots of the festival extend back to Bacchanalia in ancient Rome and Dionysia in Greece. So popular was it that those Christians developing the liturgical calendar had to include it and placed it just prior to Lent so that the bawdy partiers could repent for the following forty days. The carnival of Venice, Italy, was for centuries the most famous, replaced by Rio de Janeiro's, which is now rated as the biggest party on the planet. Carnival is still celebrated heartily in many Christian and non-Christian countries around the world. In New Orleans, Louisiana, it is called Mardi Gras.

carpenter The stagehand responsible for installing and repairing the scenery.

carpet tape Double-sided tape used to hold carpeting or decorative fabric securely to the floor so that it does not become a trip hazard for the audience or participants.

cartoon A diagram or drawing of a plan. Also an animated movie created with a sequence of drawings.

cash bar The type of bar service at a *cocktail party* or *banquet* that requires payment for each drink. It is also referred to as a *no-host bar* (or nonhost bar) and is the opposite of an *open bar*, where all drinks are complimentary or included with the ticket price.

cassis A beverage or liqueur made from hearty black currants grown in Europe. One such beverage is crème de cassis.

cast The members of the presentation or performance including speakers, special guests, actors, and entertainers.

casting The process of selecting actors or other individuals for each character of a script or part in a presentation. Typically the casting is done after the selectors have seen the possible participants in an *audition*, reading, or screen test.

caterer The individual or company that prepares and provides all of the drinks, food, and service personnel for a party, meeting, or other event. The caterer is often one of the most important and expensive elements of any event, so careful selection is absolutely necessary.

🖉 **Tips on selecting a caterer:**

✓ Should the event be in a hotel or resort, most often that facility will demand providing all catering services for the event. So the hotel's experience with the type of event desired, the *cuisine*, and the *theme* is extremely important in the selection of the facility. While many hotels say they can do anything, don't believe it! The question is, can they do it well? If not, it may be important to relocate the event or change the menu to something that the facility does well. Ethnic foods are sometimes the allowed exception for bringing an outside caterer into a hotel venue.

✓ When free to choose any caterer, ask that you attend one of their upcoming functions so that you can evaluate their food and service.

✓ Be sure the caterer's contract has exact numbers of service personnel, waiters, and bartenders. Evaluate these numbers in regard to your event to be sure the amount specified is adequate for the requirements of the event as you know them to be. For example, if hors d'oeuvre are to be passed by waiters, determine how often the waiters need to pass by each guest, how many different hors d'oeuvre are to be served, etc., to determine the number of waiters necessary.

✓ If the caterer has not been to the *venue*, make sure this happens and the caterer is satisfied that what is intended can be accomplished.

✓ Some other questions to ask the caterer:

↪ Are meal packages offered? If so, are they better priced, and what do they include?

↪ Are substitutions permissible?

↪ What does a *place setting* consist of?

↪ What are your choices of table linen colors and styles?

↪ What happens if the event extends? What time do servers go on overtime pay? What are these charges?

↪ Are there special rates for providing food and beverages for the musicians and photographers, etc.?

↪ What will the service personnel wear?

↪ Is insurance against crystal and china breakage included? If not, what is the cost?

↪ What is the last date by which a total guest count needs to be provided?

cathedral train The long, sweeping fabric behind a bridal gown that requires a very large aisle. This train requires planning in that it sweeps up flower petals, it needs assistance when the bride turns around, and care must be taken by people walking behind in the recessional. Also see *chapel-length train.*

CATV Originally the abbreviation for Community Antenna Television, the early method of bringing television to remote locations, it now generally refers to cable television.

catwalk An access way over the audience or stage area or both, used by crew or cast to cross from one side to the other. Often catwalks extend along ceiling areas, providing access to areas where lights and other equipment can be hung.

celebrity or **celeb** A person with a prominent profile and easily recognized, be it in the media, a business or profession, politics, or a community. Celebrity is hard to measure and can be at all levels from local to international. **Instant celebrity** is one who becomes a celebrity in a very short time, often by accident or infamy. The earliest recording of celebrity was at the Olympic games in ancient Greece, where winners promoted their fame by commissioning hymns praising their exploits.

centerpiece The decoration that is part of the *table setting* usually in the center of a dinner table, on a buffet table, on a table of hors d'oeuvre, or sometimes even in the center of the room. Centerpieces can take any shape and be made from flowers, candles, fruit, *favors*, or just about anything else, including recycled beer cans. A formal dinner should have appropriate floral and formal candle centerpieces. For informal and themed dinners anything can be appropriate, and its being prominent in the center of the table can effectively express the mood or design of the event.

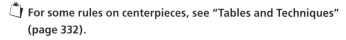 For some rules on centerpieces, see "Tables and Techniques" (page 332).

🖉 **Tips on selecting centerpieces:**

✓ For cocktail receptions, make the centerpieces and floral decorations on the hors d'oeuvre tables high because all guests will be standing.

✓ Use the centerpiece to express the event theme.

✓ If no theme exists, a seasonal centerpiece adds appropriateness.

✓ Any centerpiece higher than a foot can be problematic, blocking views of other guests, the head table, and performances or presentations.

✓ Lanterns or candles integrated into the design add an interesting visual element and set a pleasant mood.

✓ Select a centerpiece that fits the table shape—long on long, round on round, etc.

✓ Understand the amount of space the place settings will take up on the table and work in the centerpiece to fit the remaining space.

✓ The number of guests at the table and the table size also determine the amount of space remaining for a centerpiece.

✓ Consider other elements that might be necessary for placement on the table, such as favors, programs, wines, etc.

✓ Try something unusual that will make the guests talk about and remember it.

center spread Two facing pages in the center of a book, magazine, newspaper, or booklet. Called a **double-truck** when the facing pages are not in the center of the publication.

center stage The most prominent position onstage, located in the middle, equidistant from all edges of the stage area.

See a diagram of stage areas in "Tables and Techniques" (page 447).

CGI Abbreviation for Computer Graphic Illustration. Computer technology used to visually create illustrations, designs, and virtually anything that can be imagined. Used extensively in image manipulation and animation.

chain crawler The slang term for a hoist used to hang scenery, lighting, or other elements for a performance. The motor, encased in a covering, actually crawls up the chain that has been previously connected to the ceiling or something high, lifting the load. Often several are used together to lift a long *truss* loaded with lighting equipment.

chair cover Fabric sewn in various styles to fit over banquet chairs, adding color and an impressive visual to the chairs and to the overall look of the entire linen table setting. The covers are available in three styles: **standard**, which fit most banquet-style chairs rather tightly; **bag** style, which are larger and fuller, allowing for draping the chair with fabric in an elegant fashion; and **lycra**, which stretches to fit the chair tight and give it a very slick, modern appearance. Most often a *chair sash* is added to the covers.

See "Tables and Techniques" (page 386) for style suggestions.

chair dolly A dolly that is specifically designed to move a large number of chairs for setup in a banquet room or other location. Typically these dollies are designed for the specific chair, whether it is a stackable or folding chair, and they save a great amount of labor when moving a large number of chairs.

chair rail Typically in restaurants, a molding strip along the wall at such a height to stop the backs of chairs from marring the wall. But in events, it is a strip of wood tacked to the top of a platform used for a raised *dais* that prevents chairs from accidentally being pushed off the back edge—with or without the person sitting on the chair!

chair sash A fabric strip tied around the back of a banquet chair, often fashioned with a bow or other design element, adding color and visual effect to the chair. Most often the sash is used over a *chair cover*.

See "Tables and Techniques" (page 386) for style suggestions.

champagne A white sparkling wine, usually dry, produced in the Champagne region of northeastern France. Champagne, prized for its delicacy and freshness, is the drink for special occasions. Dom Pérignon, while serving as the chief cellarer of the Benedictine Abbey of Hautvillers (1668–1715), perfected the techniques for creating sparkling champagne. Sparkling wine produced in other parts of the world outside of the Champagne region cannot officially be called champagne. In America, it is referred to as wine produced in the "Champagne method." In Spain it is called Cava. Champagne is made from a blend of Pinot Noir, Pinot Meunier, and Chardonnay grapes. Both the pinots are red grapes, making champagne one of the white wines that is made using red grapes. Champagne is the greatest aperitif but also goes well with a whole range of foods including fish, shellfish, lighter meats, fruit desserts, and cheese. Champagne has an in-bottle life of four to five years if stored in a cool, dark space.

See champagnes and other sparkling wines in "Tables and Techniques" (page 318).

change order A document requesting a scope change or correction to the contract; a written change by the client, producer, vendor, or other entity affecting the event or its cost. The document must be agreed to and signed by both parties affected.

chapel-length train The long fabric behind a bridal gown, which is still grand, but much shorter than a *cathedral train*. It is the more popular, yet still formal, length of a gown train.

characterization The portrayal of a role by an actor or the defining of a person in a story by a dramatist. Humorous characterizations of well-known, important persons are often used in corporate or civic presentations.

charge-out rate A calculation of the cost of labor billed with costs, fees, and profit.

📖 See calculation formula in "Tables and Techniques" (page 326).

charger A decorative oversized plate 13–14 inches (33–35.5 centimeters) in diameter set as an underliner to the *dinner plate* to add color and decoration to a *table setting*. It is removed after the guests are seated and before food service. An alternate use is to place it under the first course dish, such as a soup bowl or salad plate, then remove it along with that dish.

charrette or **charet** An intense collaborative session where the general concepts and ideas of a project are creatively discussed. Also, a competition between several firms or individuals to come up with a solution to a given concept or design problem within an allocated time and budget.

chaser Bright music played at a rapid tempo to emphasize the end of an entertainment performance while the audience is applauding.

checklist A vital tool to both organizing and executing an event efficiently. No different from a list used by a pilot landing a plane in an emergency, a checklist for an event is a vital listing of items and action points that needs to be referred to constantly, right up to panic time when doors are opened to the audience, to ensure that important items are not forgotten. Used to actually check off items as they are attended to and to add more as necessary.

✏️ Tips about checklists:

✓ Start making one early in the production process, listing all the items that need to be purchased, accomplished, etc.

✓ Also start a second list for the day of the event. As you learn specifics during the production process that need to happen just prior to or during the event, put them on this list. For example, when you are ordering the flowers, if the florist says that because of the nature of the flowers selected they should not be placed on the tables until one hour before the event, this goes on this second checklist.

✓ Carry it with you at all times, whether it is electronic or on paper, for quick reference and adjustment.

✓ Add time notes whenever possible. For example, if the event starts at 8:00 p.m., the note about the flowers would begin with "7:00." A follow-up note might be "7:15—Check to see if flowers were put out."

✓ Always put "check on" items on the list, such as the 7:15 note above.

choreographer A person skilled in the art of designing sequences of movements in which motion and form are specified. In a show, the dance director who develops the movements and then teaches these to the dancers and stages them for maximum audience impact.

chuppah The traditional wedding canopy in a Jewish wedding. Sometimes accomplished with a floral canopy.

claque Hired members of the audience who are paid to applaud.

Clavilux The original instrument used to project various colors and patterns on a screen that changed and morphed in various combinations with the successive changes in music. This instrument has now been succeeded by more effective and controllable equipment.

clear To get rid of everything in the designated area. Also, a command given to *talent* and *crew* at the end of a broadcast or recording when the microphones or cameras are turned off.

Clear-Comm See *intercom*.

clear-span The unencumbered area between supporting columns, abutments, or posts of a structure. A structure designed and built in such a manner as to provide great open space free of intrusions. A meeting room, tent, or any structure with a long or high clear-span is easier to use than a space that has multiple supports that block views and limit the usefulness of the space for lighting, projection, and other elements of the presentation. Also see *free-span*.

clear stage A command given by the stage manager to all stage-hands, actors, and others to leave the stage immediately taking with them all tools, miscellaneous equipment, debris, etc.

clear view The unencumbered view from a seat in a theater to the stage, a seat in a meeting room toward visuals on a screen, or another location where it is important for those in the audience to see what is being presented. The opposite is an obstructed, or partially obstructed, view caused by interfering pillars, wall angles, or an improperly planned presentation. Seats in theaters classified as "partially obstructed" or without a "clear view" are seats usually on the far sides of the *house* from which the entire performance area onstage cannot be seen. Typically these seats are sold for a lower price.

closed circuit A television system within a building or space that restricts the audio and video signals to a defined meeting space, building, or area or to selected locations of a teleconference. It does not broadcast the signals to an audience outside the defined area.

close-up A camera composition in which the subject's head and shoulders fill most of the visual area. In an **extreme close-up**, the face barely fits within the boundaries of the camera frame, or just the center portion of a flower blossom is visible.

closing date The date when all copy, artwork, and photos must be in the hands of the newspaper, printer, or publication if it is to appear in the next issue, or be printed on the required date.

CMP Abbreviation for Certified Meeting Planner. The hallmark of professional achievement for the meeting planning industry, this designation recognizes planning professionals who have successfully demonstrated the knowledge, skills, and ability essential to perform all components of planning and executing meetings. Also see *ISES*.

cobweb spinner or **shooter** *Special effects* machines used to create fake cobwebs. The effect can be enhanced by hanging thin black threads from the ceiling at head height that tickle the guests as they walk through. Further enhancement can be achieved by suspending fake rubber spiders from monofilament lines running to an operator. The operator watches for opportunities to dangle the spiders in front of guests or onto their heads.

> *For Paramount Studio's premiere party for the movie* Congo *in New York City, I transformed the venue into a Central American jungle complete with thick vegetation, jungle sound effects, mist, and Native stilt dancers. The spiders and other bugs "dropping in" were a fun guest surprise.*

cocktail A beverage composed of a mixture of different ingredients, typically an alcohol spirit such as whiskey with soda or juice. A wide variety of different cocktails exist, some with very colorful names. At last count there were over eight thousand different recipes, some as simple as gin mixed with tonic water and a slice of lime as a garnish, some elaborate concoctions like a Long Island iced tea, which requires blending vodka, tequila, rum, gin, triple sec, and sweet and sour with a splash of cola, all garnished with a lemon slice. Some of the more popular cocktails are martinis, cosmopolitans, hurricanes, bloody marys, piña coladas, and whiskey sours. An event themed to a particular culture or cuisine is enhanced by offering cocktails typical to that theme, such as a tropical party with piña coladas, a South of the Border celebration with margaritas, or an Irish affair with Guinness beer, Irish whiskey, and Irish cream *liqueur.* Also see *cocktail party.*

 There are three different ways to plan cocktails for an event:

✓ Plan for every possible cocktail. This requires a very large stock of different liquors and mixes and a bartender who knows the recipes for a wide variety of cocktails.

✓ Plan for just the standard and/or currently popular cocktails. This limits the amount of liquors and mixes necessary and the knowledge required of the bartenders. But it will result in some guests taking second choices.

✓ Theme the cocktails to the event. For example, if the event is themed as a Mexican fiesta, then only margaritas could be served, or several different types of margaritas, such as regular and mango margaritas, or different types of margaritas and other cocktails made with tequila, such as a tequila sunrise.

Additional information regarding cocktails, quantities, wines, etc., is in "Tables and Techniques" (pages 303–23).

cocktail party or **cocktail reception** There are two styles of cocktail events. The first is a cocktail **reception**, an event or function in which guests enjoy *cocktails* and other beverages along with light hors d'oeuvre for the purpose of social mixing and conversation. It often functions as a gathering time prior to a larger event, such as a dinner. Ideally it is a stand-up affair of shorter duration, typically an hour or so. The second style is a cocktail **party**, better described as a party with cocktails. This event typically can last for a couple hours or more, and features cocktails along with food ranging from heavy hors d'oeuvre to a casual meal often served *buffet* style. Combined, these two styles of functions are the most popular type of social event, where elegantly dressed friends or associates mix, converse, and revel with glasses in hand. Many attribute this event type to the 1920s, when prohibition banned public drinking establishments. Unfortunately, most often these gatherings are ineffectively planned. Whether a home party or an out-of-home event, these cocktail functions require proper design, planning, and execution.

✎ **Tips on planning a cocktail reception:**

✓ Keep the guests standing. A cocktail reception where the guests sit limits guest interaction and ensures an unsuccessful event. If some chairs are required, do not line them along the wall but instead place them in conversational groupings.

✓ Ensure that the venue is adequate and the reception is not just squeezed in. If it is to be followed by a banquet or other event, ensure that there is easy access to the banquet or event area.

✓ Plan approximately 5 square feet (0.5 square meters) per person, including food and bar areas, with no chairs or tables. (Always check the legal *occupancy rating.*)

✓ Time the function so that it fits within other functions' schedules. Typically guests arrive (fashionably) about half an hour late. Yet they don't want the party to be over when they arrive. So if you want them at 6:00, start the reception at 5:30.

✓ Having waiters roam and serve hors d'oeuvre is ideal. Food placed on tables should be *finger food*, meaning that it is easy both to pick up off the serving plate and to eat using just the fingers of one hand (while the other holds the drink). A typical mistake is selecting food that must be put onto a plate and then is too difficult, or too messy, to eat while standing up holding a drink, a plate, a napkin, and fork. Plates too large add to this problem because they encourage people to load them full. Having no plates or just cocktail napkins is not only more manageable, but encourages movement around the room as guests return to the food tables for second and additional helpings.

✓ Small, stand-up cocktail tables placed in groups are helpful, allowing guests to set their drinks down occasionally. Make sure the wait staff constantly buses the tables to make sure they don't pile up with glasses, napkins, etc. Provide linen-covered trays on stands around the room to collect additional discarded items.

✓ Set a mood. Determine if it is to be loud or soft, formal, or themed. If the cocktail reception is a part of a larger event, then the mood should set the tone for the entire event. A rip-roaring Western party has a quite different mood from a formal dinner. Live entertainment at cocktail receptions is always effective. Be sure it matches the mood of the event, is not overbearing, and is easy to talk over. If recorded background music is used, it needs to be constantly monitored to keep the level correct. As more people join the event, the conversation level dictates the music level so conversation can be heard.

✓ Plan for enough bars and bartenders. One bar with a bartender for every fifty to seventy-five guests is typical, but this varies depending on guest arrival and other factors. For example, if everyone arrives at the same time, perhaps from a preceding function, more bars are necessary (to eliminate long waits). Blender drinks, such as frozen margaritas, require more bartenders—one for every forty guests (and an adequate number of blender machines).

🖊 **Tips on planning a cocktail party:**

✓ In a typical two- to three-hour cocktail party there is a central forty-five minutes, usually in the second hour, when the greatest number of guests will be present. This is not the case if there is featured entertainment or presentation that keeps the audience or if a dinner follows.

✓ Pick the right location. Look around the venue. Rather than a hotel function room it may be more appropriate and fun if it is poolside, on the beach, or in a barn, a factory, or a sales room. Select a space the right size. If the site is too small, it will be too crowded or may not hold all of the guests. If it is too large, guests will feel lost or get the impression that a lot of invited guests did not care to show up.

✓ Plan approximately 5 square feet (0.5 square meters) per person, including food and bar areas. If chairs, tables, dancing, and entertainment are planned, more space is necessary. (Always check the legal *occupancy rating*.)

✓ Budget and book enough time in the room or space for adequate setup and *strike*. Consider items that may take more time, such as extensive decorations, theatrical lighting, and entertainment (including *sound checks*).

✓ Consider other particulars of the site. Is the ceiling high enough? Low ceilings depress the crowd. Is the floor surface appropriate? Dirt or stone may not be appropriate for high-heeled shoes. Carpeting will inhibit dancing. Is there space for fireworks, or other special show or program elements?

✓ Cocktail parties (as opposed to receptions) require more food and liquor because people will stay longer. If a buffet is planned, regardless of which type of buffet, be sure to have tables and chairs for eating. If it is the type of party where people will arrive and leave at different times, fewer tables are necessary. In either case the tables need adequate busing staff to keep them clear.

✓ Plan for enough bars and bartenders. One bar with a bartender for every fifty to seventy-five guests is typical, but this varies depending on guest arrival and other functions. For example, if everyone arrives at the same time, perhaps from a preceding function, more bars are necessary (to eliminate long waits). Blender drinks, such as frozen margaritas, require more bartenders—one for every forty guests (and an adequate number of blender machines).

✓ If timing is important, perhaps because there is a presentation, state the starting time half an hour earlier on the invitation. If there is a function for the same guests immediately beforehand, than most likely all will be present from the onset.

✓ Carefully select the food to be served. Be clever with food choices and presentation so that they enhance the theme or mood of the event. Never run out of food. If a cocktail party is during dinner hours, and a full meal is not included, plan on a much higher consumption of hors d'oeuvre since guests will be hungry when they arrive and some will "make a meal" of what is served.

📖 **For food quantities, see "Tables and Techniques" (page 349).**

✓ Having a bartender at smaller parties not only controls the amount of liquor poured per drink, it also takes the burden off the hosts to watch for those overdrinking. The bartender can alert the host when there is a problem. Some hosts hold the guests' car keys and then have a fun (but serious) sobriety test before returning them.

✓ Have a plan for empty glasses and dishes, either with trays adequately placed around the space or waiters who collect the empty *glassware* and dishes.

✓ Decide on the types of drinks to be served, including whether the alcoholic beverages are standard or *brand*, and determine the proper quantities. The popularity of brands always changes, so if brands are important for image, know what is currently popular. Clever choices may enhance the mood or theme, such as mai tais at a luau or eggnog at Christmas, but may not satisfy the drink tastes of many of the guests, so options should be included. If a specialty drink is planned, ensure at least one glass per person since everyone will want to try it.

📋 See "Tables and Techniques" (page 308) for information on quantities and types.

✓ Always include sparkling water, mineral water, and sodas as an alternative to alcoholic beverages.

✓ Select music appropriate to the mood and theme of the event, be it live entertainment or merely background music.

✓ Ensure that the music is at the right level for the mood. Music too low will not make an effect. Music too loud will interfere with conversation. The volume of music needs adjusting as the crowd grows or shrinks in size.

✓ Set the light level. Lighting plays a big part in setting a mood. Use candles, tiki torches, strings of Christmas lights, or theatrical lighting for added effect.

✓ Plan the site for traffic flow. If the bars are too close to the entrance doors, congestion will occur as the guests fill only this half of the room, making it difficult for others to enter.

📋 See cocktail party room layouts in "Tables and Techniques" (page 424).

🖊 Tips on serving drinks:

✓ To make glassware really sparkle, wash in warm water, dry with a towel, and polish with a fresh dry towel.

✓ Use the appropriate glassware for different styles of drinks.

✓ Never insist that a guest take a drink.

✓ If the cocktail recipe says stir . . . don't shake. If it says shake . . . don't stir.

 ✓ To prevent a bottle from dripping, rub the lip with a waxed paper before pouring.

✓ When adding an olive or other garnishes to a drink, always pierce them with a toothpick. Use maraschino cherries with stems. Your guests will appreciate the convenience. Squeezable wedges, such as limes, should be cut prior to the event.

✓ Never reuse ice cubes when refreshing a drink. Use hard frozen ice.

✓ Hire a bartender. The cost is always worth it.

✓ Figure two to three glasses per person.

✓ Have a place for guests to place used glasses.

✓ If there is a special friend or VIP attending who has a strong preference for a certain cocktail, provide it.

✓ Check liability insurance. The host can be legally liable for an incident of drunkenness or an accident. Policies can be purchased for one-time events.

📑 **See beverage guides in "Tables and Techniques" (page 303).**

✏️ **Warning:** The laws regarding drunk driving have toughened in recent years and often the host can be held responsible. Limiting alcohol consumption is an important responsibility of the host.

Cocktail receptions can be used effectively for warming up the crowd before the main event. I once used a professional pickpocket to "work" the room. Those who had been pickpocketed (with their wallets returned, of course) then enjoyed watching him with other unsuspecting guests. All were in good spirits as they entered for the dinner. After the dinner speaker completed his remarks, the pickpocket came onto the dais and returned the unknowing speaker's wallet, then his watch, the host's watch, and finally the speaker's wallet a second time! It nicely "bookended" the event.

collateral material In marketing and sales, this is the collection of brochures, pictures, product sheets, visual aids, etc., used to support the sales efforts. It differs from advertising because it is used later in the sales cycle and is often distributed by hand.

 For *exhibits* and sales meetings, ship this heavy material to the location ahead of time.

color Various hues of the light spectrum as reflected by different materials and perceived by the human eye and brain. Various names, such as red or yellow, define each hue. Mixing paint pigments of any other colors cannot create the **primary colors** of red, yellow, and blue. All other colors (except white) are **secondary colors** and can be produced by mixing various combinations of the three primary colors. **Complementary colors** are those opposite each other on a *color wheel*, such as red and green. **Tertiary colors** are those created by mixing one primary color and one secondary color. Mixing equal amounts of the three primary colors creates black. White is the absence of any color and cannot be created by mixing pigments.

Mixing **light colors**, such as for a theatrical performance, is different from mixing paint pigments. In light, the primary colors are red, green, and blue. Adding two or more of these colors in various intensities creates all the other colors. Equal combinations of these primary colors creates white, while their absence is black. Video projectors, screens, and other electronic devices also utilize this additive method of mixing light to create various colors. Also see *color wheel* and *Pantone Color System (PCS)*.

✏ **Typically more important in shows and events is the psychological impact on the audience of the various colors. Some examples:**

✓ Pink is female and blue is male.

✓ Green is nature and blue is the sea.

✓ Warm-feeling colors are in the red part of the spectrum while cool colors are in the blue. But this can be even more subtle:

> Warm red is primary red with some yellow.
> Cool red is primary red with some blue.
> Warm blue is primary blue with some red.
> Cool blue is primary blue with yellow.

color guard In the United States and other countries, a team of military personnel carrying the national flag (referred to as the **colors**) and other flags as appropriate, typically a unit flag and department flag (for example, a navy flag). A **joint service color guard** carries the flags of all departments of the military (navy, marines, army, air force, coast guard). On each side of the flag carriers is a military person carrying a rifle. The color guard consists of enlisted personnel commanded by a senior sergeant who carries the national colors (sometimes referred to as **Color Sergeant**) and gives the commands. The formality of the uniform is determined by the occasion and the commander. Certain color guards can be horse-mounted. A color guard is a living reminder of the terrible toll of war and deserves every respect.

📖 See flag protocol in "Tables and Techniques" (page 340).

color medium A colored transparent material placed in front of lighting instruments to change the light from white to a color. The material can be glass, gelatin, cinemoid, or a number of other materials. Also see *gel*.

color pools Multiple circles of light of different colors created over a defined area. This is often done over the audience to create an atmosphere. It is also used over the audience when the audience is being televised as part of the video presentation, for example, of a concert performance.

color wash Splashing colored light of different hues over a given area or group of performers. The *focus* of the lights is nonspecific. Often the colors constantly change both in hue and intensity.

color wheel A device used in lighting to make color changes to the scene. In traditional equipment this is a large flat metal wheel with different color media mounted in a number of openings around a circle. In modern automated lights, this is a small wheel contained within the lighting instrument with several slots for placing different color modules, which can be called up by the electronic controller. A **color wheel** or **color circle** illustrates color hues around a circle and the relationships between primary colors, secondary colors, and complementary colors. Also see *color*.

 See color wheel in "Tables and Techniques" (page 358).

column inch A unit of measure in the print media equaling the width of their standard columns wide by one inch high. If it is for the placement of advertising, this is one of the units used to determine the price. Other units may include the location on the page.

comp Short for **complimentary**, it is anything received for free or for no additional cost. Often comps come with certain conditions, attachments, or hidden charges, so when discussing comps with hotels, equipment suppliers, and other vendors, keep in mind the old adage: There is no such thing as a free lunch.

compact disc or **CD**   A digital medium recording and storage device formed of a 12-centimeter polycarbonate substrate, a reflective metalized layer, and a protective lacquer coating.

C

composer   A person who creates original works, whether music, scripts, photographs, or anything else that is arranged in order to achieve an effect.

composite photo   A picture that has been altered to include several different visual elements, such as the image of a person and a company logo. This is typically accomplished with a computer program and is often used to create a press photo that conveys a specific message.

composition   The way various elements, especially those of a visual image, are combined to make a whole. The elements of composition include form, structure, or design of the group. Each is enhanced by emphasis, stability, sequence, and balance. Whether it is a photo, a flower arrangement, or individuals on a stage, one uses body position, areas, planes, levels, space, repetition, and focus to create the most interesting composition.

compote   A dessert of pieces of fruit in a seasoned sugar syrup. Originating in France in the seventeenth century, there are unlimited recipes with different fruits, some containing alcohol. A dried fruit compote is a popular Passover food. Also, a bowl with a long stem used for serving fruits, nuts, or candy.

concessionaire   A person or company given permission to operate a business or sell a product at a specified location within an event. Typically this permission is granted after an agreement is made for certain fees and operating conditions conducive to improving the event. Often events have various levels of concessionaires distinguished by the amount of space occupied, signage, location within the event, and type of business or product.

concierge   In hotels and resorts, a person who assists the guests with restaurant reservations, recommended nightlife hot spots, transportation (taxi, limousine, boats), spa services, tourist sites, and many other types of helpful information. Many of these professional concierges belong to the association called "Les Clefs d'Or" (The Golden Keys), founded in France in 1929, and wear a golden keys insignia on their lapels. Originally concierges were employees of an apartment building, and while living in a small ground-floor apartment they oversaw comings and goings, provided security, accepted packages and mail, and kept the keys to the tenants' apartments. The term evolved from the French "Comte des Cierges" (Keeper of the Candles), rcfcrring to those who attended nobles in their castles during the medieval era.

condotel Hotels and resorts that are made up of individually owned condominiums offered to convention and meeting groups as hotel rooms. The advantage over typical hotels is the size of the rooms, which are often larger with kitchens, multiple bedrooms, etc., making the rooms great for long stays and providing flexibility in the types of rooms that can be offered to attendees. Disadvantages are that they are individually owned and not always furnished to the same quality level, and they may not provide the most recent communication technology.

conductor In music the conductor is in charge of the performance of the orchestra and choir. The conductor selects the music and how it is to be artistically interpreted. An **orchestra manager** handles the business affairs, schedule, and operation of the orchestra and its members. Also, a conductor can refer to a wire suitable for carrying electrical current.

conduit A metal or plastic pipe in which wire is placed to distribute electricity from one area to another. Often this is required as a safety measure to prevent the possibility of the wire being damaged accidentally, which could create a dangerous situation.

conference A meeting of people with a common interest to discuss serious business or policy, or to share new ideas or research. Typically these meetings last for a day or more and include speakers, discussions, dinners, entertainment, and other activities.

conference center A facility, usually all-inclusive with living quarters, meeting rooms, food service facilities, and recreational activities, that caters to large groups for the purpose of having lectures and discussions. Quite often these facilities are located in remote areas to limit the distractions to those attending.

confetti Traditionally small pieces of dried flowers or petals thrown over people at festive events, but today more typically it is colored paper, Mylar, or another material that can be cut into small pieces, streamers, or various interesting shapes and shot over the audience by **confetti cannons** to create an exciting and colorful effect. The confetti cannons utilize compressed air or gas to give the confetti great height and volume when released. These cannons range in size from small handheld units to large single-release or continuous-flow units with various sizes of holding chambers. Old-fashioned paper confetti has been replaced with very lightweight paper, cut in various sizes that flutters in the air and takes its time falling. **Confetti streamers** are small rolls of paper that unfurl, creating ribbons of color in the air. These also can be shot from cannons.

 Warning: Some venues ban confetti because of the cleanup required. It also ends up in chandeliers and air soffits. In these situations, propose streamers, which are much easier to clean up. Often the audience will wrap the streamers around their shoulders and carry them away, requiring little or no special cleanup. Also be warned that confetti sprinkled on tablecloths can stain the fabric if it gets wet. Sometimes the caterer or rental company will charge for stained clothes.

connector A device that allows two cables to be put together for added length. There are a variety of different connectors available for specific uses such as audio, *lighting*, and *power* cables.

contingency An amount added to an estimate to allow for unexpected changes that may occur. It is common and practical in first-draft budgets to indicate this amount at 10–15 percent of total budget, and then reduce it as the budget is revised. Carrying a contingency that is too high may have an adverse effect on the event because too much is held in reserve.

contour covers Decorative stretch fabric designed to encase tables, chairs, flower stands, portable bars, and other banquet furnishings with color. Because the fabric is stretched to enclose the legs as well as the tops, the result of the pulled fabric is a curved, contemporary, flowing look. Many different manufacturers create these covers and add bows, ties, and other decorations to alter and enhance the look even further.

contour curtain A horizontally pleated curtain that is gathered upward from a variety of pickup points along the bottom edge to form a variety of scallops, often some larger than others, as it rises. Also see *main curtain*.

contract An agreement between two or more parties involved in a specific transaction. It can be nonwritten, but written is always better.

contract documents The forms, general and specific conditions, drawings, specifications, and addenda describing the terms and conditions of a specific binding agreement between two or more parties.

contrast The term for describing the difference in visual brightness (tone) between one part of an image and another. Normal contrast images exhibit a wide range of brightness values.

controller A person or device, either electrical or mechanical, that controls an operation, such as a theatrical lighting technician and the control board for creating lighting effects. Controllers are also used extensively onstage for rigging systems, sound systems, and stage mechanics such as turntables and lifts. A person managing, supervising, and monitoring a budget is also referred to as a controller.

convention   The gathering of people of a particular profession or common interest who meet at the same time in a designated location. **Trade conventions** focus on a particular industry or segment of an industry. **Professional conventions** focus on the concerns and advancements of a profession. **Fan conventions** are based on pop culture, including celebrities, movies, science fiction, etc. Conventions typically include meetings, seminars, training sessions, demonstrations, award ceremonies, dinners, entertainment, an *exhibition*, and a variety of other events and activities over multiple days, often for thousands of attendees. Also see *trade show*.

convention center   A large public building in an urban center designed to accommodate thousands of people for the purpose of meetings, exhibitions, concerts, dances, and other social and trade events, including *conventions*. Many such centers may be combined and include an *exhibition* hall, theater, arena, hotel complex, and numerous meeting and banquet rooms of various sizes. They also contain food service facilities, business centers, tour and information centers, equipment rental facilities, truck docks for *drayage*, and multiple parking structures. Often these centers will have multiple events happening at the same time.

🖉 Tips for selecting a convention center for an event:

✓ Ask for references of groups similar to yours in size and nature.

✓ Ask for a sample contract.

✓ Check the number and quality of hotels within walking distance.

✓ Check the distance to the main airport.

✓ What other groups will be at the center at the same time of the event?

✓ Will any construction or renovations be taking place at the time of the event?

✓ What is the hookup system for phones, computers, Wi-Fi, etc., for exhibitors?

✓ What company is furnishing the *pipe and drape* and what are their prices?

✓ Are there guidelines or restrictions on using outside vendors?

✓ How much time is included for setup and strike, and will lights, heating, and air conditioning be available?

✓ What show-management offices are available and what are the costs?

✓ If the show draws more than anticipated, is additional space available?

✓ What is the attendance history of previous exhibitions?

✓ What is the rate for exhibition space and the minimum daily rental?

✓ What is the load-in access? If by elevators, what are their size and weight capacity?

✓ Where do trucks, buses, and other large vehicles park?

copy Written text, typically in the form of a script, words for an advertising or public relations campaign, signage, display materials, etc. Or, an identical version, on paper, CD, or whatever medium of some production element, such as a *script*, photograph, *press release*, *cue sheet*, or the lighting cues.

corkage fee A per-bottle charge by many venues in return for the opportunity to bring in wine or champagne should they not have the preferred selection available or because their pricing is too expensive. Be careful: sometimes this fee will make the overall cost of the wine higher than if the venue finds the same wine and provides it.

corner block Quarter-inch-thick plywood triangles fastened to the back corners of scenery flats to hold the rails, stiles, and toggles together.

📋 See flat construction in "Tables and Techniques" (page 449).

corporate policy Many corporations have strict policies, some written, others not, that need to be considered for their events. Also referred to as the company's **corporate culture**.

✏️ Tips for corporate policy awareness:

✓ Determine the number of drinks per person the company considers appropriate.

✓ Many companies prefer having only *brand* drinks served versus *well drinks*.

✓ Determine the company's dress codes.

> *One major company I worked with required dark suits with white shirts for all employees, male or female, including the non-company event staff.*

✓ Avoid off-color humor.

✓ Determine the company's preferred formality of address.

> *Walt Disney insisted that there were only two Misters in his company—Mr. Toad (from* Wind in the Willows*) and Mr. Smee (from* Peter Pan*). Everyone else was to be addressed by their first names.*

✓ Ask if smoking is permitted in designated areas, and also ask about the policy on cigars, electronic cigarettes, and pipes. (Note that ashtrays on tables can be offensive to many people.)

✓ The type of music selected, even just *background music*, should be reviewed with the company for its appropriateness.

✓ Know the company's position on politics and whether or not it should in any way be a part of the event.

corporate show A genre of productions staged by companies, often to introduce new products and to energize internal sales staffs and associates such as wholesalers, dealers of their products, and other industry officials. Also called an **industrial**, they range from rather simple productions with a few speeches and visuals to very extravagant multifaceted and multi-day shows.

costume Clothes, accessories, and hairstyle characteristic of a period of time, a country, or an ethnic group. Garments along with mask, prosthetics, or other elements are designed to make someone, like an actor, look like something else, such as a monster, soldier, or cartoon character. A **costumer** is the crew person skilled in making and caring for costumes, while a **costume designer** creates the look and specifies the fabric of costumes.

counterweight Traditionally, canvas bags filled with sand or lead pellets, or lead weights that fit onto a holding bracket to balance the weight of a curtain or scenic piece on a stage and allow the stagehand to move it up or down easily and quickly. Also see *rigging* and *fly loft* and *sandbag*.

cover shot See *long shot*.

crane For cameras, counterweighted arms of various sizes affixed to a rolling hydraulic mount that allows the camera to swing and move smoothly. Some cranes are large enough to hold both the camera and cameraman.

crating The packaging required to move bulky show materials from one location to another. Often crates are made of wood lined with a protective material and providing points for forklifts. Show and exhibit materials typically require multiple movements by the time the materials are picked up, transported, and delivered to the show site.

crawl A list of individuals' names at the end of a motion picture, television show, or other presentation that move by on the screen, usually upward, enabling many more names to be presented then would fit on a single frame.

credits A list of individuals who participated in the creation, design, and production of a project, be it a theatrical, film, or television show; a meeting; or any other particular endeavor. Typically this list of names also includes that person's position or contribution to the project. In every industry there is an established order in which certain positions are considered more important than others and are listed first, or in larger print, or with a space before and after them. Many entertainment unions have strict rules on how credits should be given to their members. In the military, generals are listed before corporals. In corporations, presidents are listed before vice presidents. It is extremely important to understand these regulations, customs, and subtleties before presenting a list of credits.

crew briefing The meeting attended by all members of the crew just prior to the final rehearsals of a presentation to ensure that everyone understands the production and each person's responsibility, and to ensure that all production elements are assigned to a responsible member of the crew.

critical area The prime area of graphics or other visual media where the most important part of the message is placed for maximum impact. On television, due to broadcast standards, the edges of the screen lose detail and sometimes eliminate some information, making it important for vital information to be placed well within the frame.

critical path A chronological sequence of tasks that must be completed on time to meet the schedule deadlines.

critique A staff review of the event to note and rate the various elements as to their success, acceptance, and enjoyment by those attending. Also see *review*.

crop Framing the camera so that it excludes part of the view. Or when working with a photograph, selecting a certain portion of the total photo. Cropping often enhances the impact of the photo by eliminating unnecessary background and brings the subject closer, or makes a key part of the image larger.

cross fade A transition in which a dominant source is being reduced while at the same time a second source is becoming dominant. A cross fade can be between two camera shots, two sources of music, two lighting cues, etc.

cross section See *section*.

crowd control The safety and enjoyment of the attendees at an event, regardless of its size or type, depends greatly on the management and control of the crowd. Two important elements to consider are **audience profile** and **crowd dynamics**. The first is the easier of the two because the audience expected depends on the type of event, the performers, and other activities scheduled to be part of the event. The event organizers should know the age group, whether it is families or not, the amount of alcohol consumption expected, and the chance of problems such as drug use. The second, crowd dynamics, is more difficult in that things can happen at events that are unexpected. Therefore, careful planning is needed on the chance that dynamics develop that could become very troublesome. Simple things, such as lack of proper restrooms, excessive heat, lack of water, picketing, fighting, and natural events such as fire or an earthquake can be devastating to an event. Consequently, such issues as the placement and size of entrances and exits, aisle width, signage, emergency lighting, security personnel, EMT personnel, and a PA system for communication to the crowd are extremely important.

🖉 **The key to a safe event is careful planning for the enjoyment of the audience and for emergencies. Planning should be done in conjunction with the venue management and local police and fire departments. Brief all staff and those involved in the operation of the event in the following:**

✓ All exits from the venue and routes of emergency evacuation.

✓ Location of fire extinguishers, hoses, etc.

✓ To whom and how to report an incident they witness.

✓ Procedure for contacting the security team and/or police.

✓ Location of medical personnel.

✓ To whom to report a physical problem such as a toilet overflowing.

✓ How to report suspected troublemakers and what actions not to take.

✓ Understanding individual duties in case of an emergency.

✓ Familiarity with the overall site.

✓ Understanding the possible consequences if their messages are misunderstood.

✓ Have a book of emergency announcements already prepared that have been well thought out to avoid panic and be accurate in the directions given.

✓ Have a public address system that is tested and an understanding of who can use it.

✓ Have an understanding with those selling alcoholic beverages as to who can give an order to stop the sale of beverages.

✓ Have instructions for each operation person and vendors as to how they would participate in an emergency.

✓ Post emergency phone numbers in key locations.

✓ All must provide an after-event record of problems, concerns, or emergency happenings.

crowd pleaser Any element of the event that has been proven successful and well accepted by the audience. An example is *fireworks* after the dinner. The benefit of crowd pleasers is that they work and are safe. The danger of using crowd pleasers is that many of them have been seen and done before, many times, and they are not new and unique. Strive to create a new crowd pleaser.

crowd warmer A person whose job it is to "warm up" the audience or get them excited prior to the main performance. The technique is used in many ways in different types of shows, from the performing clown opening a Cirque du Soleil performance, a lesser known act before the main act at a concert, to an off-camera **warmer** for the live audience at a television show.

crow's-feet A set of bent steel tubing that is inserted inside a tubular pole to create a base to stand the pole upright.

CSEP Abbreviation for Certified Special Events Professional. The hallmark of professional achievement in the special events industry, this designation recognizes event professionals who have successfully demonstrated the knowledge, skills, and ability essential to perform all functions required in a special event. This designation has been awarded since 1993 by the International Special Events Society. Also see *ISES*.

cue   Any word, speech, move, sound, or light signal that executes action at a particular moment in a show, play, or presentation. For example, the signal can be a technical change, such as a light coming on, or a change of action, such as an actor's entrance onto the stage, a speaker beginning to speak, or the start of music. Every actual cue should be preceded by a warning cue. The shorthand abbreviation to mark a cue in a script is "Q" often followed by its sequential number, such as "Q23."

cue card   A card containing script information placed so that the actor or speaker can see it but the audience cannot. Also known as an "idiot card." See *teleprompter.*

cue sheet   A list of *cues* indicating when an action is to happen and by whom or by what. Often cues are written as notations on a script or musical score to indicate what is to happen at each point. The cue notation can specify not only the action, but also the speed, such as "slow light fade out"; direction, such as "actor moves stage right"; or simply a number, such as "Q23," that has predetermined meaning for each member of the crew and cast.

cuisine   A particular style or range of cooking typical of a restaurant, country, region of a country, or ethnic group. Generally speaking, the style of cuisine is matched to the theme of the event. **Haute cuisine** is high-quality, classic French cooking.

curtain   Any hanging drapery that conceals elements of the production or adds visual effect to the design of the scenery.

curtain call   When individuals at the end of their performance return to the stage to be recognized by the audience with applause. This is typical with musicians, actors, orchestra leaders, and even athletes at the end of a big game. Often performers will make more than one curtain call for an outstanding performance, and will continue to come back onstage as long as the audience continues to applaud.

Reportedly, Luciano Pavarotti holds the record with 165 curtain calls. In motion pictures when end credits are over, individual scenes, out-takes, or close-ups of the actors with their name captioned are referred to as a curtain call.

curtain line The location at which the *act curtain* strikes the stage floor when lowered or slides along the stage floor when drawn.

cut A command to stop all action, speech, and cues. The hand signal for this cue is to run a pointed finger across the neck as if cutting one's throat. In printing, it is a metal engraving mounted on a wooden block used for the reproduction of drawings or photographs.

cutout A piece of flat scenery having an irregular outside edge such as a tree or fence.

CVB Abbreviation for Convention and Visitor's Bureau. Each city, state, resort area, etc., has an organization of this type to promote the assets of the city in an attempt to bring conferences, *conventions*, and events of all types to the area. Usually the local hotels and attractions are supporting members. Usually these organizations are supported by hotel room taxes.

cyclorama or **cyc** A very large backing to the scenery or performance area that can be lighted to create different effects, such as the illusion of an endless sky. Typically it is seamless and all white, but it can also be all blue and used for *blue screen* effects. A hard cyc is made of solid material and is coved in shape. Often cycs will have a low matching *ground row* a few feet *downstage* so that *strip lights* or cyc lights can be placed between for added visual effect.

dais A raised platform located at the end of a large room upon which speakers and other dignitaries are placed and from which they speak to those assembled. The head table sits on the dais. Also see *head table*.

📖 **Various diagrams are shown in "Tables and Techniques" (page 426).**

dance A type of performance art that focuses on body movement, including ballet, folk, and other interpretive forms. Also an activity that many enjoy participating in at parties and events, including ballroom, hip-hop, country, disco, and line dancing. Many ethnic groups have their own favorite styles of dancing that must be a part of their function. At weddings, the **first dance** is traditional. The customary sequence is that the bridal couple starts it together. After a few turns around the floor, the bride's father takes over with the bride, while the groom dances with the bride's mother. Next the bride dances with her new father-in-law and the groom with his mother. The bride then dances briefly with the best man and ushers while the groom dances with the maid of honor and then the bridesmaids as all others join the dance floor. In some cultures the bride continues to dance with all the men present and each places money onto her gown. Also see *choreographer*.

dance floors Dancing at events such as dinners, weddings, and other celebrations is extremely popular and should be accommodated with a good surface upon which to dance. The best dance surface is a hardwood floor. Since new construction rarely features wooden floors, portable dance floors can be ordered and placed according to the room layout for the event. These portable dance floors usually consist of 3- or 4-square-foot (.278 or .372 square meter) wood-surfaced panels that lock together to make any size and can be placed on carpeting, concrete, or other floor surfaces indoors or out. They are lightweight, waterproof, and available in different styles, including raised surfaces with disco-style lighting built in. Always check the floors once installed to ensure the sections are locked solidly together with no open seams or protruding edges and that the edges are beveled smoothly to the carpeting or floor below. Failure to provide a good dance surface is both discourteous and dangerous to those guests who are dancing.

 If the event includes a dance performance, it is important to determine the construction of the existing floor and to discuss this with the management of the dance company. Professional dance troupes require an adequate floor and often will not perform without such a floor and certainly will not dance on concrete or other hard surfaces. Many stages are properly built with the wooden surface boards placed over lateral wooden beams. But many stages are not and require portable professional dance surfaces, of which there are a large variety that can be rented. Often, traveling dance troupes carry their own portable floor system.

To calculate how large a portable dance floor is necessary for the guests at a party, consider the following: on average, 40 percent of the guests will dance at the same time. If two hundred people are attending, that 40 percent equals eighty guests. Estimating a tight 3 square feet per person, that's 240 square feet (22.3 square meters). Portable floors come in either 3 × 3-foot (900-centimeter) sections or 4 × 4-foot (1,200-centimeter) sections. Therefore a 15 × 15-foot floor (225 square feet [20.9 square meters]) composed of 14 sections of 4 × 4-foot (1,200-centimeter) units, or 25 sections of 3 × 3-foot (900-centimeter) units, is barely adequate.

dancing waters Both a brand name and the most often used generic name for shows created with the combination of moving water, theatrical lighting, and music. The technique of choreographing multiple

D

jets spraying water in different patterns to music originated in Romania about 1820 and has been revised and modernized since then. One of the finest examples is the fountain in front of the Bellagio in Las Vegas.

dark The period of time when a show or function is not open to an audience.

DAT Digital Audio Tape.

dazzle To amaze the audience with a wonderful spectacle or display.

DC See *direct current*.

dead Scenery, props, and other items that are of no further use in a performance or event.

dead hung When lights, battens, or other equipment or scenic elements are hung in such a way that they cannot move up and down easily.

death march In very large events, it is the affectionate term for the dreaded walk-through by the entire staff to personally review the status of all elements. By spotting problems, and having all staff members present, there is no passing the responsibility or someone not getting the e-mail. Often these are scheduled at several critical junctures of the event production.

decibel or **dB** Commonly used in acoustics to quantify sound levels in reference to a level of 0 dB, which is the typical threshold of perception of the human ear, or in simple terms, the weakest sound heard. Extremely high decibel levels of 125 dB can be painful and very dangerous to the human ear, while other interim levels are necessary for enjoyable listening. Controlling sound levels is an absolute must, both for the enjoyment and safety of the audience. Finding the "magic" level is often a battle at events, be it the volume of a speaker or an orchestra.

Volume levels can be the grounds for audience complaints, reaction, and satisfaction as well as lawsuits. *OSHA* has established legal guidelines for sound levels.

A dB loudness comparison chart is in "Tables and Techniques" (page 359).

A dB loudness comparison chart is in "Tables and Techniques" (page 359).

Every contract with a hired entertainment group, be it an orchestra, a rock group, or even a DJ, must have a clause that gives the event organizer final control of volume levels.

decorator   The crew person responsible to find, gather, and put in place materials to enhance the visual impact or convey the theme of the event. Most often a decorator works under an *art director* or *designer* who specifies the artistic appearance required.

degrees of freedom   Directions or area in which any moving body can move. There are six degrees of freedom, defined as **heave** (up and down), **sway** (side to side), **surge** (forward and backward), **pitch** (front to back rolling motion), **roll** (sideways rolling motion), and **yaw** (rotation around the object).

delay   An audio effect that records an input signal to an audio storage medium and then plays it back, usually almost immediately. This slight echo effect adds interest to a singer's voice or musical sound. In very large audience situations, it also allows those in the back to hear the sound at the same time as those in the front. Also see *Haas effect*.

density   The calculated number of people within a defined area. At a festival or concert site, five hundred to seven hundred people per acre is a comfortable density. Crush is at 1,300 per acre, a time when it is all but impossible to move without constant bumping. Also see *occupancy rating*.

design day   The projected estimate of attendance over the parts of a day, used to calculate sizing of such items as space required, restrooms, food service, drinking water, car parking, service personnel, and emergency services.

designer A creative production team member responsible for the artistic appearance of certain physical elements. Typically a designer provides sketches of their ideas so that those in charge can review and approve them prior to execution. On any event there can be several designers, such as a scenery designer, lighting designer, costume designer, visuals designer, fashion designer, etc. A graphic designer typically lays out advertising materials, menus, signage, and other such visuals.

deuce A two-person table for eating or drinking, such as a café table.

 See various table sizes in "Tables and Techniques" (page 416).

dichroic filter A piece of glass with an optical thin-film coating that transmits certain colors (wavelengths) while reflecting the remaining colors.

diffuser A frosted glass or plastic used behind a large color transparency to distribute the light from bulbs evenly. Typically used in lighted posters and signs.

digital A discrete electronic signal represented by one bit of information.

dim To decrease the intensity of light or sound. As a command it is sometimes used in place of *fade* or fade out. Dim is also a low light setting. **Dim in** is a command to increase the intensity the same as fade in.

dimmer An electrical device used to regulate the current going to lights and change the brightness of light emanating from a fixture by decreasing or increasing *voltage*. The dimmers are controlled by a lighting control console, to *cues* set by the lighting director.

dimmer board A control panel, typically with a memory system that allows the lighting designer to preset light intensity levels throughout the performance or function or to activate the levels "on the fly" as the event happens in real time. The board allows each light or group of lights to be controlled individually depending on the operator's preference. Each controller on the board allows an intensity of one to ten and can add effects such as the lights flashing, chasing, or blacking out all at the same moment.

dinner or **dinner event** An evening meal, sometimes very formal, given in honor of somebody or something. A few common dinner occasions are for weddings, retirements, award presentations, business presentations, birthdays, religious occasions, and benefits. A formal dinner must, as tradition dictates, clearly be very formal, from the initial invitation to the appropriate *black tie* dress style, through the complete execution of a multicourse meal, all the way to the final glass of port with dessert. Informal dinners are every other kind and can be anything from semiformal or near-to-formal to casual. Unlike formal affairs, informal dinners can be extremely different and creative in the type of food served, venue, method of food service, decoration, and every other element of the event. Also referred to as a *banquet*, a dinner differs from a *buffet* or *buffet dinner* in that the entire meal is served at the table by waiters.

🖉 **Tips on planning a dinner:**

✓ Plan, plan, plan. A well-executed, successful dinner requires extensive planning.

✓ First determine your budget. Dinners can be extremely expensive. A well-planned reception is better than a poorly executed dinner.

✓ Determine the type of dinner, formal or informal. Consider what best meets the purpose of the dinner, the dynamics of the guests invited, the capabilities and opportunities of the *venue*, and the presentations that may be required.

✓ Decide on the serving style early on. Determine if it is to be a sit-down buffet, a standing buffet, a sit-down dinner with waiter service, or a family-style dinner.

✓ For sit-down dinners, with proper staffing, plan thirty to forty minutes per course to serve, eat, and clear. In America, a three-course meal usually takes 1.5 hours from appetizer to dessert and coffee. This pace can be relaxed somewhat to make the event more leisurely. Typically other cultures take longer. A formal dinner can take much longer.

✓ Plan an interesting *menu*. Not just the ordinary.

✓ Whether your dinner is at a professional venue like a hotel or at home, check your liability insurance. The host can be legally liable for an incident of food poisoning or accident. Policies can be purchased for one-time events.

📖 **For helpful information on dinner planning, including linens, place settings, food quantities, etc., see "Tables and Techniques" (pages 344, 380, and 397).**

dinner plate The main course plate, typically 10–12 inches (25.4–30.5 centimeters) in diameter. Traditionally these plates are round, but a variety of shapes are now available to enhance the *place setting*. A **buffet plate** used for dinner tends to be larger at 11–14 inches (28–33.5 centimeters).

diorama Three-dimensional full-size scenes of exquisite detail designed to re-create moments in time or places such as historical happenings, folk life, or animal habitats, typically found in museums, theme parks, and other venues. Often they use a modified scale of objects, painting techniques, and other illusions to enhance the depth perception. Dioramas can also be in model form. They were invented by Louis Daguerre and Charles-Marie Bouton. The **Daguerre dioramas** were a popular entertainment form that originated in Paris in 1822, requiring a very specialized theater. Carl Akeley is credited with creating the first full-size diorama in 1889. Also see *panorama*.

direct cost Cost that can be directly attributed to a particular item of work or service. See *budget*.

direct current or **DC** A form of electrical current that constantly flows in one direction, from positive to negative poles, processing a voltage of constant polarity. It is typical of batteries where there are positive and negative terminals and in most low-voltage applications for consumer electronics. It is the original type of electricity developed by Thomas Edison in the late nineteenth century, but he lost the battle to *alternating current (AC)* for general use. Also see *alternating current (AC)*.

directing/director The member of the creative staff responsible for providing the overall leadership and artistic value of a performance or event. The director's role varies widely. Some directors are exclusively creative, while others are the head of management and finance. More typically, the director is the person who effectively brings the entire event, or show, and its many pieces together with the supporting help of a business team, creative team, assistants, and support staff.

> 🖊 **Before contracting a director, it is important to determine what is required and to specify the exact duties for which the person will be responsible. A misunderstanding of this key role by either side can be disastrous and expensive.**

disc jockey or **DJ** A person who selects and plays recorded music for an audience on the radio or at an event. At nightclubs and discotheques the DJ often adds their own expertise to the music by adding delay, reverb, and other synthetic audio effects to enhance the sound while mixing lighting effects.

dish paper Used on serving dishes and platters to collect crumbs and spills. Typically oval-shaped and solid (unlike a lace-like *doily*) but often embossed with a pattern.

display A visual arrangement of materials such as flowers, graphic materials, photographs, etc. For example, an exhibit booth display can include a mix of any number of items, including photos, text, backgrounds, videos, and graphics all combined for effective impact on the potential customer walking by. Or, flowers can be displayed in a vase.

display advertising The type of advertising that typically includes text, drawings, photos, or other images all artistically combined for visual effect. Contrast this with classified advertising that is only an arrangement of words.

dissolve A change from one scene to another in which the outgoing and incoming visual images are superimposed or blended together for a discernible period of time as one scene fades out while the other fades in. Also see *cross fade*.

distributable A cost item that is spread over other cost items rather than managed as a separate account. See *budget*.

distribution panel A component of an electrical supply system that divides incoming electricity into various circuits as needed for distribution to various electronic devices. It also provides an on/off switch and a protective fuse or circuit breaker for each circuit.

dock On a stage, the area where odd scenery is stored and often painted. At other locations such as exhibit halls, the raised area trucks can back against for easy unloading of equipment and supplies.

doily or **doyley** Decorative paper for use on plates under food, especially desserts, or other plates, usually in lace patterns. It is available in a wide variety of shapes and sizes and is required in formal food service. Also see *dish paper*.

doing the magic Making the project exciting to the audience.

dolly The movement of the camera across the floor. The camera can dolly in or out. A sideways movement is called a *truck*. A dolly is also the mechanism the camera is mounted on that allows the movement to happen smoothly.

door flat A scenic flat containing an opening into which the door-frame with the door is inserted.

dove release White doves soaring into the sky at a key moment in a ceremony. This has been accomplished effectively at many events, from the Olympic Games opening ceremonies to weddings. It is always a crowd pleaser. Sometimes the dove has thin ribbons attached, creating a colorful trail behind it. The key is to find a bird handler who is well experienced, because often the birds do not want to fly when the cage is opened, so they must be coaxed to leave quickly in order get the dramatic visual effect. Also see *butterfly release.*

One of the more infamous dove releases was at the opening ceremony for the Olympic Games in Seoul, South Korea, in 1988. The birds were released on cue and the hundreds of white doves soared in a beautiful cloud around the stadium. However, many of them paused for a landing on the tall structure that held the cauldron for the Olympic flame. Moments after the release, the cauldron was lighted in an enormous burst of flame. Consequently, many of the doves sitting on the cauldron rim were also lighted, and burning doves went flying in all directions. Everyone watching in the stands and on television saw what happened. One can imagine the big story of the day in the press. I felt sorry for the planner who should have anticipated the problem.

down and under (or out) An audio cue to lower the level of the music under the dialogue or vice versa. Or, it may be taken all the way out.

down center (DC) The area of the stage closest to the audience and in the center of the stage. It is the ideal area to use for fights and crisis scenes. Also see *stage areas* and *stage mood*.

 See stage directional chart in "Tables and Techniques" (page 447).

down left (DL) The area of the stage closest to the audience on the right side of the stage as viewed by the audience. It is the ideal area to use for scenes of conspiracy and hard business matters. Also see *stage areas* and *stage mood*.

downlight The light emanating from theatrical instruments directly above the stage area that strikes the performers on the tops of their heads or the top surface of scenic elements. These lights are often used for a special visual effect.

down right (DR) The area of the stage closest to the audience on the left side of the stage as viewed by the audience. It is the ideal area to use for intimate love scenes and long narratives. Also see *stage areas* and *stage mood*.

downstage The edge of the stage closest to the audience. Traditional stage floors were raked at an angle from the audience upward. The purpose of this rake was to increase the perspective of the picture created on the stage by scenery and actors. An actor would literally walk down the rake as they moved closer to the audience.

drapes Fabric that is hung on a stage to mask areas or elements not to be viewed by the audience. Also referred to as curtains. A standard stage arrangement has an entire system of drapes, including the main drape or *main curtain*, *tormentors*, *teasers*, *legs*, *tabs*, and *borders*.

The various drape positions are illustrated in "Tables and Techniques" (page 446).

draw curtain The style of curtain that is suspended from a track and opens either in the middle or from one side. Also see *traveler curtain* and *main curtain*.

drayage The carting of an exhibit into and out of the exhibit hall by companies contracted by the exhibit hall management. Additionally these companies will unload the crates arriving on trucks, hold briefly until the scheduled *move-in*, and then cart each exhibit's crates to the appropriate location of the exhibit floor. After the exhibitors crew has emptied the crates and begun the *setup*, the empty crates are removed by the drayage company. After *run of show*, the reverse takes place. The cost for this service can seem outrageous, so always get a quote ahead of time. Portable fold-up exhibits that are carried by one or two individuals are exempt from the drayage rules and costs. Often drayage companies are contracted to handle the entire shipping process of exhibit material, products, and collateral and sales material from point-of-origin to show or exhibition site and back by a mutually selected means of transportation. The goal is to get all the required materials to the site on time and at a reasonable cost. You don't want to be an exhibitor whose materials haven't arrived when the exhibition opens. The least expensive shipping method is usually motor freight, which is either standard trucks, referred to as common carrier, or dedicated moving vans. Truck shipping rates often are based on classification of materials. Exhibits are at a different rate than *collateral material*. Considerable money can be saved by properly identifying your crates by what they contain and specifying such on the labels and bills of lading.

D

✎ **Tips about drayage:**

✓ Plan ahead to avoid costly last-minute "emergency" shipments and extra drayage fees.

✓ Ship it to arrive on the day assigned for the "timed" move-in of the exhibition.

✓ Carry sufficient insurance on loss or damage.

✓ Keep a complete inventory of everything you shipped, including how, when, and by whom, and contact name.

✓ Keep an individual tracking form on each separate shipment.

✓ Be prepared for any necessary minor repairs.

✓ Use distinctive crate and package markings.

✓ Be on site when your material is scheduled for arrival.

✓ Have the return or next location shipping labels on site.

dressing room A space for cast members, musicians, brides, or presenters to prepare themselves before a performance and to change back afterward. This includes changing into costume, applying makeup, fitting wigs, and whatever other preparations are necessary. Also see *quick-change room.*

✎ **Tips on adequate dressing rooms:**

✓ Ensure enough space for the number of people required for the performance and the required equipment.

✓ *Celebrities* and *headliners* will require a private dressing room separate from other members of the cast, with a private toilet, shower, and a couch plus comfy chairs for relaxing. Also see *rider.*

✓ A bride's dressing room can never be too large. Often they are accompanied by an entourage and need space for practicing the "walk" with the dress.

✓ A toilet should be immediately adjacent to the dressing room. Showers are appreciated.

✓ Mirrors and adequate lighting are necessary for applying *makeup*. Ideally the mirrors should have incandescent lights surrounding them to light faces and should be located above a table to hold makeup supplies.

✓ All dressing rooms require a full-length mirror.

✓ Racks need to be available for hanging costumes and the performers' street clothes.

✓ Lockers are necessary for members of the cast to secure personal belongings.

✓ Ongoing shows require an adjacent seamstress room for making repairs to the costumes.

✓ All dressing rooms need to be at locations convenient for the performers' stage entrances without passing through public space.

dress rehearsal The final rehearsal of a performance conducted in *real time* with all *cues*, full crew, and the entire cast in full *costume*. The dress rehearsal is run just a like a performance except that there is no audience present.

drop A large painted canvas hanging from a batten onstage as part of a *set*. If it is the background to a setting, such as a sky drop or woodland drop, it is commonly called a *backdrop*. Drops can be of all types, including onstage and in other environments, such as a frame for a video screen.

drop curtain Fabric that is *rigged* to fall instantly on *cue* to *reveal* with a flair something special, such as a new product. The curtain is suspended by a system of electrical solenoids that can release the curtain at the touch of a button. The older way is to run a tie line through grommets attached to the curtain that are quickly pulled out, allowing the curtain to fall.

drum kit   A collection of drums, cymbals, and other percussion instruments such as tambourines, chimes, cowbells, woodblocks, and drum stands all required by a drummer. Each professional drummer has different requirements for specific equipment and quantity and requires the event organizer to provide the specified list.

drum platform   A *riser* commonly used by bands that is large enough to accommodate the drummer and the *drum kit*. Its purpose is to raise the seated drummer.

Dubonnet   A sweet *aperitif* made from a blend of herbs, wine, and spices including a small amount of quinine. In 1846 Joseph Dubonnet won a competition by the French government to create a drink with quinine for the French Foreign Legionnaires fighting in Africa to reduce malaria among the troops. It is rumored that the Queen of England's favorite drink is 30 percent *gin* and 70 percent Dubonnet with a slice of lemon over ice.

dummy   An artist's rough version of an advertising piece, booklet, etc.

duplication (dupe)   The process of making copies of recorded video and audio information. Also called a dub.

dutchman   A fabric strip usually about 3 inches wide used to cover the crack between two adjoining flats. When masking tape is used for this purpose it is referred to as an **instant dutchman**.

Duvetyne   A soft fabric with a fine nap that is commonly used in display work to cover *backgrounds*, stage structures, and just about anything else. It is relatively inexpensive, available in many colors and widths, and cuts are smooth and do not unravel.

DVD Abbreviation for Digital Versatile Disc, which is an optical disc storage media format. DVDs have a higher storage capacity than **compact discs** (CDs) while having the same dimensions. Prerecorded DVDs, known as DVD-ROMs, are mass-produced using molding machines and can only be read, not written or erased. Blank DVD-R and DVD+R discs can be recorded on once. Rewritable DVDs— DVD-RW, DVD+RW, and DVD-RAM—can be recorded and erased multiple times.

easel A portable stand, typically three-legged, for supporting and displaying a piece of art, sign, drawing pad, dry erase board, or any of a thousand other items. Forget the flimsy wooden types and select a well-made, strong, adjustable easel. Outside, easels need to have a weight suspended between the tripod legs to hold them against wind.

editing, edit, editor In film or video it is the process of placing one scene after or before another, each arranged for storytelling and impact. In print it is the review of a document for accuracy, *syntax*, spelling, and overall content. An editor is the person or persons actually performing these tasks.

effect Something that produces a desired impression or response in the mind of the audience, adding to the realism or theatricality of the presentation. Some typical effects are a rainbow created with lights, a fog filling the air, an explosion, twinkling stars on a backdrop, *water cannons*, and laser animation on water. Sometimes referred to as a **special effect**, these should be used to create a special impact or spectacular moment in the presentation.

effects generator or **effects machine**   A wide variety of mechanisms that create the illusion of rain or snow falling, clouds, rippling water, fire, crashing glass, smoke, or another special *effect*. Also see *fogger*, *laser*, *snow machine*, and *hazer*.

electrician   The member of the stage crew responsible for most things electrical, including power, lighting instruments, and operating the lighting control console.

elephant doors   Large tall doors designed for loading scenery onto a stage from outside of the building. Also see *loading doors*.

elevation or **elevation view**   Scaled drawings of sets, stages, daises, scenery, buildings, and other elements of the production as seen from the audience's point of view. The purpose of this view is to show heights and widths as well as a view of what it will look like when constructed. For example, a drawing of a building front is an elevation. Also see *plan*, *section*, and *scale*.

elevator stage   A section or sections of the stage floor that can be raised and lowered by some mechanical means. In many theaters, the orchestra stage is an elevator, allowing it to be raised to different elevations. Hotel ballrooms sometimes have a section of the floor that can be elevated when necessary to form a stage platform.

eleventh hour   A time that is nearly too late. Many events come together in the eleventh hour simply because they are events and that is the nature of the business. Only proper planning and excellent coordination make the eleventh hour workable and the event a success. The term originates in the Christian Bible in the book of Matthew, referring to workmen being hired late in the day.

embossed or engraved   A type of printing used for invitations. The process involves the letters being etched into a metal plate that is then rolled with ink and wiped off. The ink remains in the etched area of the plate and when pressed to paper leaves a slightly raised letter. Only black ink is considered correct for formal invitations.

See standard embossed font styles in "Tables and Techniques" (page 369).

emergency lights All lights used to light the stage and auditorium as well as exits in case of an emergency. The electrical crew and light board operator should know where the controls are located, test them, and have access to the controls during the performance.

encore A repeat or additional performance based on the strong positive response by the audience to the performance, such as a *standing ovation*. Traditionally at the end of a concert, the spirit of the audience determines if the performer returns for one or more additional songs that were not on the *playlist* for that concert. It is the performer's show of gratitude for the audience's appreciation of the performance. Nowadays, most encores are planned, but unplanned encores still happen. Encore stems from the French word "encore," which means "again."

ensemble A group of dancers, actors, musicians, etc., who perform together with roughly equal contributions from all members.

entertainment Anything that is performed or produced for the enjoyment of an audience. Generally entertainment falls into three categories: **presentation**—such as an actual show, concert, or keynote speaker; **atmosphere**—such as strolling musicians, a background piano player, or a sleight-of-hand magician moving table to table; and **participation**—such as karaoke or team-building activities, where the audience is involved and entertaining themselves as well as others. An event may have just one or all of these types either at the same time or spread throughout the duration of the event.

🖉 **Tips on planning entertainment:**

✓ Select the moments in the overall event when entertainment will add to the guests' experience.

✓ Enhance the event theme with the right type of performers. Hula dancers at a barbecue don't make it, unless it is a Hawaiian barbecue!

✓ Surprise the guests with different entertainment than what they would expect. If the event is annual, and they have had a folk dance ensemble each year, consider another type of entertainment.

✓ Sometimes lots of inexpensive *beer talent* is better than one expensive performer.

✓ Multiply the effect.

✓ Know the entertainment savvy of the audience. A highly experienced audience will want a much higher quality performance.

✓ Plan where the entertainment will be staged or positioned within the venue for maximum effect.

✓ Unless it is strolling atmosphere entertainment, wherever entertainment is positioned, adequate power will be required.

✓ Entertainment is expensive. Be sure to include the cost of the entertainers and all additional expenses related to presenting that entertainment. See *rider.*

✓ Keep the atmosphere going by alternating two or more bands or a band and a DJ. Or alternate with a different style or type of entertainment.

✓ If a certain piece of music is required, make sure the musicians selected can play it or how long it will take to have them prepare it.

📝 **Tips on selecting entertainment:**

✓ Know your target audience and what type of music or performance they enjoy.

✓ Good entertainers book up fast, so place your order well in advance of an event date.

E

✓ Always see a performance of the band, dancers, or whoever is performing before booking it.

✓ Check the quality and appropriateness of the costumes to be worn. Are there extra charges for wearing formal attire?

✓ Some performers take long breaks between *sets*. Often this loses the atmosphere created. Negotiate short breaks or no breaks.

✓ Agents and bookers of entertainment are a great aid, but their fees add to the cost.

✓ Discuss with a band their *repertoire* and your "*playlist*" and "don't play list" before hiring.

✓ Do they have a *gig* before or after, and are they willing to play longer if necessary?

✓ Is it necessary to rent a piano (upright, grand, or baby grand) or do they bring an electric keyboard? Large orchestras may require other rentals, such a *drum kit* or *drum platform*. What other equipment may be required?

✓ If an older well-known group is desired, be sure to check on who the actual current band members are. Oftentimes the band names are sold and no original members are involved.

📝 **Tips on presenting entertainment:**

✓ Control the volume. Have it worked out with the entertainer so you know who has control and which persons on the staff can give volume directions during the performance.

✓ Control the length of the performance. All too often the entertainment goes on much too long. If three musical numbers are agreed to, ask the duration of each number.

✓ Some entertainment, such as bands, have a lot of unsightly equipment. Work with them to keep their setups as visually clean as possible by putting cases and unnecessary equipment away, hiding speaker stacks (which can be done with *flats* covered with speaker cloth), and positioning mixers out of sight.

✓ Enhance entertainment with *scenery*, lighting, and other theatrical elements, including special *effects*.

✓ Consider new ways of presenting entertainment at standard events. Perhaps at a wedding the *vocalist* strolls through the audience with a wireless microphone while singing the bride's favorite love song.

✓ Keep the overall *pacing* of the event in mind, adding stronger entertainment elements after weaker ones and building to the most exciting.

✓ Keep in mind the ol' entertainment axiom: "Have a strong opener and even stronger closer and everything in between will work."

✓ Stipulate no eating, drinking, or smoking by performers while performing.

✓ Stipulate the amount of talking a performer can do between musical numbers, and what can and cannot be said. Having them mention the person or occasion being honored may be a plus.

📖 See entertainment setups in "Tables and Techniques" (pages 428 and 440).

For a snow skiers' event called Winterfest, I organized a collection of winter and alpine entertainment, including German folk dancers, a polka band, Swiss Alpenhorn blowers, cowbell ringers, a yodeler, a John Denver tribute singer, snowman makers, ice carvers, live reindeer, snowball tossing, a tuba quartet, "winter" songs background music, and performing ice skaters. The overall effect was much stronger than the individual parts, and together they created a big impact on the audience throughout the duration of the event.

E

entrance When an actor, performer, or speaker moves out onto the stage or platform.

entrée A dish served as the main part of a meal. In a formal dinner, the light dish served before the main course, often between fish and meat dishes, is also referred to as the entrée.

epilogue A scene that appears after the end of the play.

Equity Another name for *AEA*.

escalation Provision for an increase in the cost of equipment, material, labor, etc., over the cost specified in the *contract* due to price-level changes over time.

escort card A notice handed to guests arriving for a dinner telling them what table they have been assigned to. Typically it is a small card, about 2 × 3 inches, upon which the *table number* is written. The difference between an escort card and a *place card* is that the escort card tells the guest which table while the place card identifies the seat at the table. The cards are distributed at a reception table outside the room. If there is a cocktail reception prior to dinner, some find it more effective to have the reception table in the cocktail area. Placing it outside the cocktail area has three advantages: first, it is hard to be missed by arriving guests; second, often guests get involved in conversation and mingling during cocktails and never get their cards; third, with the cards picked up before entering for cocktails, by midparty the cards remaining indicate no-shows, thus affording the opportunity for the headwaiter to remove extra *place settings* prior to the guests entering the dining room. The cards are taken by the guest so that they can be referred to when searching for the table. Usually about half as many cards are needed as the number of guests because couples receive only one card.

 Place the escort card with the table number written on it inside a small envelope with the guest's name on the envelope. This allows for last-minute seating adjustments by just changing the card in the envelope.

E-stop An emergency stop.

ETCP Abbreviation for Entertainment Technician Certification Program, the association that certifies theatrical *riggers*.

evaluation The process of examining all elements of an event to judge its value, quality, successes, weaknesses, and impact on the attendees. The evaluation should be held immediately after the event with input from the client, staff, and key attendees. All aspects of the event should be discussed and reviewed, including venue, food service and quality, entertainment, duration, busing, parking, program materials, audience reactions, etc. Each item should be listed on an evaluation chart, rated on some scale, and noted with appropriate comments, becoming a valuable document for future events.

event The reason for this book.

Event Safety Guide Originally published as "The Guide to Health, Safety and Welfare at Pop Concerts and Other Similar Events," it was well received and adopted as the standard for planning health and safety at these events. However, this is a British document, and while it is excellent for planning, codes and regulations may be different from those in the United States or other countries. It can be found free online at www.city.ac.uk.safety. Also see *Life Safety Code.*

excitement Something that engages people's attention or emotions in a lively and compelling way. A key element in every event!

✎ **Some elements that can be utilized to create excitement:**

✓ Surprise—something totally unexpected.

✓ Something new—such as a new product or the announcement of a new president.

✓ Celebrity—the appearance of someone famous or very important to the audience.

✓ Audience involvement—participation can be very invigorating.

✓ The unusual or unexpected—totally different from the norm.

✓ Anticipation—the buildup and waiting for something to happen.

exclusive vans Resorted to by the exhibit manager primarily when his company has a prototype or special product and desires to make sure that it will not be viewed by another firm or exhibitor prior to the time it arrives at the exhibition booth. Also, when exhibitors want total control of their materials and want to use as much space in the van as they desire. With exclusive vans there are no other pickups and no stops along the way.

exhibit A visual presentation to be admired by others. For example, art at an *exhibition.* Or, a display of services, products, or skills by individuals or companies at a *trade show.* Trade show exhibits are small to large depending on the space rented and allocated by the exhibition management. Typically the small, basic exhibit spaces are 8–10 feet square and arranged in rows with two spaces back to back and an aisle in front of each. Larger exhibits can take any multiples of these basic spaces and use them together. The spaces that are more sought after are those at the end of the aisle adjoining a cross aisle. Here the two end spaces (and the two behind them) can be effectively used with a larger exhibit that faces three sides, thus attracting more visitor traffic. Regardless of the size of the exhibit, great care should be taken in its design to effectively present what is being offered. Often trade shows are part of a larger event or *convention*.

E

✎ **Tips on getting good exhibit results at a trade show:**

✓ Be sure the exhibition is right for your product. Check to see what kind of buyers will come, who they are, and how many will attend the show.

✓ Select a good location on the exhibition *floor plan*. Be where most of the attendees will be, either because they have to walk past that location repeatedly, or because it is across from a food location or a very popular exhibitor.

✓ Evaluate the space size best suited for the product, display, and impact intended.

✓ Leave the front area open so that passersby can easily come into your space even if it is just 10 × 10 feet.

✓ Have a strong graphic or large video monitor on the back wall to catch the passerby's eye.

✓ Make sure the staff operating the booth are well trained and know the key words to generate further discussion on the product or service being offered.

✓ Notify in advance and invite prospective buyers before the show, specifying the booth number and location.

✓ Buyers walking the floor are often foot-sore and thirsty. If space permits, provide a seating area with simple refreshments. Keep them moving so that others can use the space.

✓ Have the *collateral material* easily available for take-away.

✓ Always make notes on buyers' business cards as to what they need or are interested in for follow-up later.

📖 See layout suggestion for a trade show exhibit in "Tables and Techniques" (page 335).

exhibition   An event that is a public showing or display of a collection of special-interest materials, usually for a limited period of time. Exhibitions can be of trade, art, particular skills, crafts, sports, etc. Sometimes the exhibition is open only to those within the special area of interest or business, and sometimes it is open to the general public. Each can be local, regional, national, or international in scope. Often exhibitions are part of a broader event such as a *convention*. See *expo* and *exhibit*.

📖 Suggestions for a simple exhibition display can be found in "Tables and Techniques" (page 335).

exhibition center   A venue designed and built to effectively conduct large exhibitions of many different types, providing the support necessary, including parking, power distribution, ancillary meeting rooms, and visitor control.

exit   When an actor, performer, or speaker moves off the stage or *platform*.

exit show   A major show held once a night just prior to closing in theme parks and other attractions. Its purpose is twofold: to keep the audience in the venue longer, and to serve as a *finale* to the day, creating a last positive impression.

exit survey Asking the audience exiting an event some predetermined, brief questions about the event, various elements of the event, their opinions, what they liked best and least, whether they would return next year, etc., all for evaluating the success of the project and planning the next one.

expo A large internationally sanctioned exposition, sometimes referred to as a **world's fair** or **universal exposition**. Most are designed to show off the world's latest technology, utilizing experimental architecture, fantastic entertainment, and dramatic exhibits. There are two types of expos, "registered" and "recognized," with the latter being smaller in scope, investment, and duration and not exceeding 25 hectares (61.5 acres) in size. The main attractions are national pavilions presented by participating countries. The largest expos are designed to attract millions of visitors over the predetermined duration of time and to leave behind something permanent as a lasting remembrance, or icon, of the event. For example, the Eiffel Tower was built as the entrance arch for the Exposition Universelle of 1889 celebrating the centennial of the French Revolution. For the World's Columbian Exposition (World's Fair) in Chicago in 1893 it was the first Ferris wheel (even though it wasn't officially part of the Fair). See *exhibition*.

exposition A large *exhibition* or *expo*.

exposure The total amount of light allowed to fall onto the photographic medium, be it film or image sensor. It is measured in lux-seconds. The camera's shutter controls the amount of light through an adjustable combination of time, **shutter speed**, and size of the opening, the **aperture**. **Multiple exposure** involves a series of brief exposures.

exterior The outdoors, or a scene or setting that represents the outdoors.

extravaganza See *spectacular*.

eyelet Small metal or plastic rings embedded in fabric, vinyl, or paper to add strength to fastening points where string or wire will be used for hanging or attachment.

fabric structures See *tent*.

facility manager The person at the event's venue who needs to know every detail about the plans for what will happen. Most often these people are responsible, excellent facilitators and work well with event planners. However, keeping little secrets, or forgetting to mention items to them, can be troublesome. Often, anticipated difficult issues can be discussed and resolved. Either present this person with a sketch as to how the room should be set, or discuss it and ask that they generate a sketch for review.

fade The gradual increase (or decrease) of the level of lighting, volume, or projection. The cue can be a fade-in or fade-out.

fail-safe An attribute of a system, component, or circuitry such that every single point failure and critical multiple point failure that may occur in the system, component, or circuit, results in a safe state.

fair, faire, or fayre A temporary gathering to display or trade animals, produce, homemade food, or other goods, including farm machinery. Traditionally a **market fair**. In the twentieth century, fairs were expanded to attract a more diverse audience and often include performances, *carnival* rides, commercial *exhibits*, flower shows, horse races, and many other elements.

fairgrounds The venues for *fairs*. Designed to accommodate large crowds, they combine both permanent and temporary structures as well as the necessary requirements for housing livestock. Most fairgrounds are utilized for both the short run of an annual fair and for multiple other uses such as *exhibitions* and concerts throughout the remainder of the year.

false proscenium An inner frame within the proscenium designed to mask equipment or to reduce the size of the stage opening. Also see *proscenium*.

fanfare A musical salute, often with a trumpet flourish that stirs one's soul. Very accepted as an indication that something special has just happened or is about to happen. Often orchestral fanfares are followed by a tympani **drum roll** under an announcement to introduce someone or something. A **fanfare trumpet** is a standard trumpet with a long extended bell upon which are rings to hang a decorative banner, often with a crest, logo, or national colors. The musical composition of fanfares often features trumpets playing different musical parts to give the sound a harmoniously rich, dynamic feeling. Also, to do something **with fanfare** is to make it showy or a big deal.

farce A dramatic presentation designed for laughter and entertainment in which ordinary people are caught up in extraordinary goings-on.

fashion show A popular type of event that utilizes the presentation of models wearing new fashions as the entertainment. It is used extensively as a *fund-raiser* because the models and fashions are often donated by local retail stores, keeping the presentation costs low. Typically the models are accompanied by music and a verbal description of the fashions. Unfortunately, these have become very clichéd and often are presented with little or no *dazzle*.

 Some tips on presenting a fashion show:

✓ Make the fashions unique, something worth seeing.

F

✓ Add more interest by using members of the presenting organization as the models.

✓ Add some special effects, like flashing lights, smoke, pyro, or other elements to make it exciting.

✓ Choose a theme for the event.

✓ Choose music appropriate to the audience and/or the theme.

✓ Stage it differently, perhaps by placing three or four smaller runways in different parts of the room.

✓ Be different, not the same old fashion show!

favors Gifts given to attendees at an event. Traditionally these were small tokens of remembrance of the occasion, often with a company, organization's *logo*, or bride and groom's names, but in recent times the emphasis seems to be on expensive gifts and often more than one. If many guests have traveled from afar to the function, select favors that are easy to pack and won't cause problems with airport security.

> At the Academy Awards and other major events, each attendee is given a large shopping bag full of expensive gifts often valued at hundreds of dollars. Typically manufacturers provide these gifts as promotional items and some even pay the organizers a fee to place their products in the favors bag. The end result is good for the audience, the manufacturers, and the event.

feast A large meal with much splendor. Also see *festival*.

feedback The loud, harsh squeal emitted from an audio speaker when the volume is too loud or when a microphone is incorrectly placed, normally in front of the speaker.

festival or **fest**   An event usually staged by a community that celebrates and centers on some aspect of that community. Originally, a festival, or **fest** or **feast**, was religious, such as the Feast of the Nativity of Our Lord (Christmas) described in the original Christian liturgical calendar, and the event was designed to offer a sense of belonging. Ancient Egyptian festivals celebrated military victories. Today there are festivals for everything imaginable, but all feature the same traditional elements of food, entertainment, and most certainly *audience participation*. A **movable feast** is a festival that is not on a specific date but varies by the calendar. In Christianity these are based on the date of Easter each year, which is determined by a complex formula and is itself a movable feast.

festival seating   A seating area without chairs. Typically it is a section of raised or sloping lawn upon which the audience sits on blankets, their own portable chairs, or just the grass to enjoy what is being presented.

festoon   An ornamental chain draping of flowers, leaves, ribbons, or fabric, such as *bunting*, hanging in a loop or curve between two points. This makes an ideal decoration for *head tables*, speaker platforms, and other elements of an event. Festooning is accomplished easily by using a measured stick indicating both fabric length (at the end of the stick) and the shorter mark (on the stick) indicating the length of the festoon. Also frequently referred to as *garland*.

fête   A party and celebration often honoring somebody or something. A feast.

film library   See *stock photos*.

final count   The final total number of guests who will be attending a dinner, cocktail party, or other event. Usually caterers require this count at a certain deadline, allowing them enough time to purchase supplies and prepare for the event. Once the final count is given, it determines the final total cost, even if fewer actually attend. If more attend than the final count given, there could be no table space or dinnerware left over, but often good caterers plan for a few extra of everything just in case.

finale The end, finish, or climax. In theater, it is the last scene. In music, the last piece performed. It is also the last in a series of events. Typically finales are the grandest, most exciting, most poignant part of the event, performance, or function, and they are orchestrated to leave a strong positive impression with those attending.

Some tips on structuring a finale:

✓ Don't leave them wanting more; give it all to them.

✓ Structure the event with high and low moments, allowing the rhythm to build to the finale. If everything is grand it is hard to top it with a finale. On the other hand, if everything is low, there may not be an audience by the time of the finale.

✓ Don't stop at one; build one finale upon another so that when the audience thinks it's over, it's not.

finger bowl A small bowl of warm water brought to the table after the serving of a messy food such as raw oysters, steamed lobster, or barbecue. At formal *dinners* it is placed at each *place setting* just prior to dessert. It is also a traditional part of the place setting in some Asian cultures.

See formal place setting in "Tables and Techniques" (page 398).

When using a finger bowl it is appropriate to touch one's lips with moistened fingers if they feel messy. It is not appropriate to dip a napkin into the water and wipe hands, lips, or face.

finger food Food served at a function that does not require a plate and can easily be handled with one's fingers, such as hors d'oeuvre.

Finger food is often served at *cocktail parties*, *high teas*, and other functions where limited food is required. Also see *buffet*.

fire curtain A curtain made of nonflammable materials hung imme-diately behind the *proscenium*. The curtain is designed to come down in an emergency, separating the stage from the *house* to protect the audience from smoke or fire originating in the stage area and keeping the high fly loft from serving as a draft to pull the fire up quickly. Originally these curtains were made of asbestos or steel. Modern the-aters have different types of systems that provide the same function. Also see *asbestos curtain*.

fire marshal The safety control officer assigned to oversee the enforcement of all public safety ordinances. Typically they represent the local fire department and have the responsibility of ensuring the event is set up to be as safe as possible. Should fireworks or other pyro be used, special permits will need to be secured beforehand from this official and will require special preparations and high certificates of insurance.

fire ratings See *capacity* and *flameproofing*.

fireworks Explosive pyrotechnic devices used for entertainment purposes. There are two types of fireworks, consumer and profes-sional. Only professional will be addressed here. A combination of different types of fireworks, sometimes enhanced by music or other elements, create a **fireworks display**. Invented in China in the twelfth century to scare away evil spirits, fireworks are made of gun-powder and other chemicals depending on the visual effect desired. In a fireworks display there are two types of visual effects, low-level or **ground effects** (not exceeding 100 feet [30.5 meters]) and high level or **aerial shells** (bursting up to the 300-foot [91.5-meter] range). An excellent display combines both, and different countries have different favorite combinations. Low-level shells consist of rock-ets, Roman candles, fountains, spinners, mine bags, fire falls, and whistles. Also popular are **set pieces**, which are images such as logos, flags, and other designs, constructed of bent bamboo on frames with pyrotechnic lances that burn for a period of time, creating dazzling visual pictures. Effectively combined they can produce a stunning display. The shells for aerial shows have two explosive parts to the shell, one to lift the shell into the air to the desired height and the second being the exploding visual effect. These shells vary in size from about 3 inches (7.6 centimeters) in diameter to 14 inches (35.5 centimeters). The larger the shell, the larger the visual effect. The most common visual effects are called Peony, Chrysanthemum, Willow, Palm, and Ring, each name describing the basic visual. Salutes are very loud reports without a visual but designed to add excitement.

Pyrotechnic devices are also used extensively as *special effects* in motion pictures and other live shows to create fire, smoke, flash, and other visuals. The U.S. classification for display fireworks is Class B explosives.

Tips on presenting a fireworks display (or show):

✓ Contract a reputable fireworks company. Keep in mind that many of these companies only have the knowledge to "throw a bunch of shells into the air," lacking the creative *showmanship* to create a really stirring show. So it is important to work with them to do something different and appropriate to your event.

✓ Secure insurance for the display. This typically can be done through the fireworks company.

✓ Don't go for the thirty-minute show syndrome. Fireworks get boring. The best shows are short but packed with lots of effects. Many people see Disney parks fireworks shows and rave about them, not realizing that they are only five minutes long.

✓ A company logo blazing brightly as a set piece with Roman

candles firing behind can be very exciting, and much less expensive than an aerial show. It can be placed very close to the audience.

✓ Add music to the display. Work with the fireworks company to create a musical track appropriate to the audience and occasion, add an opening announcement, and finish with a bang.

 ✓ Notify local fire authorities well in advance to gain permission and to know their requirements.

✓ Work with the fireworks company and fire department to create a safety zone around the firing site free of any spectators. The size is determined by the type of fireworks selected.

✓ Placing the audience close to the fireworks, yet in a safe area, creates maximum impact. Be sure the audience is not downwind of the display to avoid falling ash.

✓ Support the pyrotechnics with other *special effects*, such as dancing water fountains, lights panning the sky, or *laser* lights shooting overhead.

✓ Carry the pyro theme through the dinner by featuring a flaming dessert, a fire dancer onstage, or fiery hot visuals on the projection screens.

✓ Even sparklers are considered fireworks by the fire department and require special use permits.

first impression Make it great! It not only sets the guest's attitude, but also often becomes the lasting memory of the event. What they experience first—the lighting, color, decorations, music, aroma, etc.—all has a powerful impact on the success of the event.

✐ **Tips on creating a great first impression:**

✓ Don't open the door to the event until everything is absolutely ready.

✓ Create something of visual interest right inside the door. Maybe guests will walk through arches of flowers or pass a gypsy violinist.

✓ The room should attack the senses, creating a mood through the use of lighting, color, aroma, and theme.

✓ Cordial greeters with big smiles add friendliness and warmth.

✓ Waiters bearing drinks and food add a sense of hospitality.

fitting The trying on of costumes by a performer to determine the final size or adjustments required. Referred to as a **fitting session**, it often requires payment to the actor for the time required.

fixatif An aerosol clear lacquer spray applied to artwork to prevent smearing, protect it, and give it a finished look. Available in glossy or matte. The matte helps to prevent glare or light reflection from the "fixed" art.

flag protocol or **flag etiquette** The proper use and display of the national flag of a country. The rules for national flags vary by country and as to whether the use is ceremonial, official, or casual. The United States has a code of law for the flag. Improper use of the flag is illegal and considered disrespectful, which can be embarrassing to the organizations associated with an event.

For a complete set of rules for how to display the American flag, see "Tables and Techniques" (page 340).

Tips in regard to the American flag at an event:

✓ Is it okay to use flag napkins or plates? No. Section 8i of the flag code reads that the flag "should not be printed or otherwise impressed on paper napkins or boxes or anything that is designed for temporary use and discard."

F

✓ Is flag cake decoration ok? Nothing specific to cake decorating is in the flag code. However, it does say "No disrespect should be shown to the flag of the United States of America" and "It should not be . . . printed or otherwise impressed on . . . anything that is designed for temporary use and discard." The icing on a cake would generally be eaten, digested, and "discarded." It is generally suggested that this is an inappropriate display of the flag.

✓ Is it appropriate to use mints wrapped in a flag print wrapper? No. This, and any similar usage such as flag T-shirts or scarves, is considered trivializing the flag.

✓ The flag cannot be used for advertising. Section 8i of the flag code reads: "The flag should never be used for advertising purposes in any manner whatsoever."

✓ It is improper to have people sign a flag. It is acceptable to sign the canvas strip along the side that holds the grommets.

✓ What is the proper method of showing respect to the flag during the national anthem, Pledge of Allegiance, hoisting or lowering of the flag, as the flag passes in a parade, or other presentation of the flag? Americans should stand silently at attention facing the flag with the right hand over the heart. When not in uniform, men should remove any nonreligious headdress with their right hand and hold it at the left shoulder, the hand being over the heart. Persons in uniform should face the flag and render the military salute. Veterans who are not in uniform may also render the military salute. Those who are not U.S. citizens should stand at attention.

✓ "Presentation of the **Colors**" is often used in event programs. When is this appropriate? In formal and military contexts, the American flag is called different names depending on where or how it is displayed. For example, it is called an "ensign" when it is displayed on a vessel. It is called "*colors*" when it is carried by foot, as by the infantry. It is called a "**standard**" when it is displayed on a car or an aircraft and carried by the cavalry.

✓ The flag does not have to be in the triangular fold for normal storage. If the flag is affixed to a staff, the flag may be rolled around the staff for storage.

✓ What is the red cap placed over the top of the flag when it is retired or put away? The tradition of the Phrygian cap or *liberty cap* evolved as a symbol of freedom during the Revolutionary era in America. Today the cap (which has a specific design—it resembles the Smurfs cap) is still often used to show respect to the flag.

✓ The flag is never to be used as decoration. Instead, festoons, rosettes, draping, and buntings of blue, white, and red should be used.

✓ When in doubt it is best to be conservative with the use of the flag of any country.

📖 See parts of a flag in "Tables and Techniques" (page 339).

flambé or **flamed** A dramatic way to present a food course, such as a dessert. The flame is accomplished by sprinkling certain foods with liquor, which is ignited immediately before serving. Sometimes the flame is created by a liquor-soaked sugar cube or bread crouton placed in a small dish in the center of the food. Bananas flambé is a fun way to end a luau dinner. Then there is Baked Alaska. Don't forget to turn the lights down before serving.

flameproofing The process of reducing the flammability of many materials used in events, including fabrics, scenery, carpeting, tents, and many other items, to meet local fire marshal requirements in both interior and exterior venues. Since flame "proofing" is almost impossible with most materials, the goal is to make them **flame retardant**, meaning more resistant to fire or taking longer to burst into flame.

Scenery, for example, or other noncertified items necessary for the event, can be sprayed with certified solutions after construction to achieve the *ASTM* (or other testing company) standards rating required. Typically fire marshals will not allow scenery, decorations, tents, bunting, or other items to be used in an event unless they bear a flame retardant certification stamp or label. Often fire marshals will do their own on-the-spot test by simply holding a match to the item to see how it responds. If it doesn't pass the test, they can order it be removed or even close down the event.

 Always contract for a flame retardant certificate from builders of scenery, tent vendors, decorators, etc., and receive it before delivery of the goods. Keep this certificate available during the event in case the fire department has any questions.

flash pot A pyrotechnic special-effect device that creates an instant large burst of smoke, flame, or both depending on what ingredients are loaded inside. These are used by many magicians. Typically it is attached to a lighting circuit and executed on cue by the *lighting director*.

flat A basic element of scenery that is itself without depth but can be in different shapes and sizes and painted to look like almost anything. A traditional flat is made of wood framing with *muslin* stretched over its surface, while others have a thin wood covering. Flats are usually hung from *battens* or lashed with others and supported by a *stage brace*. Flats are designed to be lightweight so they can be easily moved, and usually not wider than 5 feet 9 inches (1.8 meters) so that they can go through standard doorways.

See diagrams of a flat in "Tables and Techniques" (page 449).

flat ride A circular spinning carnival-type ride that stays horizontal on the ground, such as a carousel.

flatware All standard utensils used for eating, including knives, forks, and spoons. Commonly called silverware. Also referred to as cutlery or placeware. Flatware is made of various metals, the most expensive being *goldware*, followed in cost by sterling silver, silverplate, and *stainless steel*. The style, or pattern, of flatware and the quality selected for a dinner event should reflect the occasion and type of dinner, be it formal, themed, or casual. Flatware is always placed on the table in order of its use, starting from the outside in, moving toward the plate. Occasionally dishes that are flat or relatively shallow, such as plates and saucers, are also referred to as flatware. Also see *hollowware* and *tableware*.

📖 See "Tables and Techniques" for flatware styles (page 404) and place setting examples (page 397).

flex space Most newer hotels and conference centers design their banquet and meeting area to be utilized in flexible ways by changing the size and shape of the space. This is accomplished by opening sliding walls, removing panels, or hanging curtains. Flex space is also any area that can be used for different functions, whether a meeting, *cocktail party*, performance, etc.

float A decorated moving vehicle used in a parade or show. Also, extra time available for an activity either to begin or end because it is not part of the *critical path*. This is also called slack.

floodlight Commonly referred to as **floods**, these light instruments create a diffused widespread light effect for general lighting. Also called *olivette* lights.

floorcan A spotlight that sits on the floor shooting up to light key elements. Also see *parcan*.

floor cloth See *ground cloth*.

floor manager In television production, it is the person in the studio who generally oversees the activities and relays the director's orders to the on-camera talent, often by using hand signals.

floor plans See *ground plans*.

floral foam Used in centerpieces and other floral arrangements, this foam is designed to hold water and yet be strong enough to support flower stems and other decorative items inserted.

flow The manner in which guests move through an event environment. Planning adequate guest flow from the entrance, to the various event activities, and to the exit is essential to avoid bottlenecks, dead ends, and uncomfortable and unsafe situations, and to ensure a successful guest experience. Flow also describes the manner is which an event is structured from beginning to end to incorporate all the event elements in an effective and impactful progression.

flowers by month Every month has a flower commonly associated with it, making that flower an ideal decoration for a birthday party or other events falling in that month.

fluorescent paint A specially formulated paint that changes color when illuminated with ultraviolet (UV), often called *blacklight*. The paint is available in several different colors. Scenery painted with this can be visually effective and completely changes appearance when the lighting switches from normal to blacklight. Signs, logos, and other elements can be very effectively visually enhanced. Haunted house events rely heavily on this paint.

to fly To move battens, lights, scenery, or actors vertically on the stage. Or, to hang something above the stage or presentation platform.

fly The length of a *flag* from the side where it attaches to the pole to the opposite end. The distance varies with different flags. The fly of the

American flag is 1.9 times the *hoist* or flag height. British and Canadian flags have a fly of twice the hoist.

📖 **See parts of a flag in "Tables and Techniques" (page 339).**

fly gallery Traditionally the pin rail used to control the flying of scenery on a stage. Originally it was located in the flies high above the floor; later it was moved to an easy-to-use level just above the stage floor. In most modern stages it is eliminated by an automated rigging control system.

flying The technique of making a performer or object appear to be moving through the air, sometimes above the audience. This *special effect* is achieved by a special apparatus *rigged* into the fly loft or ceiling. It takes a *flyman* to operate the system during a performance.

fly loft or **flies** Commonly refers to area above the stage and below the roof that scenery and other elements move into when lifted above the stage. This area is often referred to as the flies or *loft*.

flyman The member of the stage crew responsible for *to fly* scenery, props, or a person. In theaters with new fly systems, this position is replaced by automation.

fly over Bring the sky into the show or event by featuring a low-flying aircraft. The aircraft featured can be anything from antique planes to the latest stealth bomber. Most popular are four fighter jets that break off into different directions trailing colored smoke. A blimp with specific messages on lighted screens can be very effective at night.

For the grand opening of Canada's Wonderland theme park in Toronto I arranged two Canadian Airline 747s to fly over very low with wings almost touching. To the guests they appeared enormous and the roar was so loud that the guests were aghast and cheered wildly after they passed. For the opening ceremonies of

> World Cup USA, I arranged for dozens of World War II and earlier
> fighters to fly over in tight formation. What made their appear-
> ance so special was that they filled the sky and moved overhead
> slow enough to overwhelm the audience.

fly rig A device designed to fly a person over a stage or audience that utilizes a harness connected to thin cables hanging from an overhead track. It allows for movement of the person both vertically and horizontally.

fly through A computer-generated motion graphic that visually moves the viewer through a still illustration as if the viewer is literally flying around and through buildings, trees, etc., in the drawing.

focus The direction to which a lighting instrument is aimed. Also, the arrangement of individuals and items onstage for *composition* and emphasis.

fogger A machine that create smoke to simulate fog for performances. There are two types of fog units. One heats a special mineral oil to create a very lightweight fog that floats freely in the air. These are used extensively in theater and with performing bands because they can quickly cover an area with fog that is easily lighted with colored lights, providing a colorful atmosphere around the performers. Other devices are available to burst the fog or to create smoke rings. The other type utilizes dry ice in a barrel to make dense, heavy, low-hanging fog to cover the ground up to a height of about performers' knees. This type of fog looks like a heavy ground fog and can also be easily lighted for the desired effect. Often the two different units are used together. Also see *hazer*.

fog screen Controlled falling fog, created by specially designed foggers, upon which images can be projected. Sometimes used with a performer coming through the projected image.

foley The *postproduction* process of adding sound effects created in the studio and additional dialog to enhance film, motion pictures, television, video games, and radio shows.

foliage Virtually any type of plant, be it plastic, silk, or real, including blossomed plants. Foliage is an ideal way to add visual interest to a stage, speaker's platform, or room or event space. By renting foliage such as large ferns, potted trees, flowers, etc., quick decoration can be achieved with little cost. Silk flowers can be added to green plants for added effect. And because it is typically delivered and picked up by the supplier, foliage is easy to execute. Also see *greens*.

foliage border or **cut border** A border of which the lower parts have been cut into an irregular design, such as tree branches or foliage.

follow spot A spotlight with a strong narrow beam of light capable of being moved by an operator to follow action by a performer or actor onstage. Often more than one follow spot is used at the same time either from different angles and/or to color the performer's costume while highlighting his or her face. Automated follow spots that automatically follow the movement of the actor or performer are also available.

Fome-Cor Original trade name for a laminated, featherweight board ideal for signs, mounted artwork, charts, and just about anything else necessary as display pieces for a meeting or other event. Commonly called **foam core**, it consists of thin porous polystyrene foam sandwiched between white cardstock-like paper.

font Style and size of type used in typesetting for printing or computers. A full alphabet with a particular lettering style. There are three general categories of fonts: Serif, Sans Serif, and Script. A serif font has added structural details at the ends of the strokes that make up the letter. These are used for traditional printing such as in books and newspapers. Sans Serif fonts are considered more modern and easier to read. Script is stylized handwriting or *calligraphy*.

 **See classic fonts in "Tables and Techniques" (page 369).**

foot-candle The unit for measuring illumination, the amount of light given off from one candle that will fall on a surface 1 foot away.

footlights or **foots** A row of lights located on the *downstage* edge of the stage. Usually these are *strip lights* sunk into a trough at the front of the *apron*, but in old theaters they were individual instruments, or more traditionally lanterns, spaced along the front of the stage with reflectors to keep the light from striking the eyes of the audience. Like most strip lights these are wired in three circuits to enable the light to be colored appropriately.

forced perspective The process of building or painting background objects smaller in scale than those closer so that they appear further away. Often the perspective of the visual created with scenery onstage is forced to make the scene look larger or more interesting. The addition of *wings* on the sides and *borders* above greatly enhances the effect.

formal dinner See *dinner*.

format The organization, plan, style, margins, and other specifications of a script, series of advertisements, schedule, budget, show, or presentation. For example, if the function is an awards presentation, a format would be established as to the sequence of awards, the direction from which recipients enter and exit the stage, who presents each award, the length of each presentation and acceptance, etc. Or, to organize a CD or computer program properly to accept data.

form of address A formal designation attached to a person or family by virtue of office, rank, education, hereditary privilege, or marital status. Correct usage of titles is extremely important in addressing individuals both in spoken and written form. An *invitation*, formal and informal, must be addressed to individuals with their proper titles.

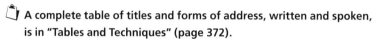 **A complete table of titles and forms of address, written and spoken, is in "Tables and Techniques" (page 372).**

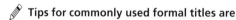 Tips for commonly used formal titles are

Note: The traditional rules are constantly changing. Always check directly with the person to find the individual's preference.

Mr.—Proper for a male of any age above thirteen.

Master—Still appropriate in formal correspondence for males under the age of thirteen. Some argue it is appropriate until a boy graduates from high school.

Jr.—The title for the son of a father with the same given name. It is proper to use "Jr." after the son's name as long as his father is alive. It is his choice after his father's death.

Miss—Proper for all females under thirteen and all unmarried women. The plural form is Misses. For young women over the age of thirteen, either Miss or Ms. is appropriate.

Mrs.—The title for a married woman. Correspondence should be addressed "Mrs. (husband's first name) (married family name)." This includes a widow, who keeps her husband's name unless she remarries.

Ms.—The title for a female that denotes no marital status. Some married women prefer this title while other married women dislike it. The plural is Mses. or Mss.

Husband and wife—Use Mr. and Mrs. followed by the husband's first name and the married family name.

Separated, not divorced woman—Use either Mrs. followed by

husband's full name, or either Mrs. or Ms. followed by the woman's first name and husband's last name.

Divorced woman—Use either her first name and her ex-husband's last name preceded by either Mrs. or Ms. (this is often preferred by women with young children) or Ms. with her first name and Maiden name.

Dr.—A person with an MD in the medical field is addressed as "Doctor" professionally, and usually socially, as well as in written correspondence. A doctorate of divinity, literature, philosophy, etc., is introduced either as "Mister" (or appropriate woman's address) or to show respect, "Doctor." However, for social correspondence it is generally correct to use "Mister" (or the appropriate woman's address).

Alternate lifestyle couples—For those with different last names, use Mr. or Ms. followed by the full name, the word "and" (to signify their partnership), and then Mr. or Ms. followed by the partner's full name, all on the same line. For a couple sharing the same last name, use Mr. or Ms. followed by one person's first name, the word "and" (to signify their partnership), and then Mr. or Ms. followed by the first name of the partner followed by the last name.

to foul To tangle the lines supporting different elements such as scenery and light instruments as they are being moved up and down.

fourth estate A political force or institution whose influence is not officially recognized. It is accepted to be the *press*. The term comes from old England where the three estates of Parliament were Lords Spiritual, Lords Temporal, and the Commons, but it was claimed that the real power rested in the reporters' gallery, thus the fourth estate.

fourth wall The imaginary side of the room toward the audience that has theoretically been removed so that the spectators may look in.

frame The basic time period for the recording or playback of show data. For example, 16 frames per second would indicate that show data is stored a maximum of 16 times per second and playback is at 16 times per second. The standard for video stored and played back is 24 frames per second, while the standard for 35 mm film is typically 30 frames per second.

free-span The volume of open space under a roof uninterrupted by support columns or other structural elements. Large event spaces, such as *convention centers* or ballrooms, are designed with high ceilings and all the support structure at the outer walls, leaving the interior space visually uninterrupted.

Fresnel The type of *lighting* instrument that utilizes a stepped lens, similar to the type designed for beacons in lighthouses. A standard theatrical light used for many years, it can be recognized by the concentric rings of its lens. Named after the French physicist who invented the design. The lens produces an even field of light with soft edges.

front curtain See *main curtain*.

front light The light emanating from theatrical instruments that strikes the front, or audience, side of the performers or speakers. Most often front light is actually two lights placed at a 45° angle out from each side of the actor and 45° up from the actor's face. The sideways angles allow the performer or speaker to be lighted as they turn their head from side to side. The upward angle illuminates the face in the most natural way while highlighting under features such as eye sockets and nose.

front scene A scene played in front of a full stage set or an *act curtain*. Sometimes the full set has been darkened or colored so that the visual emphasis is on the front scene.

front-surface mirror A piece of glass with an exposed broadband reflective optical coating on its surface. Light does not have to travel through the glass to reach the reflective coating as it does in typical mirrors, allowing it to reflect up to 99 percent of the light. These mirrors are typically used to reflect laser beams in various directions.

fund-raiser Any event with the primary purpose of raising money, whether through sale of tickets to the event, donations collected at the event, an auction, or even an investor meeting.

FX Abbreviation for *effect* or *special effect*.

gaffer An electrician on theater or film crews.

gaffer's glass A small round glass with a filter that allows a lighting director, gaffer, or technician to look safely directly into the light from a theatrical instrument. This makes it possible to locate exactly the hot spot in order to accurately determine where to aim the light to achieve maximum coverage for that instrument's assigned area.

gaffer's tape Duct tape. Used extensively for all types of purposes, from marking positions onstage to doing emergency repairs of many things. Available in multiple colors, it is one of the necessary items to have on hand for any event.

gag Any kind of special effects trick. In a cartoon film it is when the anvil misses the roadrunner and falls on the coyote's head.

gala A festivity, celebration, party, or ball that is grand in its scale and exciting to attend. An affair to remember.

Gantt chart A scheduling tool that uses horizontal bars, spread over a dateline graph, to show the amount of time a task is estimated to take.

garland A wreath or *festoon* of intertwined flowers, leaves, paper, or other festive materials hung as a decoration. Often garland is swaged from point to point or laid on a tabletop or other surface. Garlands are standard wedding decorations, but are also used extensively to decorate many different events. Garland is also a wreath worn as a sign of honor or for ornament.

gate A control point or an entry way or portal. For events it is the position that the audience must pass to surrender their tickets, receive programs, and be admitted. Since most people arrive at the prescribed or scheduled time, planning the operation at the entrance is critical. While a large crowd needs to be processed quickly, **gate crashers** and unwanted people must be recognized and dealt with effectively. It may be necessary to have well-marked secondary gates for members of the press, stand-by ticket holders, and *VIP*s.

gathering court An area behind the entrance in which the audience or visitors are able to gather prior to entering the complex, theater, park, or festival.

gauze A large seamless mesh curtain, generally stretched tight between top and bottom battens. It is used to create "visions" or a dissolve effect between scenes by changing the intensity of the lighting in front and behind. If used in front of backgrounds, it gives the illusion of the background being more distant or more real.

gavel A small mallet typically made of wood used for ceremony in meetings, courts of law, and public office. While it is used to mark the beginning of a session, it is also used to bring order or to mark a final judgment. Originating in medieval England, the gavel would sound the transaction of a deal when a tribute or payment was made with something other than cash. *Robert's Rules of Order* provides guidelines for the use of a gavel.

gel or **gelatin** A thin transparent piece of colored material used to

G

give color to the light emanating from a spotlight or other lighting instrument.

gel frame A device usually made of thin metal designed to hold the *gelatin*, or color medium, for attachment to the light instrument. It is also known as a color frame.

general conditions The portion of the contract documents that states the responsibilities and relationships of all parties to the contract, as well as any conditions applicable to the contract.

generator A mechanical device that creates electricity. Often needed in many events where the power source is nonexistent or does not have a large enough capacity to meet the needs of the event. Available in all sizes and rentable. Quiet or silent operating generators are always preferred. The event electrician and/or lighting director can calculate the projected power requirements necessary. When budgeting, be sure to include the setup and rehearsal days in the amount of time the rental generator is required.

genre The scope of the word is usually confined to music, literature, and art and defines some loose set of criteria to create categories. For example, a story about crime may be categorized in the genre of mystery, or romance if there is a strong love affair between the lead characters. While genres are not precisely definable, genre considerations are one of the most important factors in what a person decides to read, listen to, or see.

ghost A streak of light that falls where it is not wanted. Most often this is on projection screens.

gig A slang term for a scheduled performance or booking. Musicians typically use it when referring to a paid performance.

gin A popular alcoholic beverage whose flavor is derived from juniper berries, often with other botanicals added for enriched taste. Different varieties of gin include London gin, sloe gin, distilled gin, and Slovenská borovička. Its origins are in the Middle ages.

glassware or **drinkware** All the vessels used for beverages. The range of design for different purposes and types of drink is quite extensive, including wine glasses, pilsners for beer, and martini glasses, just to name a few. The shape of the glass and the density of the rim determine how and where the liquid flows onto the tongue, affecting the taste. It is also said that the shape of the glass intrigues the eye and adds mystique to the drink. Classic **barware** is glassware typically used in most bar setups, including beer steins and shot glasses. A glass raised from its base by a stem, or foot, is called **stemware**, such as a flute, goblet, chalice, snifter, or wine glass.

G

A guide to glassware is in "Tables and Techniques" (page 305).

glitter Small pieces of reflective material, such as Mylar, used to reflect light. Glitter adds sparkle to centerpieces, signs, and many other such decorative items. Also, dazzling glamour such as the glitter of an outstanding performance at an opera.

glitz or **glitzy** Flashiness or ostentatious showiness. Over-the-top. Can be used effectively in performance and decoration to make a statement and get a reaction.

goblet A footed, or stemmed, cup used for drinking. Also called a chalice. Throughout history this style of cup has been used for ceremonial drinking. Also see *glassware*.

gobo A metal cutout used with a spotlight to project a pattern on a surface.

gofer A production assistant who is responsible to "go fer" whatever is needed. Also see *runner.*

goldware *Flatware* that is plated first with sterling silver and then with gold. The silver base is necessary to chemically bind and strengthen the soft gold. Goldware adds an unusually rich look to a *table setting* and is ideal for formal dinners.

goodies A list of program elements that may be in the *candy store.*

"go with God" An expression meaning that the presentation is impromptu or unrehearsed. The production management and crew do not have a script or any idea of what is going to happen onstage, and so they must be prepared for any action.

grand drape See *main curtain.*

grand opening A very common event designed for three purposes: to announce an opening; to gain *publicity*; and to thank or honor those involved in completing the project. In the motion picture industry it is called a **premiere**.

✏️ Tips for grand openings:

✓ Make sure the activities planned take place at the location of whatever it is that is opening. This provides an appropriate background for pictures and familiarizes the press and invitees with the site and the company's business and products. This seems obvious, but often that is not the case.

✓ Stage the event so that the front of the building, the sign, or whatever is most important can be easily photographed. Ideally the speaker and building, or whatever is being opened, can be captured in one powerful photo.

✓ Make the event worthwhile. After all, the press and important people have been invited, so make their valuable time well spent.

✓ If having the press attend is important, do everything possible to get them there. All too often they say they will attend, but then never show up.

✓ As with all events, take the ordinary and make it extraordinary.

Since this type of event is so common, it is especially important to do something different and memorable.

The grand opening celebration of Walt Disney World that I produced was three days in duration and included multiple extravagant dinners, a performance of the World Symphony Orchestra, thousands of performers, dozens of celebrities, a network prime-time television special, incredible fireworks, and hundreds of special guests all mixed with in-park audiences exceeding one hundred thousand persons. Its task was to tell the world that Walt Disney World was fantastic and open for business.

G

grandstands A structure, whether permanent or temporary, designed for seating spectators. It is unlike a stadium in that it does not wrap all or most of the way around the action area. They have individual chairs or bench seating, sometimes covered and sometimes not. A variety of portable grandstands can be rented or constructed, typically out of scaffolding. They are also called **bleachers**, but typically bleachers are far more basic and single-tiered. Also, overacting is called **grandstanding**.

grass mat Canvas, burlap, or plastic backing to which a material representing grass has been adhered. Handy material to cover large unsightly areas onstage or off, out of doors, or in large convention spaces. It is relatively inexpensive and reusable, and with a few plants or other decorations placed on it the visual effect is convincing from the audience point of view. The old style made with a paperlike fabric for the grass has a much better appearance than the newer plastic type. Also called **funeral grass**.

gratuity A gesture or payment for extra good service, commonly called **tips**. Practically, in America gratuity has become standard additional payment for many services, whether the service is good or bad. Most caterers, hotels, limo companies, etc., have a set amount they charge on top of regular charges. Tips can be a large budget line item, so plan them carefully. At a restaurant or for a hired caterer, the following positions are typically tipped: head-waiter, wait staff, bartender, bus staff, coatroom attendant, wash-room attendant, and doorman. Often these companies will automatically bill additionally a prearranged amount for the gratu-ity for all of their staff. Verbal commendation directly to those who deserve it is also always appreciated.

green room A waiting or reception room located backstage where talent, actors, dignitaries, or others on the program can relax before and after their appearance. A green room is usually stocked with food and beverages, is decorated with bouquets, has a restroom nearby, and is hosted by a responsible individual. It is not a dressing room.

greens The reference term for all plants and floral foliage for theatri-cal, film, and other events. The *foliage* may be artificial or real or typ-ically a combination of both. A **greensman** is responsible for procuring and placing the greens as necessary or as directed by the art director or director. Often greens are as large as full-size trees, or as small as a branch mounted on a stand to be foreground for a camera shot.

For a premiere party for the Paramount movie Congo we actually created a jungle in a soundstage in midtown New York City. We gathered plants from theatrical prop houses and nurseries all over the city, including tall palm trees, tropical flowers, low palms, mulch for the ground cover, and even some Venus Flytraps. The walls were hung with large jungle scenic drops. Entering, guests really felt like they were emerging into a dense jungle. Native huts decorated bars and food stations. Native dancers on tall stilts performed. To add further realism, we had stagehands on ladders behind the scenic *drops controlling rubber spiders on invisible monofilament lines, dropping them down onto a guest's shoulder or head. Rubber snakes lurched from tree branches. Paramount asked us not to use the mechanical rats.*

green screen A technique for compositing two images together in which one color is removed from one of the images, making that area transparent. For example, an actor, photographed in front of a pure green background, is placed over the picture of a castle, creating the effect that the actor is at the castle when the green is removed. Typically green is the color removed because it is furthest from skin tones, but blue is also used. Also called **chroma keying** or **color keying**.

grid or **gridiron** A steel framework system hung above the stage area from which battens, rigging systems, and other elements of the show production are hung. Often this system is hung just far enough below the ceiling to provide access for crew through a system of catwalks.

grip A member of the stage crew who assists in the movement of materials and settings onstage. A stagehand.

ground cloth A fabric covering, usually canvas, for the floor of the stage. Often this cloth has a pattern, design, or logo painted on its surface. It can also be a rug or carpeting. Also referred to as a **floor cloth**.

ground plans Scaled drawings of a floor or ground area showing the location of the *set*, projection screens, staging, and other elements of the production. Also referred to as floor plans. Also see *plan view*.

ground row Long, low, free-standing scenery that typically represents bushes, rocks, or other such visuals. Often these hide lights and other equipment. A curved ground row in front of a cyc blocks the view of the bottom edge of the cyc and conceals strip lights used to light the bottom portion of the cyc, all of which aids in creating the visually seamless background.

grouping   The placement of items or cast on a platform, dais, stage, display, video shot, or photograph. Emphasis can be achieved for one or more of the subjects depending on how the people or items are placed. Typically the center is the strongest position but, for example, two on one side and one on the other makes the lone one stronger in the grouping . . . unless that one is turned looking at the other two who are looking straight ahead, which gives the emphasis to them. Consider the impact of grouping items carefully.

group shot   Two or more individuals or items framed in the same photograph or video take.

guest list   When people invited to the event acknowledge their acceptance of the invitation, they are grouped alphabetically on a listing for easy reference and count. This list also should contain their contact information, relationship to the event, and other pertinent information that can be used for both follow-up prior to the event and for future *invitation lists*. Some events with multiple functions, where different people are invited to some functions and some to all, require individual guest lists per function and a master list that meshes the various functions lists together.

   Apps are available to manage guest lists with a variety of special features. The most important feature is that they make check-in much easier than going down lists. My favorite feature is that an app can alert event management immediately via phone when selected *VIP*s arrive.

guidon   A regimental flag or pennant, or the soldier who carries it.

gun salute   The tradition of firing cannons or firearms as an honor is believed to have started when defeated naval warships were ordered to fire all their remaining loaded cannons to signify that they were no longer a threat, similar to a soldier dropping the point of a sword. This tradition evolved into firing cannons to honor heads of state at ceremonial events. The first international recognition of the United States as an independent republic came in 1776 when the American ship *Andrew Doria* fired thirteen salutes to a Dutch colony in the Caribbean, one for each American colony, and the Dutch fired back nine, the traditional salute to an independent republic. The U.S. tradition of firing one salute for each state continued until the British tradition of a twenty-one-gun salute recognizing sovereign countries was adopted. The twenty-one-gun salute officially became the "President's Salute" in 1842 and continues today as the gun salute of highest honor in the United States. It is rendered on the arrival and departure of the U.S. president in concordance with four "*Ruffles and Flourishes*" followed immediately by playing "Hail to the Chief." The first cannon shot is fired on the first ruffle and flourish. At a presidential state funeral, the salute begins at precisely noon with one shot every minute.

 A three-volley rifle salute is an honor given at military funerals.

 Other gun salutes are given in the United States as follows:

19 Salutes—Vice President, Speaker of the House, Chief Justice, Cabinet Officers, State Governors, Ambassadors

17 Salutes—Governor of a U.S. Territory, General, Admiral

15 Salutes—Vice Admiral, Lieutenant General

13 Salutes—Rear Admiral, Major General

11 Salutes—Chargé d'Affaires, Brigadier General, Rear Admiral

7 Salutes—Consuls accredited to the United States

5 Salutes—Vice Consuls

Many countries use gun salutes as an honor.

> *When I staged the state funeral of President Richard M. Nixon I experienced how dramatic the effect of cannon salutes can be. Each shot is so loud and earthshaking, emphasized by the wait and anticipation of the next. It is very emotional. Followed by the playing of "Taps" by a lone bugler, and a slow flyover by a squadron of fighter jets in the "missing man" formation, the impact was unforgettable.*

Haas effect A psychoacoustic trait of human hearing distinguishing the first arrival of sound as the source, whereas slightly delayed sound simply reinforces the volume. This important phenomenon was first described by Helmut Haas in 1949 and is a key in modern sound reinforcing in very large audience performance spaces, indoors or out. In these large venues, in addition to sound-reinforcing audio speakers being placed at the stage in front of the audience, they are also placed along the sides, in the depth of the audience area. By delaying the reinforcement sound emitting from these side speakers long enough for the sound from the stage speakers to strike the ear first, the audience believes they are hearing all the sound directly from the stage.

"Hail to the Chief" The musical composition reserved for the entrance of the president of the United States at public functions. It is typically preceded by "Ruffles and Flourishes." The march was written by James Sanderson as part of melodrama. It was first used in association with a president in 1815 at the occasion to honor both George Washington and the end of the War of 1812, and it has been used for most presidents since. Its official status was established in 1954.

halftones A cut or an engraving of an illustration having shades or tones like a photograph. Made up of a series of dots for reproduction by printing methods.

halyard A rope used to raise the flag on a pole.

handicap requirements See *ADA*.

handshake A method of two systems verifying the integrity and operation of the other system. For example, the light dimmer system connected successfully to the lighting control board.

hang points Positions in the ceiling of a banquet room or other *venue* designed to be structurally capable of holding the weight of hanging heavy objects such as *scenery*, curtains, or a pipe batten of theatrical lighting instruments. Most modern meeting rooms, ballrooms, banquet rooms, and theaters have such locations identified and hidden when not in use. Often these points also have electrical service to power theatrical lights, sound speakers, *chain hoists*, and other electrical equipment. Should a prospective venue not have such points, rigging of this equipment is impossible, or it is much more difficult and requires the services of a professional *rigger*.

hard wired The installation of electrical or electronic equipment where the connecting is by a wire versus radio transmission or other means. Typically this may not be as convenient but it provides less chance of error during performance.

hazer A special effects device that creates a fine, light fog in the air. Hazers are often used in laser and light shows because unlike a *fogger* that creates large amounts of smoke, a hazer creates just a thin haze, or mist, in the air that is almost invisible until the vapor particles are struck by the beams of light. Without this haze, laser light beams would be invisible.

headaddress A decorative covering worn on the head for ceremonial purposes, as a sign of rank, as part of a costume, or as personal display.

Many traditional headdresses are very specific in design, with each element having meaning or purpose.

header   The beam across the top of an opening such as a doorway, large window, or small performing area. A **display header** is the horizontal component of a display or exhibit that is across the top and often bears the product or company name.

headliner or **headline talent**   A performer who is very well known to audiences and whose name will attract large audiences and numerous ticket sales. Also sometimes used to denote which performer, of a group of performers on a program, is considered the best or most important.

head table   The table at a banquet or meeting at which the dignitaries, speakers, and other people key to the event are positioned. Often this is a long table on a raised *dais* set so that everyone attending can easily view those at the head table. When two or more rows of chairs are required, each row is raised higher than the preceding one, allowing for easy viewing of those at all tables. Sometimes a tabletop lectern is placed at the center of the table, or a stand-up lectern is used at one end of the platform. If there are two or more rows, the lectern can be placed at the center of either of the rows. If there are decorations on the tables and dinner is being served, the tables must be deep enough to accommodate both. The head tables are always skirted on the audience side to hide the legs of those seated.

See head tables in "Tables and Techniques" (pages 333, 404, and 426) for helpful planning suggestions.

Since the popularity of head tables varies, another technique at a dinner is to place the head table in the center of the room to establish a closer relationship with all those attending. In this case the head table is more elaborately decorated than all other tables, has a larger or different centerpiece, could or could not be on a low riser (*dais*), or may have some other distinguishing features that makes it different from all other tables in the room. This technique also leaves the stage available for performers, speakers, or other presentations.

While many feel it is an honor to sit on a dais at the head table, they are understandably the worst seats in the house. First, there are all those people staring at you while you eat. Then you can only view the speakers from the side and often can't see visuals being presented on screens. Finally, if your position is at the end of the table, you only have one person to converse with during dinner. Another way event planners can help this situation is to have the VIPs eat at different tables in the room then call them up to the dais for the presentations after the dinner is eaten. This can be done with an introduction of each.

✎ **Tips on organizing the people at the head table:**

✓ Convene them in a *green room* where they can meet one another and be comfortable prior to the start of the event.

✓ Use this time in the holding room to give them necessary instructions, review the schedule, etc.

✓ Line them up in the order they will be sitting at the table. This will allow them to march to the dais and take their seats without confusion.

✓ Each chair on the dais should have a card on the seat with the name of the person to sit there in large letters, so that they can read them while standing.

✓ Arrange for someone to escort their spouses to their seats at other tables if they are not to be on the dais.

✓ Instruct them beforehand as to what they should do at the end of the event, how they should leave the dais together, and where they will find coats or other belongings.

head room The amount of space between the top of a person's head and the top frame of the camera picture both in video and still pictures. This space needs to be a compromise between too little, where the frame seems to be pushing down on the head, and too much, where the head appears too low in the picture.

heads up A danger-warning phrase that an object is being lowered or moved overhead or falling from above.

hertz (Hz) Equivalent to cycles per second, as in an audio sound wave. Humans perceive the frequency of sound waves as pitch. Each musical note corresponds to a particular frequency, which is measured in hertz.

high definition or **high def (HD)** A technique used in digital television systems, in which a substantially higher resolution image is produced by millions of pixels per frame rather than the several hundred projected scanning lines used in the old analog systems. The term was first used in the 1930s when the number of scanning lines went from 30 lines of resolution to 405.

high tea An early evening meal typically eaten between 5:00 p.m. and 6:00 p.m., usually followed by another light meal a couple of hours later. High tea consists of cold meats, eggs or fish, cakes and sandwiches, and, of course, tea. The name refers to the table at which it is eaten, which is a standard dining-style table. Also see *afternoon tea.*

hit it hard The expression used to designate a strong entrance or beginning; for example, when the music is first heard, it is heard very loud and fast.

hoist The short side, or height, of a flag. This is one of the measurements that determines the proportions of flags. The other is the flag's length or *fly.*

See parts of a flag in "Tables and Techniques" (page 339).

A hoist is also a portable mechanical device, either electrical or hand-pulled, that when fastened to the ceiling of a venue is used to lift, and then hold in position, heavy objects such as lighting instruments. Also see *chain crawler.*

hold To pause the show or presentation either to build emphasis at a particular moment or because of a problem.

hollowware *Tableware* that is deep, or hollow, such as soup bowls, cups, vases, and serving items such as teapots, creamers, sugar bowls, pitchers, platters, and serving bowls. It is not another word for *flatware* as is commonly mistakenly thought.

See flatware styles and appropriate placement in "Tables and Techniques" (page 404).

hologram A light-sensitive film that captures and plays back light wave interference patterns. One of the most striking results is a true three-dimensional statue of the re-created holographic image.

home run An electrical or control *cable* that runs straight from a power or control source to the equipment, without being interrupted, split, or diverted to other pieces of equipment along the way. The advantage of such a line is that it is less subject to interference, drop in signal strength, or interruption. For example, home runs from the control and power to a projector are a safety measure to help ensure that the connection will not fail during an important presentation.

honey wagon Affectionate name for a mobile toilet.

honor guard A ceremonial military unit often used as "guardians of the colors" to display and escort the national flag on ceremonial occasions. See *flag protocol.*

See flag protocol in "Tables and Techniques" (page 340).

horns   The brass instruments of an orchestra, including trumpets, trombones, and tubas. Also see *loudspeaker.*

hors d'oeuvre   Small, savory appetizers served before the meal. Typically they can be hot or cold and one- or two-bite size. They are customarily served with cocktails or *aperitifs.* While it is most effective, visually and practically, to use circulating waiters to serve the hors d'oeuvre on small trays, it is also common for them to be placed on decorated tables. Hors d'oeuvre (technically both the singular and plural form of the translation, but commonly an "s" is added for the plural) can be in the form of fancy *canapé* or simple crudités (raw seasonal vegetables).

 Tips on planning hors d'oeuvre:

✓ Mix them up. Select items that have different flavors, temperature, or texture.

✓ Forget the old standards like Swedish meatballs and cheese chunks on crackers. Try new recipes that offer a different appearance, color, and ingredients. Or select items that support the function theme. Make them a conversational topic.

✓ If it is a stand-up cocktail reception, make sure the hors d'oeuvre are not messy to eat and are small enough to handle with one hand while holding a drink in the other. See *finger food.*

✓ If waiters are passing the items, have enough waiters so every guest is served and re-served in a reasonable amount of time. Waiters are also needed to pick up debris like used napkins, toothpicks, and unwanted beverage glasses.

✓ If plates are used, provide flatware and a place for the guests to put the plates, flatware, and spent napkins when done. Also, if plates are used, most guests expect a place to sit, or tall tables to stand at while eating.

✓ If serving shrimp, understand that it is a favorite and a lot is necessary.

✓ If the event is held during regular lunch or dinner hours, and no lunch or dinner is being served, many guests will make a meal of the hors d'oeuvre, so plan on much larger volume consumption.

✓ Remember vegetarians.

✓ Supplement the main items with fillers such as nuts, olives, bread-sticks, chips, and dips.

✓ All items need to be 75 percent prepared before guests arrive in order to meet the demand.

📋 **See quantity charts in "Tables and Techniques" (page 349).**

hospitality suite A separate location, such as a hotel suite, at large conventions or trade shows where companies host select vendors, customers, VIPs, and associates for more comfortable conversation, meetings, and intense marketing. The suite should be enhanced with niceties such as flowers, company logos, snacks and beverages, and coatracks and umbrella stands. An adjacent area should be equipped with paper, pens, a computer, printer, copier, and other necessary supplies.

host, no-host bar Defines whether the bar beverages are complimentary or are included in the price of the event. A no-host bar means that each drink must be purchased. For planning, anticipate that the quantities required will increase with a hosted bar.

hot A situation where too much light is falling on one individual, or object, or portion of the stage.

hot spot A place on a projected image where the brightness is measurably different from that on other areas. Often this spot can be bothersome to the audience viewing the image. By relocating or diffusing the hot spot, it is possible to make the visual more effective.

house The part of a theater, arena, or other venue that holds the audience.

house curtain See *main curtain.*

house left The left side of the audience area when standing in the auditorium facing the stage.

house lights Lighting fixtures existing in the venue that provide general illumination in the area of the audience such as the auditorium, banquet hall, or meeting room. Also, existing theatrical lighting fixtures, either already hung in position or available for hanging. For a presentation or performance these lights need to be controlled by the lighting technician. Ideally they would be on dimmers or controllable by the lighting console.

house management The process of effectively executing the audience-related tasks of box office, ushers, program distribution, refreshments, merchandise sales, emergencies, and other such tasks in a theater or other *venue.*

house right The right side of the audience area when standing in the auditorium facing the stage.

hub and spoke A circulation system in which the visitor reaches the core of the complex or event and radiates out to other areas or zones. This technique creates added interest and natural crowd flow and can be effectively utilized for everything from a cocktail party to a large festival.

HVAC Abbreviation for Heating, Ventilation, and Air Conditioning. Anytime a lot of lighting instruments, projection, and large audiences are combined in a space, HVAC becomes an issue that must be planned for in advance.

IACC International Association of Conference Centers. The IACC has more than three hundred member facilities worldwide.

IATSE The abbreviation for the International Alliance of Theatrical Stage Employees, the labor union of stagehands and technicians, including sound and light technicians.

ice sculpture Sculpture made by either freezing water in special molds or carving blocks of ice into a multitude of shapes, all used as decoration at an event. Typically used to decorate buffet tables or hors d'oeuvre tables at a cocktail party. Often the image relates to the event, such as a company logo, a number for an anniversary, or an appropriate symbol. Ice molds of many different images are available and just require filling with water and freezing, but an appropriate size freezer is required. The sculpture requires a pan under it when on display to catch the melting water. Colorful lighting on the ice enhances the appearance.

At a martini party I attended, the hosts featured a large block of ice with a clear tube curled inside so that it was invisible. Flowers and other décor elements were also frozen into the ice block, making it quite beautiful. On top of the block was a funnel-shaped depression connected to the top of the hose. At the bottom a niche was carved below where the hose ended. The niche was large enough to place the martini glass. The bartender mixed the martini to order and gave it to the guest in a small glass. The guest first placed their martini glass in the niche below and then poured the mixed drink into the depression in the top of the ice block. The beverage flowed down, around, and through the ice, becoming very cold before pouring out the bottom and filling the martini glass in the niche. Great fun!

IEEE The abbreviation for the Institute of Electrical and Electronics Engineers.

illusionist See *magician*.

image magnification or **image mag** or **I-Mag** Typically refers to a live image or video that is enlarged greatly for easy viewing by a large audience, such as on giant screens at a rock concert. This technique is often used effectively for a speaker in a large venue, for demonstrations of smaller activities such as sewing technique, or to enhance a performance with close-ups of the musicians or singers.

impedance, low and high Impedance is the resistance of a circuit to alternating current, such as an audio signal. Microphones, guitars, and some other electronic elements including *loudspeakers* have different impedance. The matching of impedance within an audio system was impossible, but now different advantages can be achieved with different combinations. This all gets very technical and is best left to an excellent audio engineer.

impromptu A presentation, such as a speech, that is not planned in advance or is unrehearsed. Or it may be that it was planned, but a script does not exist. Such a presentation is very difficult for the production crew to manage and often forces them to *"go with God."*

incentives Extra services offered by hotels and resorts to planners giving reasons why a meeting or other event should be held at their location. Sometimes these are special activities they have available, including everything from swimming with dolphins to tours of interesting surroundings. Sometimes the incentives are special price deals on VIP rooms, food and beverages, or other legal financial advantages.

indirect costs All costs that are not part of the specific project budget such as start-up costs, insurance, taxes, and administration. See *budget*.

industrial Term used for a high-production corporate show such as a new product introduction. Also see *corporate show*.

inflatable Air-inflated structures. Very large character images, logos, and other visuals are created utilizing a plastic coated material and filled with air for display purposes. A wide variety of children's play units, including slides, jumping and bouncy structures, and even *laser* tag housings are inflatable.

in house Materials, food stocks, and other items that are already owned and on the premises. The term is also used for work and tasks to be accomplished by staff and existing personnel instead of by hiring a vendor.

inner proscenium See *false proscenium*.

"in one," "in two," "in three" Phrases used to designate different areas of the stage determined by the distance back from the *main curtain* and coinciding with the placement of the wings. "In one" means the prime area across and downstage of the first set of *legs* just upstage and center of the main *curtain line*; "in two" the second legs, etc. "In one" is the area most often used on a stage.

instrumentation A particular combination of musical instruments employed in a composition or utilized in a band or *orchestra*. In written music it is determined by the *composer*, *arranger*, or orchestrator, who in turn determines what instruments the orchestra must have. Also see *arranger*.

insurance Event insurance is necessary, often hard to secure, and expensive. Different events require different insurance. For example, if flame or fireworks are being used, a special policy is necessary. Or, if helicopters, high-wire acts, or large animals are being used, a special policy is necessary. The best advice is to discuss the details of the event with an insurance agency well in advance.

intellabeams *Lighting* instruments that can be preprogrammed for direction, color, size of beam, and other features such as rotation and effects so that when the *cue* is given, they automatically perform the prescribed function and then set themselves for the next cue.

intellectual property Creative works such as a script, design, musical composition, or painting for which ownership has been claimed and protected through a patent or a copyright. The owner of the intellectual property may or may not be the creator. To use such material in an event requires permission from the owner, which may require a fee. Always seek permission, or check to ensure that permission has been granted, before utilizing such properties in a public event. Noncompliance could result in a lawsuit and/or fine.

interactive Any activity that induces the audience to become involved. These experiences can be physical, mental, touchy-feely, etc., and they can aid in getting a message across or they can be just for pure fun.

intercom A communications system between all production personnel. The system can be wireless or wired with a headset for hands-free use. During performances, most prefer a wired system so that there is no chance of breakup, which might cause missing a cue. During setup, a portable wireless system is preferred for constant and easy communication over wide areas. Often referred to as Clear-Com, which is a leading brand name.

interiors Theatrical sets designed to represent indoor or interior scenes such as a room, a laboratory, or a cave.

in the round A theatrical presentation that takes place on a stage or performing area completely surrounded by the audience. Some directors prefer to have a live audience as the *backdrop* instead of settings or drapes. Some presenters prefer this setup because they believe it makes the audience more involved in the presentation.

intoxicated The condition of those who drink too many alcoholic beverages. All waiters and staff should be alert to someone becoming intoxicated but instructed not to say anything directly to the guest, or cut the guest off, but rather inform key staff or the host so they can handle the situation. Suspicion of drug usage or being under the influence should also be reported.

introduction The beginning of a piece of music, performance, or presentation. Or, the act of presenting someone to an audience. Also, the presentation of somebody to somebody else. At gatherings, certain social precedents require proper sequences of introduction. Women take precedence over men, such as "Susan, this is Mr. Jones. Mr. Jones, this is my wife Susan." Likewise older people take precedence over younger ones. Guests are always presented to the hosts, such as "Mr. (host), this is Sally Smith." The same is true with dignitaries or high office holders. Also see *reception line.*

invitation A means to ask those you want to come to your event. The basic tool for securing attendance for an event. Formal or informal, expensive or simple, the invitation gets the message to those you specifically want to get it to, quickly and efficiently. The invitation is the first exposure the guest has to the event. Consequently, it immediately creates an impression of the event. The receiver reads into it things like how dressed up one will have to be, how much it will cost, the importance of the event, how much fun it will be, whether it will be worth the time, whether one must go, and what other people will likely be there. An invitation may or may not require a reply. See *R.S.V.P.*

Timing of the invitation is critical. Invitees need a comfortable amount of time to respond. An invitation received too late gives the impression to those invited that they were invited as an afterthought or that the event has been hastily or carelessly thrown together. Late invitations also cut down on attendance because potential guests may have already committed to another function. An invitation sent too early appears almost as an imposition or demand, and often people forget about the event by the time it comes around. For most situations, mail the invitation four weeks before the event. Never mail less than two weeks ahead. During extremely busy holiday periods, or when the majority of guests are located out of town, more advance notice is appropriate and necessary. While there are many electronic delivery systems, invitations *must* be mailed by postal service.

At the time of this writing, it is acceptable to send e-mail invitations only for the most informal of events.

📓 **See invitation schedule in "Tables and Techniques" (page 369).**

Select the style of invitation appropriate to the event. It may be a *formal invitation* or an *informal invitation*.

📓 **Examples of invitations are found in "Tables and Techniques" (page 361).**

✏️ **Tips for information to include on an invitation:**

✓ Purpose of the event.

✓ Date and time.

✓ Dress.

✓ Exact location.

✓ Whose event it is.

✓ Whether or not a response is required, and if so, whom to respond to and when.

✓ Ticket price or donation required.

✓ Whether or not children are invited.

✓ Necessary items to bring to the event (such as *BYOB*).

✓ Time the event will end (particularly for young people's events—so the parent knows when to pick them up).

✓ Whether the event is a surprise party.

✓ Theme of the event or party.

✓ A meeting place, if special transportation is planned.

✓ The menu.

✓ If cocktails are being served, and whether it is an open (free to the guest) or cash (pay) bar.

✓ Ensure that each person's *title* is correct when addressing an invitation.

✓ Vary the type of invitation if it is being sent to the same guest list repeatedly. A different invitation alone can add interest to an old event.

invitation—formal The style of invitation traditionally issued for official functions, business functions, debuts, weddings, bar mitzvahs, anniversaries, formal dinners, and balls can be appropriate for almost any event. It requires a traditional format and must be engraved (or handwritten—never typed or computer printed) on fine white paper stock. Simply adding a logo to the invitation changes it from formal to informal.

✎ **A formal invitation may consist of some or all of the following elements:**

✓ An outside envelope, with the return address of the event and the address of the recipient.

✓ An inside envelope for the invitation (bearing the guest's name handwritten; if the invitation is for a married couple, address it "Mr. and Mrs. Smith." Intimate relatives can be addressed "Grandmother" or "Aunt Sue and Uncle Joseph).

✓ The invitation.

✓ Reception invitation in a separate envelope.

✓ A tissue over the invitation to protect the engraved printing.

✓ A response card for acceptance or regrets.

✓ A return envelope for the response card (which is addressed and stamped).

🖉 Tips for a formal invitation:

✓ All formal events, regardless of how few people attend, traditionally require a formal invitation.

✓ The form needs to be exact.

📑 See form examples in "Tables and Techniques" (page 361).

✓ Spell out completely all first and last names, days of the week, time, the word "and," and all directions, such as "West Street." It is correct to use "Jr." when appropriate.

✓ Write formal invitations in the third person.

✓ Be sure to take all elements to the printer at the same time so that they will all be consistent and fit in the envelopes.

✓ Write out all years, such as "Two Thousand and Fifteen."

✓ Children over thirteen years old should receive their own invitation. Younger children should be part of the family address on the outer envelope, such as "Mr. and Mrs. Smith and Susan" or "Mr. and Mrs. Smith and Family."

✓ The post office demands that outer envelopes have a return address.

✓ Select an appropriate *font* style that is easy to read.

📕 **Examples of type styles are in "Tables and Techniques" (page 369).**

✓ Either print in the *engraved* style, or handwrite. See *calligraphy.*

✓ Invitations to single adults may be addressed, "Mr. Paul Jones and Guest."

✓ Do not put phone numbers on the invitation.

✓ Do not run the wording together as if it were a sentence, and do not use sentence punctuation. Instead, break it into phrases.

📕 **See examples of phrasing in "Tables and Techniques," page 361).**

✓ Determine if a response is necessary.

✓ On wedding invitations:

  ↪ Always put the bride's name before the groom's. When the groom's parents are hosting the wedding, the rule is reversed. This conveys who is hosting the wedding.

  ↪ While Mr. is always used with the groom's name, do not use Miss or Ms. with the bride's name.

  ↪ Use military titles for brides and grooms on active duty. Fathers may use their military titles at any time.

  ↪ Use professional title (Doctor, Judge) for grooms. Do not use professional titles for mother of the bride or bride, except that when both are issuing the invitation the bride may use such titles.

A formal *invitation response* is required for all formal invitations.

invitation—informal Every style of invitation that falls outside the strict guidelines of the formal invitation is considered an informal invitation. The range is as broad as the imagination, from formal invitations printed on color-tinted paper stock to an invitation printed on a drinking straw. The addition of simple elements like a logo, phone number, or e-mail address on a formal invitation changes it to informal. **Novelty invitations** are informal and are often well accepted. They can be anything from a "pop-up" type paper-crafted image of the invitee's product to a physical item appropriate to the event such as a note attached to a flower lei for a luau-themed party.

Tips for an informal invitation:

✓ Traditionally, if more than six persons are invited, the event calls for an invitation.

✓ Be creative—try to develop an interesting, intriguing invitation that catches the potential guest's interest and makes them want to attend. Be different.

✓ Set the mood of the event with the invitation.

✓ Use the invitation to establish a new logo or slogan.

✓ Don't be restricted by form.

✓ Be specific with the details of the event—the time, date, place, etc. Most people prefer to know the exact time, such as 7:00 p.m. to 9:00 p.m.

✓ Provide a means for responses if necessary—mail, phone number, e-mail, etc.

✓ Write the invitation in the first person and use any form desired.

✓ Do not overdo it or mislead the guests with the invitation. Make the invitation representative of the event.

The response to an informal invitation varies. No response is necessary if an R.S.V.P. is not stated in the invitation. A stated R.S.V.P. requires a response, be it an acceptance or a regret, by mail unless otherwise stated. If "R.S.V.P. Regrets Only" is stated on the invitation, then a response is required only from those declining. Also see *invitation response.*

invitation—multi-function events An invitation with two or more separate invitations. Large events may have any number of small functions that together comprise the overall event. For example, there may be a ceremony, a VIP area for the ceremony, a cocktail party, a dinner, and an after-dinner party. If everyone is invited to all, one invitation works. This invitation should list all of the events complete with time, dress, etc., for each event. When different people are invited to only certain functions within the overall event, a **multiple-function/ multiple–*guest list*** invitation is required.

🖊 **Tips to accomplish a multiple-function invitation:**

✓ Use one general invitation, which has multiple pages. Each page is for a different event with all the appropriate information. Another option, less expensive, is to create a general invitation that states basic information about the overall event but does not list the various functions, and place it in the envelope with it a smaller invitation card for each additional function. Each card has the details of that particular function. The card may also serve as a ticket to that function. If so, it should state that on the card. R.S.V.P. information would be on the general invitation.

✓ This also works for the multiple-function/multiple–guest list invitation where selected guests are invited to different functions. Insert the smaller cards only for the events that guest is to attend. For example, for a political fund-raiser, everyone gets the same invitation, except there is a special invitation inserted for the largest donors' private pre-event, and a special invitation is inserted with these guests' general invitations, plus other selected guests' general invitations, for a post-event photo opportunity with the candidate in the garden outside. This card may also serve as the ticket for admission to the garden area.

 **See example in "Tables and Techniques" (page 370).**

✓ Tickets add another complexity to multi-function events. Should tickets to the individual functions be required, the appropriate tickets for each function would be included in the invitation packet. Or, the invitation card would be designed as a ticket to all events, stating that it is a ticket and the number of people it admits. If tickets are to be more tightly controlled, or if an R.S.V.P. is required, the tickets would not be included within the invitation packet. Rather, the invitation packet would list the events and state the number of tickets available to each invitee and ask the recipient to state the number of tickets requested on the R.S.V.P. response card. It must also be stated that either the tickets will be mailed after receiving the response card, or will be available for pickup at a point central to all the functions, or will be at the door of each function.

Multi-function-invitation events require extensive record keeping and excellent coordination to avoid confusion and embarrassment. The objective is to get the right people to the right event without them knowing that they are not invited to other events. Those receiving the guest's responses, and who answer phone questions, must have quick reference to the matrix of who is invited to which functions. They must communicate with the invitee in a manner that makes the invitee feel they are special and are invited to all the events, even though they are not.

invitation—multiple hosts When several people are hosting the event, there are no strict requirements for the sequence of the listing of hosts on the invitation. Typically the eldest host, or the host whose home the event will be at, or the chairperson of the event, will be listed first. It is important to indicate which host is the one to contact for acceptance and request.

See example in "Tables and Techniques" (page 362).

invitation list A record of who is invited to an event or multiple events. The invitation list is a seldom-recognized valuable tool to the success of any event. If proper thought, foresight, and courage go into its composition, it will bring the people you want, or need, to your event. If it is an annual event, or a series of events, with the proper pruning and nurturing this list will grow and be an even more successful tool as time goes on. This list is not to be confused with the *guest list*, which lists those actually attending the event.

Tips for a successful invitation list:

✓ Be sure it includes the number of people you want or need to attend.

✓ Question if these are the right people to invite. Should any names be removed from the list?

✓ Anticipate how many will respond favorably. Is it enough?

✓ Ask for a response if you feel the information is valuable.

✓ Be sure those invited will enjoy the nature of this particular event.

✓ Invite those who need to be invited or expect to be invited.

✓ There is no quicker way to make an enemy than to *forget* to invite someone.

✓ Invite some new people if you want to grow the list in the future.

✓ Invite the press or media if appropriate.

✓ Are there community or business leaders, politicians, or other VIPs that should be invited to help your cause, or event, become more prominent and grow?

✓ Decide on the appropriate style of invitation for the event.

✓ Ensure that attendees' titles are correct. They change often.

✓ Review the list for deaths, divorces, or retirements that may prove embarrassing.

✓ Are the addresses up-to-date?

✓ Keep records! It is amazing how quickly it can get confused as to who was invited to what.

✓ After the event, review the list, note attendees and nonattendees, and make notes for the next time the list needs to be used.

invitation response The form of the invitation dictates the form of the response. All invitations that request a reply require a response. However, it is accepted as courteous, and is appreciated, to respond to *all* invitations. A **formal invitation response** is the return by mail of the preaddressed and stamped response card included with the invitation, or if one was not enclosed, a handwritten card stating the invitee's intention. An **informal invitation response** is required only when the invitation carries an *R.S.V.P.* or an *R.S.V.P. Regrets Only*. The reply to an *informal* invitation is the return of a response card if included, or it can be done in a number of different ways, including phone or e-mail, as requested on the invitation. Some hosts prefer "Acceptances Only" on informal invitations. Formal or not, in this day and age, because of so many late responders, it is often necessary to put **Respond by [date]** on R.S.V.P. cards.

📖 **See an example in "Tables and Techniques" (page 361).**

Managing the responses, particularly for a large *multi-function event* with different people invited to different subevents, and turning these responses into a *guest list* for each event, can be a tremendous challenge. The best way to handle the task is to assign a group of staff in one room with phones and computers to coordinate and log each response. All responses need to go directly to this room. This can be accomplished by using a code on the response card such as the address followed by "Room 200," so that whoever opens the mail recognizes that this is an invitation response. Another way is to establish a code name. For example, all responses are addressed to a person, such as "Miss Windsor." An e-mail address can function the same way. This enables the mailroom, the company phone receptionists, whoever is checking the e-mails, and even the executive's assistants and secretaries, to know what to do with a call asking for Miss Windsor. And everyone taking reservations by phone answers the phone by the name, Miss Windsor, so that the caller feels they are getting personal attention from the key person. Many business associates will call the executive they work with, or that person's assistant, and say "count me in." Such a response has a good chance of getting lost. So all should be instructed to tell that caller to speak with Miss Windsor.

✎ **Regardless of what social media system might be used for reservations, many people want to actually speak to someone about making their important reservations, because they often have questions and want to make sure they are included.**

"Miss Windsor" was the name I used for reservations for the grand opening of Walt Disney World. Not only were there twenty or so different events over a three-day period with different people invited to some and not others, Hollywood stars were being booked on various charter flights, different people had different classes of hotel rooms over different dates, and certain tickets were assigned seats for the major events. Yet the system worked perfectly, almost!

iris A mechanical or electronic device used to fade a light source such as a projector. This is used at the end of a presentation so that the image doesn't harshly appear or disappear, but rather fades in or out.

iron ride A generic term for any metal-framed style amusement ride typical of those used in a *carnival*.

ISES Abbreviation for the International Special Events Society. This professional association for those in the special events industry's mission is to educate, advance, and promote the industry and its network of professionals while cultivating high standards of business practice. For more information see www.ises.com. Also see *CSEP* and *CMP*.

jack A triangular frame made of wood and hinged to the back of a set piece or *ground row* to brace it from behind. Also, the female half of a connector (audio, video, telephone, etc.) that mates with a *plug*.

jell To come together. Typically used in events to describe the status of the project, or elements of the project, when everything is being worked out successfully.

jeroboam A size of *champagne* or wine bottle that holds four bottles or 3.2 liters.

See chart of standard bottle sizes in "Tables and Techniques" (page 306).

jigger Generally used to measure liquor, this small shot-size measuring glass usually holds 1.5 ounces of liquid. Jiggers are also available in 1-once and 2-ounce sizes, and some are made with different sizes on each end, making bar measurements for different drinks quick and easy.

jog Any flat that juts out at approximately a right angle to the perpendicular flat going *upstage*.

Jumbotron The trade name for a very large video screen, typically mounted to a semi-truck trailer, that is bright enough to be viewed in sunlight. The old technology screen is composed of a system of tiny lights while the new uses *LED* lights.

junket A **press junket** for events it is a trip made by the public relations and publicity team to other locations for the purpose of promoting and gaining press for the event. A movie junket is when entertainment journalists are invited to see a movie for the purpose of giving it *publicity* and writing reviews.

karaoke Interactive live entertainment in which amateur singers sing along with pop song music that is prerecorded and excludes the lead vocal. Usually the lyrics are displayed on a video monitor with a visual indicator to guide the singer. A **karaoke machine** is the device that stores and plays back the music and video on command. It is believed that this device was originally created in Kobe, Japan, in 1971. The person announcing the next singer and operating the machine is a **karaoke jockey** or KJ. While most associate karaoke with music, it is also commonly done by speaking lines of popular movie scenes. This is called **karamovie** or **movieoke**. Karaoke is different from *lip sync* in which a performer mimes to a previously recorded song with the lead vocal intact.

keep alive To store props, visuals, scenic pieces, or other materials so that they are readily available if required.

key art The poster for a film. It contains the film title, a designed graphic, and the titles and positions of key individuals important to the film. The term is sometimes used for event posters as well.

key light The primary light on the front of the speaker or actor. Most often this light will come from two directions at about 45° to one another, allowing the subject to be seen nicely from the audience on both sides. The key light is balanced with the *backlight* coming from behind.

keynote The most important speech or presentation given at a dinner, conference, or other gathering. The **keynote speaker** or **keynoter** delivers this address and is often the reason many of those in the audience choose to attend. At a banquet, place the keynote speaker at the head-table with other dignitaries to both emphasize his importance and so that all in the audience can see and relate to the person.

✎ **Tips on hosting a keynote speaker:**

✓ Ask them for their exact title and how they wish to be introduced. Also ask which items in their curriculum vitae they prefer to have mentioned in their introduction. And don't forget to get the speaker's preferred pronunciation of their name.

✓ Provide a place for the speaker to rest quietly, such as a *green room*, prior to their presentation.

✓ Provide a written thank-you for their efforts, ideally a letter signed by the highest officer in the organization.

✓ Pay them promptly. Offer to repay their out-of-pocket expenses immediately upon receipt of receipts.

✓ Give them special treatment while at the event.

All of these tips will help in booking the next speakers. They all talk among themselves.

keystone A distorted projected image (typically wider at the top than the bottom) because of the angle the projector is placed to the screen. To eliminate the keystone effect, ensure that the projector is perfectly square with the screen. Another method to eliminate "keystoning" is to enlarge the image so that the edges of the visual fall outside of the screen limits, but this method will not straighten words or lines of copy. Sophisticated video projectors have an adjustment to correct for the keystone effect. This distortion is named after the shape of a keystone at the top of an arch. Also see *scenery*.

kibitzer A character who verbally interferes or gives unwanted advice. Often this device can be used to add comedy or advance a story through humor. It can also be an unruly audience member, planned or not, particularly in a comedy performance.

kill To remove an item from the stage such as a prop or piece of *scenery*, to extinguish lights, or to stop the audio or effects.

kir A white wine that is flavored with either *cassis* or *champagne* and served as an *aperitif*.

kissel A dessert soup made of fruit popular in northern and eastern Europe and Russia.

kompot A nonalcoholic clear juice drink obtained by cooking fruit in water; popular in Poland and Balkan countries.

lamé A shiny glitter fabric used for theatrical curtains. There are many variations but all integrate metallic fibers to sparkle light and are available in many solid colors. Some are iridescent.

lamp A source of light such as the bulb in a lighting instrument or the carbon arc in a follow spot.

laser A device that produces a coherent beam of light that remains parallel for long distances and contains one or more extremely pure colors. The term is derived from Light Amplification by Stimulated Emission of Radiation. A **light-show laser** usually consists of gas-filled tubes using high-voltage current to cause the gas to glow. The type of gas used determines the color of the light beam.

laser light show A presentation where laser light is the primary attraction, creating beam effects in the air, moving graphics on screens or surfaces, and abstract patterns, all in combination and set to music.

✎ **Many large lasers are water-cooled and require a reliable, continuous water source.**

✎ **Keep in mind that laser beams can only be seen when the light hits something such as dust or moisture particles in the air. Since these cannot always be counted on, *hazers* need to be used to add these particles, and they need to be placed upwind. Also, lasers are most impressive shooting toward, but well over the heads of, the audience.**

✎ **Warning:** Do not allow laser beams or projections to shoot into an audience. They can cause blindness. Always keep the beams well above the heads of the audience. U.S. federal law also requires all laser beams to be terminated against a solid surface, such as a large wall. Shooting unterminated beams into the sky is illegal and subject to heavy fines.

I contracted a reputable laser company to provide a permanent laser installation as part of an exterior show we were doing for a casino. Apparently while setting up, they allowed a beam to shoot into the sky. I was called by the casino management, who said they had received a letter from the federal government stating that they would be taken to court and issued a fine, because apparently the beam hit a fighter jet and was reported by the pilot. Because we were still

> *awaiting the license for the laser from the Federal Department of Health (where all laser installations are regulated), it was my responsibility to resolve the issue. To do so, I had to make a trip to Washington, D.C., to meet with the one person who issued the letter and who issues the licenses. He was tucked away in a tiny office in a very large building and was the only person doing this job. The office was stacked floor to ceiling with so many manila file folders of applicants for lasers yet to be approved that there was not space for a chair other than his. Finally, after a two-hour meeting during which we explained the error, apologized, and made a case for our license, he dismissed the matter and issued the license. Whew!*

lash To bind two *flats* together with a rope through *lash line cleats* on the back frames of the flats. The rope used for this purpose is called a **lash line**.

lash line cleat The metal device attached to the back of a scenic flat to which the lash line is fastened to securely hold two or more flats together.

lasting impression An impact on a person that will stay in that person's mind for a long time. It is also what every event must create. In my opinion, an event is not successful unless it accomplishes this. It can be in the form of a wonderful feeling, a sustainable visual, a first experience, or a combination of all. It is what those attending tell other people about the event and something they may remember for the rest of their lives.

layout The plan as to how all the components of an event or show are distributed and arranged over the space available. The best layouts are scaled-drawing floor plans; others simply indicate approximate dimensions and distances. The more information available on the layout, the better.

✐ **Situations that require a layout are**

✓ Cocktail reception—showing location of bars, entertainment, food tables, and decorations.

✓ Musical presentation—showing the location of piano, drums, other instruments, microphones onstage, and the space required for and between each.

✓ Speaker's platform—the position of the lectern, props, steps, screens, and other elements required on the platform.

✓ Theatrical presentation—the plan for the scenery, entrances and exits, drops, lighting, and furniture and props.

✓ Dinner—the plan for the tables, stage, screens, speakers, and special entertainment.

L

📋 **Examples of these and other layouts and plans can be found in "Tables and Techniques" (page 415).**

✐ **Items often overlooked on the plan that can cause a problem at the last minute are**

✓ Cable runs and places where safety coverings of the cables are required.

✓ Floral or decorating elements delivered at the last moment.

✓ The locations of speakers or performers onstage in relation to where lighting can realistically be mounted.

✓ The placement of video cameras.

✓ What is required onstage given the platform and ceiling height.

✓ Large chandeliers, other built-in fixtures, support columns, or other inherent problem sight-line elements in the room or the space being utilized.

lead-in The opening portion of a newscast, in which the reporter typically sets the story and location of the event.

leadsheet A piece of sheet music that contains the basic melody, chord changes, and lyrics of a musical composition or song. Also see *score*.

lectern A slender stand with a slanted top on which a book, notes, or other materials can be placed before a standing speaker. Also referred to as a *podium*. Some lecterns are shorter and designed to be placed on a tabletop. Good lecterns also have lights built into them to illuminate the papers on top and attachments for microphones. Another important element of a lectern is for it to be adjustable for different heights of the speakers. Some have motors and can be adjusted by an offstage *crew* member between speakers so that it is at the right height for the next speaker.

L

✏ **Select a lectern carefully.**

✓ While lecterns come in all styles and sizes, it is important that they function as necessary and "fit" the speaker. For example, a large man looks uncomfortable behind a thin lectern, a small woman looks dwarfed behind a large lectern, and a very important person requires a substantial lectern.

✓ Know the heights of the speakers. Some may require a small platform behind the lectern to raise them to an appropriate height. An ideal solution is an adjustable lectern that moves up and down electronically and is controlled by an *offstage* device. By rehearsing with the speakers, you can determine the heights and make notes so that during the speaker's entrance, the lectern can be adjusted.

✓ The front of the lectern is an ideal location for a logo, seal, or other visual element that will make a statement both to those attending and in press pictures. A common mistake is to not remove the venue's signage, such as a hotel's logo, from the face of the lectern and replace it with something identifying the event. But check your contract with the venue before doing so.

LED The abbreviation for bulbs made of Light Emitting Diodes with electrical circuitry that converts energy into light. Theatrical lighting instruments utilize these bulbs, replacing traditional incandescent bulbs, because they have intense light and can remotely be controlled to change to any color all while using much less electricity. Other advantages are that the instruments are lighter to carry, have much longer bulb life, and afford the lighting designer much more control over the lighting while utilizing fewer instruments. Ideal for parties are battery-operated color floods, which add colored light to any object.

leg drop One or more vertical pieces of scenic material with battens at top and bottom. Often used for a group of tree trunks or similar types of scene elements.

legs Vertical pieces of either scenery or drapes placed on the sides of the stage performing area to block audience viewing into the side *backstage* areas. Most often legs are placed or hung from battens one behind the other and are flat so that in between the cast and *scenery* can be easily moved on and off the stage from side areas. If the leg is scenic, such as the trunk of a tree, it is referred to as a leg drop.

Leko The common style of lighting instrument that uses an ellipsoidal reflector to create a spotlight effect. Originally a brand name, but now a generic term. Lekos have been the most common style of theatrical lighting instruments.

lens An optical glass that is used to gather or disperse by refraction rays of light that pass through it. It is an essential element of a *spotlight*.

level The intensity of a light or audio source. For example, the level of the background music in a *cocktail party*. Also, a platform of various heights and sizes; when placed together, they create a group of different levels to vary the performing areas onstage.

Liberty cap or **Phrygian cap** A small red cap placed over the top of the flag staff when the flag is retired or put away. The tradition of the Phrygian cap or liberty cap began in ancient Rome where it was given to a slave upon manumission—a sign of his freedom. It evolved as a symbol of freedom during the Revolutionary era in America. The picture of Liberty on early silver dollars shows her wearing a Phrygian cap and today it is seen on the seal of the U.S. Army. The cap, which has a specific design—it resembles the Smurfs cap—is often used to show respect to the flag as it is put away.

license The granted right to use material owned by another. For example, to use material out of this guide in one's own presentation would require securing a license from the publisher, which is granted with a written contract stating the uses permitted and the costs needed to be paid to the grantor. For example, to use an existing piece of music requires a license from the publishers, secured through *ASCAP*. Photos, comedy routines, book passages, etc., all require a license for usage. *Stock photo* libraries and music libraries make the process very easy and inexpensive.

L

 Do not assume that it is okay to use someone's material without obtaining permission and/or a license. There have been many lawsuits resulting in large payouts over usage thought to be "nonconsequential."

Life Safety Code Guidelines and regulations for planning audience safety at major events and event venues. Published by the National Fire Protection Association, it is the national safety codebook for any public gathering in the United States. Many of the same code issues can also be explored with local fire departments. The guide is available for a fee at www.nfpa.org/catalog/product. Also see *Event Safety Guide*.

light area The spot on the stage that could be covered by one light, but typically that spot, or light area, would be covered by four lights: from the front, one center, one from 45° left, and one from 45° right; and from the back, one center. A small stage could have six light areas: three in a row across the downstage area (Down Left [DL], Down Center [DC], and Down Right [DR]) and three in a row across the upstage area (Upstage Left [UL], Upstage Center [UC], and Upstage Right [UR]). Since every stage and every production is different, it is the *lighting director* who determines the light areas and the number of instruments required to meet the demands of the production.

📖 Examples of stage areas and basic lighting can be found in "Tables and Techniques" (page 448).

light bridge A long, narrow platform suspended by adjustable lines directly over the inner proscenium opening or any other portion of the stage. On this are placed the spotlight for the upstage areas, special spots, and effects projectors.

light curtain A stage curtain embedded with small light bulbs, usually colored, and lighted or flashed on cue to provide dazzle to a scene or performance. The light patterns can take the form of a logo, stars in the night, or various geometric patterns and designs. The curtain lights are connected to the lighting control board and controlled by the lighting director.

lighting Any presentation can be greatly enhanced through effective, appropriate, and creative use of theatrical lights. Lighting ads color, effects, and most importantly directs the audience's attention to where it needs to be. Lighting is also used to illuminate people and their faces at press events, speeches, and most other event activities. Lighting also sets the mood of the event, be it bright and colorful, or stark and somber, or dramatic. Consider lighting as the most important visual element of any event.

🖊 **Tips on lighting that may be helpful:**

✓ Insist that all lighting be done the night before and be prepared to spend most the night worried, frustrated, and wondering if it will ever get completed.

✓ Have a mini-flashlight with you during the lighting procedure. The lighting director always wants everything dark.

✓ Don't ask for a change unless you are willing to spend a couple hours making it happen.

✓ Never use rope lights. They are much too overused.

✓ Insist that all key lights, those most important, have new bulbs inserted. All too often these will be the lights that blow a bulb during the first few minutes of a presentation.

✓ Always explore what can be done with existing *house lights* prior to contracting a *lighting designer*.

lighting director The key member of the creative production team responsible for the theatrical lighting of the presentation or performance. Referred to as the LD, this person plans the placement and usage of the theatrical lights by developing a *light plot*, specifies the power source, and determines cable runs to the lights, the dimmers, and the control board. The LD manages his team of technicians who hang the lights, place *gels*, and provide the labor for all other lighting activities. The LD will also activate the lighting *cues* during the performance.

light plot A scaled plan drawing of the stage or presentation area indicating the *light areas*, positions of lighting instruments, cable runs, type of mounting and color *gel* for each instrument, follow spotlight positions, and all other details of the light design. All documents are created by the *lighting director*.

limbo The type of setting where the background seems to go on forever or is totally black.

limo or **limousine** Large, luxurious automobiles. Usually ultra stretched to accommodate a group of people or *VIPs*. Traditionally only prestige automobiles were used as limos, but now all types of vehicles are available, including Hummers, Jeeps, classics like vintage Rolls Royces, cowboy pickups, Batmobiles, and even military Ducks.

> One of my corporate clients, a leading beer maker, insisted that every guest (of which there were several hundred) invited to the event be picked up at the airport, chauffeured during their stay, and returned to the airport in only Mercedes-Benz stretch limousines. To accommodate this request, Mercedes limos and their drivers were brought in from all over the western United States. Of course, each was stocked with the company's brands on ice.

line of sight See *sight lines*.

line or **lines** The written material of a speech or performance. Also, the ropes attached to the top of flats, pipes, or battens that go up through pulleys to the gridiron and are counterbalanced. The scenery and lighting can be raised or lowered by manipulating these lines. See *line set*.

line drawings Simple drawings from which scenery, props, platforms, or other items can be constructed. These drawings usually are not drawn to scale and have no reference to other specifications.

linen The general term for all the fabrics used for dining or a banquet, including tablecloths, napkins, runners, skirts, chair covers, and place mats. For home parties this may extend to towels in the bathroom.

Linens are made from a wide variety of fabric types in many colors, patterns, and styles. Also see *place setting* and *tabletop.*

📖 **For a complete list of linen sizes see "Tables and Techniques" (page 380).**

line set A group of *lines* that are short, center, and long, in one horizontal row or plane, used to lift a *batten* or unit of *scenery.*

Linnebach projector An old-style projector used to create large scenic backgrounds onstage. It utilizes a painted image on a large glass slide as the source for the visual. See *Panni projector.*

lip sync When a performer's mouth movements are matched to previously recorded dialog or lyrics they are not actually speaking or singing. Some major performers have been denied legitimacy for lip syncing their performance.

liqueur An alcoholic beverage, such as rum, whiskey, or brandy, with sweetened and flavored roots, leaves, fruits, seeds, and other such ingredients. While some liqueurs are generic, others have secret formulas that have been guarded for centuries. Some were originally used as a medicine. The alcohol content ranges widely from around 15 percent (some Irish creams) to 55 percent. Traditionally liqueurs were served as an after-dinner drink, but today many are popular as cocktails, either by themselves or mixed with other spirits, and are required for a complete bar. Cream liqueurs are mixtures that have been homogenized with cream, but they require no refrigeration. Liqueurs are different from eaux-de-vie, fruit brandy, and flavored liquors that contain no added sugar.

The popularity of individual liqueurs changes constantly, but a few of the standards are anisette, Cointreau, crème de cassis, crème de menthe, Drambuie, Goldwasser, Grand Marnier, Irish cream, Jagermeister, Kahlúa, Midori, ouzo, sambuca, Tia María, and triple sec.

Examples of beverages favored by geographical area can be found in "Tables and Techniques" (page 322).

liquor An alcoholic beverage, especially of the type produced by distillation, such as vodka, rather than fermentation, such as beer or wine.

live A band, entertainer, or complete show performing in-person in real time as opposed to a recording. Also, the condition of a microphone when it is turned on. Also, a newscast that is being fed directly to its home base, usually via microwave, and being immediately broadcast out to the audience.

load-in The process of moving all of the required equipment, scenery, risers, and other materials into the theater, exhibit hall, ballroom, or other space that is the venue for an event.

loading doors Very large double doors through which scenery and other large materials are brought backstage or onstage from outside. These doors typically are tall enough to bring in large scenic pieces without having to fold or disassemble them.

load-out The process of removing all of the equipment, scenery, risers, and other materials from the theater, exhibit hall, ballroom, or other space at the completion of an event.

lobby The part of a theater, ballroom, or other public space immediately outside of the main space. This area is often used for events preceding the main event, such as a cocktail party, a receiving line, a preshow, or many other such activities.

loft An upper floor open to the main floor of a church, auditorium, or other structure. In a church, this area is used exclusively for the members of a choir, and possibly the organist, as their performance area. Also see *fly loft*.

logo A symbol, emblem, or insignia of an organization, such as a company, club, association, or military unit. Company logos are typically a legally owned mark of the company and are rigorously controlled so as not to be distorted or misused. All uses of a logo must have the owner's prior permission and contain the legal designation of the mark, such as ® for registered, © for copyrighted, or ™ for trademarked.

long shot (LS) A camera lens angle that is very wide and includes the entire scene. It is used to establish a location or to aid the viewer in knowing where they are within the area.

loose pin hinge A hinge whose pin is not permanently inserted but can be removed to separate the two parts. It is commonly used onstage to connect two flats together. This technique allows for quick assembly and disassembly of the flats or scenic elements.

loudspeaker A device that converts electronic analogue or digital signals into physical wave forms for audible sound. Available in many different shapes, sizes, and qualities and often designed for different sound reproduction purposes. For example, lower or bass sound, around 40 hertz (Hz), is best reproduced by electrodynamic drivers in large cabinets called **woofers** and placed at the bottom of a sound stack. The midfrequency range and high frequency **horns** vary greatly in shape and are placed in the middle and top of the speaker stack, respectively. Augmented to this standard audio loudspeaker stack are **tweeters**, designed to reproduce the high frequency sounds in the 2,000 to 20,000 Hz range, which are in the upper end of human hearing, and **subwoofers**, which reproduce the lowest level frequencies in the 20 hertz Hz range for augmented bass response.

magician A performer who creates illusions of seemingly impossible feats. Often referred to as a stage magician or **illusionist** to distinguish them from one practicing paranormal or ritual magic. One who specializes in escapes from restraints is called an **escape artist**.

mailing list A list of people contacted for a specific event. It can be a publicity list of press to contact for event promotion, a list of invitees, a list of donors from which to gain funds, or a list of VIPs who must be contacted. Traditionally, materials were mailed by post on a planned scheduled to people on the list or lists, but much of this is now done by e-mail. These lists are extremely valuable for repeated events, each time reviewing the responses to eliminate the nonresponsive while updating the lists with new names.

main curtain Also referred to as the front curtain, grand drape, house curtain, or act curtain. It is the curtain hung immediately upstage (behind) the *proscenium* arch, which frames the stage. Only limited performance takes place in front of the main without it being opened.

✎ **There are different types of main curtains:**

✓ Guillotine, which is a single curtain that lifts vertically up into the *fly loft* to reveal the stage. (Named after the execution device!)

✓ The wipe style, a single curtain that moves sideways to reveal the stage.

✓ A tab or tableau, which gathers the two halves, pulling each up and to the side.

✓ An Austrian or contour, with a characteristic set of folds, that is suspended from an overhead *batten* behind the proscenium. When pulled up it collects the folds one after the other, creating a visually interesting reveal of the stage.

✓ Smaller theaters typically have a traveler style, with two halves that pull apart toward the sides.

📖 **See diagram in "Tables and Techniques" (page 446).**

main event In wrestling it is the most prestigious matching of the event, the reason most of the audience attended. Also sometimes used in championship boxing.

maítre d' The host. The person responsible for guest interaction and satisfaction. Often a headwaiter or house steward. Also referred to as a **maítre d'hôtel**. This person is an important asset when you are planning a function at a hotel or restaurant. Close planning with the maítre d' is essential for everything from the food and beverage menu to the reception of your guests at the door.

make fast To make secure or **to fasten**.

makeup The art of improving or changing the appearance of an actor or others for the purpose of dramatic effect. A **makeup artist** utilizes a wide range of chemicals in different shades along with other materials to deepen, highlight, or cover facial characteristics. Often these changes are subtle, intended to just add a glow and eliminate blemishes, while special effect makeup can completely change the facial appearance through the use of artificial hair, prosthetic appliances, skin-safe silicone rubber, and paints.

manual mode A mode in which the human operator is in direct control of a system's functions with a minimum of interlocks.

manuscript See *script*.

marmite A tall-sided soup bowl. French onion soup is typically served in a marmite.

marquee A large and often decorative sign outside a venue such as a theater that displays what is currently performing, sometimes with a scrolling message. Also, a large tent erected for the purpose of the event.

marquette A miniature sculpted figure, often used as a model before producing a larger-scaled sculpture.

mask To conceal any equipment or area that is not to be seen by the audience. Also, a covering for the face that creates a different appearance. Sometimes a facial mask accomplished with *makeup* alone.

masking Anything used to hide or disguise something not to be seen by the audience. Onstage this is typically accomplished with a piece of scenery or *drapery*, either vertical or horizontal. Also see *mat*.

 See examples of stage masking in "Tables and Techniques" (page 446).

 master control The location during a show, performance, or event that is manned by the key operators, including lighting, sound, projection, and the person giving the cues. It can be in a control room, in the middle of an auditorium or arena, or backstage, but regardless of where it is located it is the heart of the operations. Also, the handle, dial, joystick, or other device that controls a series of individual switches or dimmers that have been interlocked so as to act as one unit. For example, to perform a lighting blackout, all of the individual light controls are interlocked to the master control lever so that the operator needs only to turn down this one lever to make all the lights fade out.

master of ceremonies or **MC** The person who introduces other participants on the program or parts of the show.

mat or **matte** A device, such as a paper or electronic frame, obscuring part of the image, permitting only the portion desired to be visible.

mechanical effects Also called physical effects or practical effects, these are essentially used to describe devices or props that are manipulated manually. For example, during a performance a painted moon is lowered by its supporting cable so that it appears to sink behind a flat shaped and painted like a mountain.

media The various means of mass communication, including newspapers, radio, magazines, and television, and the people involved in their production. Also see *press* and *publicity.*

media advisory A brief announcement to the media, usually via fax or e-mail, about an upcoming event or activity. It outlines in one page the schedule, the key people involved, and other details with the desired effect of generating press coverage about the event. Also see *press.*

media alert A notice sent to all general media announcing a press conference or *media event.* The purpose is to inform the news services of a newsworthy event and to encourage them to send a reporter and video crews to cover it. It states the time, place, and reason for the event.

📋 See sample form in "Tables and Techniques" (page 412).

media event Any kind of function that is arranged specifically to attract great attention from the mass *media.* Typical media events include a press conference, grand opening gala, political rally, awards presentation, groundbreaking, product introduction, VIP reception, or sales event.

📋 See media event layout in "Tables and Techniques" (page 411).

✏️ Tips for a successful media event:

✓ Start on time. Nothing can create a negative response from the media faster than having to wait for the event to start.

✓ Do everything possible to ensure that the media will show up to the event by following up the alert with phone calls, personal visits, or whatever it takes.

✓ Select the right day and time for the event. Most media don't attend events on the weekends, in the evening, etc. Talk with the media you are interested in attracting to find what is the best time for them to attend.

✓ Have preprepared copies of the speeches, data, names and titles of speakers, or other materials that will be verbally presented to hand out to the press upon their arrival along with a *press kit*.

✓ Have the podium, stage, and background well lighted so that good pictures and video can be easily taken.

✓ Ensure that the *public address system* is more than adequate and that there is a way that multiple video cameras and recorders can be easily connected. See *mult*.

✓ It is extremely important to have a live audience that is enthusiastic, represents local ethnicities and interests, and has key people the media recognizes who support what is being presented. Often the media will do interviews with these people after the presentation.

✓ Place a card on each chair onstage with the name of who sits there so that each VIP onstage knows his or her assigned seat.

✓ Add something special to the presentation that will ensure the press will report the story and event.

When I was working on the Ronald Reagan presidential campaign, at some point the very large traveling press corps was no longer interested in reporting basically the same speech every evening, so one of my responsibilities was to plus, or add something of interest to each of the rallies. At a very large rally in a packed arena in Newport, Virginia, as I was standing backstage with Reagan while the pre-speakers were talking, I spied a young child in the first row of the audience dressed in an Uncle Sam outfit, complete with the tall striped hat, and an idea hit me. I pointed out the child to Reagan and suggested that I send him out to him, carrying a small American flag, at the completion of his speech. "Good idea," he said. "I can work with that." So as Reagan went onstage to speak, I subtly went over to discuss it with the child's mother and brought the child backstage with me. Then the hard part . . . I had to find a small flag! I did, and while I was waiting at the bottom of the stage steps, I explained to the young boy what to do. At the conclusion of the speech I sent the child out onstage to take the flag to Reagan. Reagan turned to the child, shook his hand, and then lifted him up for all to see. The photo of the candidate holding the cute child in the Uncle Sam outfit waving the little flag hit the front page of almost every newspaper and was the lead video on all the news channels that evening! Later the picture was used in pictorial summaries of the campaign and other publications.

M

media kit See *press kit*.

media placement The actual location of an advertisement in print media such as the back page, or the time of day of radio or television commercials. Also, the act of purchasing advertising space in newspapers, periodicals, television, radio, etc.

medium shot (MS) A camera lens angle that is between a *long shot* and a *close-up*. An example is a person sitting in a chair where both the chair and the person are included.

meet and greet A reception to allow attendees to introduce themselves to each other and to key officials prior to the actual start of the event. Usually light refreshments are served.

meeting A gathering of people for a discussion. Meetings have traditionally been at a venue with all invitees present, but are also held via the Internet, or a combination of both. Regardless of the format, a meeting must have a stated purpose to achieve results. Also see *conference* and *meeting room*.

✎ **Tips for a successful meeting:**

✓ Define the purpose of the meeting. It can be to reconcile conflicting views, solve a problem, provide training, receive reports, or organize a plan.

✓ Be thoroughly prepared with an *agenda*, previous notes, materials to be used, an *audiovisual* presentation, and key guest participants.

✓ Each person attending should have been told what is expected from them and what topics they are to be prepared to present.

✓ Arrange for lively participation by structuring the meeting with a combination of reports, presentations, and discussion topics.

✓ Be conscious of how long a visual is left on the screen. It should be long enough to comfortably read, but not long enough to distract from the oral presentation.

✓ Make sure all visuals are large enough for everyone in the room to comfortably read.

✓ If the participants are all together in one location, be sure the *venue* is appropriate and the room is properly set up, with the appropriate audiovisual equipment working properly.

✓ Recap the key points, summarize the decisions, and bring the meeting to a definite conclusion in some memorable way.

📑 **Complete guides to meeting setup and audiovisual and other aids is in "Tables and Techniques" (page 430).**

Meetings that last for an entire day, or multiple days, require the above, plus food and beverage, *cocktail receptions*, hotel and travel arrangements, and other activities all carefully planned to keep the attendees interested, enthusiastic, and benefiting from the information exchange.

meeting location See *meeting room* and *venue*.

meeting room A space, typically in an office, hotel, or conference center, set up for a comfortable exchange among several people with the added aids of an easel pad, wall-mounted *whiteboard*, and audio-visual equipment such as a projector and speaker phone. Larger meeting rooms would also have a sound system and *lectern*.

🖉 **Tips for meeting room preparation:**

✓ Select a venue that specializes in meetings. It is just easier.

✓ Select a cozy room for the meeting, one that is not too large. If expecting one hundred participants, don't book a room that holds three hundred. Participants will feel lost.

✓ Set the tables and chairs in the most effective manner, be it schoolroom, round tables, theater style, or conference table.

✓ Make sure meetings in adjacent rooms are not bothersome, meaning they cannot be heard.

✓ Arrange to have ice water set on every table and see that the room is refreshed during breaks.

✓ If candy is provided, be sure it isn't cellophane-wrapped.

✓ If pens are provided, make sure they don't click.

✓ Preset and test all audiovisual equipment, including projection systems, audio systems, easels, whiteboards, markers, and whatever else.

✓ Have a tall stool for the presenter.

M

✓ Keep refreshments outside so that presentations are not interrupted with people getting more coffee or food, and so that
the supplies can be refreshed during the meeting without
interrupting.

melodrama An exaggerated play that is exciting, romantic, improb-
able, humorous, and often involves participation by the audience. In
old-fashioned melodramas the audience cheers the hero and boos the
villain.

menu A list of food and beverages available or selected for presentation. An **à la carte** menu is a list of all items available from which the
guest can choose any number of options. Originally in France, diners
were offered a choice of prepared items listed on a small chalkboard,
which in French is a "carte." So à la carte is "according to the board."
A **table d'hôte** menu is a preestablished list of courses to be served.
Early European restaurants offered set dishes the chef or proprietor
decided to prepare that day for a fixed price. Or they would offer one
complete dinner for a fixed price. Later in the eighteenth century a
table d'hôte establishment would offer a selection of dishes available,
each with its own price, and then cook each dish when it was selected.

✐ Tips on planning a menu:

✓ Go seasonal. Think about the food of the season and select dishes
to reflect the fresh vegetables and ingredients available.

✓ Remember vegetarians and dieters. Plan the menu so that people
can select items that they prefer and yet make a full meal of what
is selected.

✓ Do old favorites with a flair. If it is as basic as steak and potatoes,
find recipes that give each item a different look, taste, or zing.
Maybe the steak is cooked Brazilian style and sliced off large
skewers.

✓ Mix it up. Select recipes to offer different flavors, temperature, or texture throughout the meal. This will keep your guests from getting bored with the same old, same old.

✓ Keep the menu manageable. If you are preparing the food yourself, don't plan more than what can be accomplished. Plan to have 75 percent of the menu items prepared in advance.

✓ At banquets, when people sit down to eat and they see roast chicken with peas and potatoes, many automatically think the event is going to be bad, regardless of what happens later. If this is all the budget allows, find recipes and substitutions that cost the same but offer a different approach.

menu card A small card in a holder at each place setting on a table that lists the sequence and the food being served for each course. Only the name of the course item is listed ("Herb Roasted Chicken Breast with Garbanzo Bean Glaze") for each course. The cards can be hand-lettered or printed. At formal dinners it is only a white card with black printing in a classic *font*. At informal dinners it is appropriate to place one card between two place settings. At certain events, such as a retirement dinner, it is appropriate to have the retiree's name, the company logo, and the years worked, making it a **souvenir menu card** with the intent that attendees will take the card as a memento.

mezzanine The audience area of a theater that is either the first, or lowest, balcony or the separated first few rows of the balcony when there is only one.

mic, **mike**, or **microphone** A device, or transducer, that converts acoustic sound into electrical signals for the purpose of reproducing, broadcasting, or recording the sound. There are many different varieties, including condenser, dynamic, ribbon, carbon fiber, fiber-optic, and laser microphones. Also there are many different patterns of sound detection, including omnidirectional, unidirectional, bidirectional, and shotgun, and each is designed for specific ways to effectively collect the sound. The first microphone was a condenser style created in 1916 by Bell Laboratories. An *audio engineer* is responsible for selecting the correct microphone to match the usage and audio system.

mic flag A small *logo* sign attached to a *microphone* to identify the radio or television network or other *media* representative conducting the interview.

MIDI Musical Instrument Digital Interface, a hardware and software specification for the exchange of information between different musical instruments or other devices.

milestone A key point in the progress of a job or project, such as the completion of planning and beginning of production, client progress reviews, and press release dates.

military color guard See *color guard*.

mime A performer who tells stories through body motion without the use of speech, which is the art of **pantomime**. Mimes use subtle, expertly choreographed visual gags. A popular art form for street theater and *busking*. The most famous mime was Marcel Marceau in his character of "Bip."

miniatures Small-scale models of landscapes, buildings, vehicles, animals, and even people. Skillfully photographed, they can be strikingly effective in shots where it is not practical or possible to use the real thing.

mirror ball A special-effect device that creates multiple bright rays of light in a space, either stationary or turning, resulting in light dots wherever the beams end. The effect is made by the light from spotlights bouncing off a ball whose surface is covered with small pieces of mirrored glass. Also called a disco ball, even though mirror balls have been used widely long before disco became popular. Often used over dance floors.

mobile stage A platform of varying size and configuration mounted on a trailer that can easily be brought to the venue, opened up to create a performing area, and, after the event, folded down and taken away. Typically mobile stages have a roof over the performing area capable of holding a few lighting instruments, a *backing*, and platforms on the sides for stacking *loudspeakers*.

mocktails Cocktails without liquor, such as a virgin mary. These beverages have become increasingly popular because of new liquor laws, designated drivers, and the trend among young people of not being interested in alcoholic beverages. An entire line of new recipes, most featuring fruit, is now available, ranging from the traditional Shirley Temple to an apricot mint julep, elephant charger, and lemon daisy.

M

 Since most mocktail recipes require ingredients not typically used by bartenders, special prearrangements are necessary with those providing the bar service. A quick solution is to offer two or three different mocktails along with the standard bar beverages.

mock-up A rough version of an advertisement, collateral, or other visual piece to give the impression of how the final version will appear.

monitor To observe an action in progress, such as watching a video feed on a screen as it is recorded or transmitted. Also, the device, be it a screen, meter, etc., that indicates the volume or intensity of sound, light, video, and other production elements. Also, audio speakers that are placed onstage, or near a podium, facing toward the performer or speaker so that they can hear the audio.

monogram A person's initials placed together in an artful design used to decorate an object. Typically it is three initials, unless they spell a word. The most common for a married couple has the last name initial in the center and the wife and husband first initials smaller on the sides. A single woman or man uses their last name initial in the center with the first and middle smaller on each side.

mounting The overall procedure of organizing all of the elements for a show, presentation, event, or other production. Also, the process of securing photographs and visuals to stiff paper boards or other materials for the purpose of display.

move-in The process of actually setting up a show, event, or other function at a venue.

moving lights Also referred to as intelligent lights, these theatrical lighting fixtures have many features such as movement in any direction, color changing, and changing the size of the beam of light, all automatically, either by instant commands or by preset cues through a controller. These lights often replace the traditional theatrical lighting instruments, such as *Lekos*, because of their advanced capabilities. Often one of these lights replaces several traditional lighting instruments.

MP3 The digital audio encoding format common for consumer audio storage, transfer, and playback of digital music on audio players. Also referred to as MPEG.

mult or **multbox** An electronic box with multiple audio *jacks* of different styles that allows the press corps and other media representatives to plug in their audio recording equipment to receive a direct audio feed from the microphone of a speaker. This eliminates the need for a mass of microphones attached to the speaker's lectern. The box has a *home run* directly from the microphone's amplifier ensuring strong, clear sound. The mult is located in the press area of the event, and the event host is responsible for providing it.

multimedia Any of a wide variety of equipment, old or new media, used for presentations, including standard or video projectors, video and screens, sound systems, audio players, computers, electronic pads, and telephones. Also, presentations composed of multi-content materials combining still images, animation, text, video, audio, and interactivity.

music An important element of many events, whether it is pre-recorded or a live performance by a band, orchestra, or choir, used for dancing, to play on and off speakers, or just as background to a lovely dinner.

🖉 **Tips to consider when selecting music:**

✓ Choose music appropriate to the event and the event's theme.

✓ Choose music appropriate to the audience. Consider their gender, age, and why they are assembled.

✓ It may be important to mix musical styles at different times in the event. The right classical selections with the right pop music can be very effective. Be clever with your choices.

✓ Review musical styles and selections with the client. Music is very personal.

🖉 **Classic musical selections for a Christian wedding ceremony:**

"Joyful, Joyful, We Adore Thee" (Beethoven)

"Liebestraum" (Liszt)

"Jesu, Joy of Man's Desiring" (Bach)

"The Lord's Prayer" (Malotte)

"Ave Maria" (Schubert)

And for the processional, "Wedding March" (a.k.a. "Here Comes the Bride") (Wagner)

✐ **Tips to consider when presenting music:**

✓ Music is always better when performed by live musicians, even if it is just a single harpist or guitar musician.

✓ If music is continuous, or *wall-to-wall*, it can be less interesting than if it is used as a highlight or at important moments.

✓ Always control the volume and be sure there is an understanding beforehand with those presenting the music as to who has final control of the volume.

✓ Few things ruin an event faster than music played over a poor sound system. Audiences are too accustomed to hearing great quality music reproduction.

muslin The ideal fabric to use on scenic *flats* and as *backdrops* because it is easily painted on and will shrink when *sizing* is applied. This sturdy cotton fabric is available in natural and black and in many widths.

napkin fold A presentation of the napkin as a decorative touch to a *table setting* or items being served. Dinner napkins can be folded in various fancy and interesting ways such as a rose, bishop's hat, swan, and many other shapes for both the casual and formal dinner.

📖 **See examples and instructions for traditional folds in "Tables and Techniques" (page 386).**

napkin ring A circular device made of silver, wood, porcelain, or many other materials designed to add decoration and form to the napkin. Also called a **serviette ring**, its original purpose was to identify the napkins of different households between washdays. The French began using the idea as a *place setting* decoration in the 1800s. Often napkins are monogrammed. Today they are available in an endless variety of styles, colors, and materials.

narrator A performer who delivers lines, tells a story, gives an account, or makes introductions. Often this is done from offstage. Also see *voice-over.*

negative image A condition in which the polarity of a picture is the reverse of normal. In standard nondigital photography, negatives are used as a basis for final prints.

network television A national affiliation of local television stations, such as the American Broadcasting Company (ABC), or program delivery companies that broadcast over many cable television systems, such as HBO or the Disney Channel.

NFPA Abbreviation for the National Fire Protection Association, the publishers of the *Life Safety Code*, which specifies safety policy for all events.

no-host bar The style of bar service at a *cocktail party* or *banquet* where each drink must be purchased. It is the opposite of a hosted or *open bar*, where all drinks are complimentary. Also see *cash bar.*

noise Electrical interference that causes inaccurate signals in sound, lighting, and other production systems, resulting in hum, inaccurate movement, or other problems. Also, any unwanted sound that interferes with a presentation.

notices Press criticism and clippings from newspapers and periodicals. Also see reviews.

NTSC A nondigital video playback and transmission standard used primarily throughout North America and parts of Asia.

OCC Operator Control Console. Any of several consoles that exist to provide select modes and initiate *manual* and local control of functions.

occupancy rating The number of people permitted by law to be in any given area based on space usage. For example, the room occupancy rating for a stand-up cocktail party is different from a banquet. The local building codes and fire regulations determine room occupancy based on a number of factors, including the location and number of exit doors, other function rooms in the area, and other conditions. Occupancy rules need to be strictly adhered to. Also see *density*.

offline Refers to a programming or monitoring system that is not currently operating.

offstage Any area outside of the acting or performance area of a stage. Also see *backstage*.

olio curtain A curtain that rolls up, usually from the bottom. Often it will be painted with a scene. Also, it refers to a backing, flown halfway between "*in one and in two*," giving a greater space for the actor to perform than "in one" and yet leaving the "in three" space for the next scene.

olivette See *floodlights*.

onstage The area of a stage or riser used for acting, performance, or other presentations or that is within the *sight lines* of the audience.

open bar The type of bar service at a *cocktail party* or *banquet* where all drinks are complimentary or included with the *ticket*. This is also referred to as a *host* or hosted bar and is the opposite of a *no-host* or cash bar, which requires payment for each drink.

open cold To open a show or other performance or presentation without an overture, musical number, announcement, or other type of introduction.

orchestra The lower floor or separated first rows of the auditorium. So named because these are the seats closest to the musicians immediately in front of the stage. Also, a group of musicians, especially a fairly large number, hired to perform music for the show or event.

orchestra lift An elevator located in an orchestra pit that is used to lift and lower the floor of the pit. Often these lifts are designed to create an apron in front of the stage area when in the uppermost position.

orchestra pit A recessed area in front of the stage used by the musicians to perform the score to the production onstage. Usually, access to the pit is from under the stage so that the audience does not see the musicians enter or exit. Often the base is a lift designed to raise and lower the orchestra or to serve as the front part of the stage if no orchestra is being used.

orchestration See *instrumentation*.

orchestrator See *arranger*.

order of events The sequence of individual occurrences during the actual overall event. It differs from a *schedule* in that these are only the occurrences that are pertinent to the specific event, such as the banquet. It includes a sequential list of such items as when food service begins, when toastmaster begins, the toastmaster's introduction of the speaker, speaker musical play-on, speaker play-off, presentation of an award, etc. Typically, along with the description of each occurrence is the planned time for it to happen and who is in charge of making it happen and other appropriate notes. While much of the same information may appear on the event planner's master schedule, the order of events is distributed to different individuals than is the more comprehensive schedule. Such individuals would be the toastmaster, the musician, the sound engineer, the host, etc. It becomes each of these individual's working guide to the flow of the event.

An order of events could be a sequence as tight as this:

8:00 p.m. Main course is served.

8:40 p.m. Final dinner plates are removed. Give stand by to MC and bandleader.

8:45 p.m. Musical fanfare with announcement.

8:46 p.m. Master of Ceremonies at podium for opening remarks.

8:50 p.m. First VIP at head table is introduced and moves to podium with musical play-on.

8:51 p.m. VIP begins remarks.

8:56 p.m. VIP's visual projections begin.

9:00 p.m. VIP finishes remarks, play-off over applause. Projection screen goes dark.

9:01 p.m. Master of Ceremonies provides background of second VIP.

9:05 p.m. Second VIP at head table is introduced and moves to podium with musical play-on. Give stand by to performers.

✎ While it can be planned this tightly, rarely does an order of events actually occur as scheduled—except if it is being televised.

order-of-magnitude estimates Price, quantity, or volume projections made without detailed data and specifics. Often experts can make these guesses based on past projects or their general experience but will not be responsible for their accuracy. Also called **ballpark estimates**. Also see *WAG*.

OSHA   Abbreviation for the Occupational Safety and Health Administration, a U.S. federal agency that regulates workplace safety and health hazards. The agency also has influence on many items included in events. Therefore, familiarity with OSHA regulations is recommended to avoid possible fines or other legal action.

out-of-home entertainment   All those entertainment activities that a consumer must leave home to do, such as live concerts, festivals, dances, etc.

overhead   An expense inherent in a project for general items not specific to the project and that must be allocated on some arbitrary basis believed to be equitable.

overhead projector   Rapidly becoming obsolete, these devices enable graphic material produced on a transparent film, pages of a book, or other printed material and placed on its lighted surface to be projected onto a *screen* for display. A big advantage is that the presenter can write over the graphic image on the transparent film and it is visible to the viewers in real time. Also see *whiteboard*.

P

pacing the event   The tempo of the event elements from beginning to end of the planned sequence. Long segments should be mixed with short. Exciting elements mix with short ones. In any kind of event, the overall energy of the elements should build, one upon the next, each getting shorter and more exciting until the finale.

pageant   A large-scale play often representing a historical event with lots of spectacle. Also, an elaborate procession or display. For example, a beauty pageant. Also see *parade*.

paging   Utilizing an event-wide sound system to make announcements for public safety or information.

paging the curtain   Opening the center of a *traveler*-style curtain in such a manner as to allow a single actor or presenter to pass through by utilizing a stagehand on each side to pull back each half just far enough to allow access, then reclosing it.

paint frame   A frame onto which fabric is fastened for painting. It may be stationary and require ladders for the scene painters or it may be movable up and down through a slot in the floor, allowing the painters to remain on the floor. Traditionally backdrops for Broadway shows are painted by laying the paint frame flat on the floor, with the stretched canvas attached. The painters walk over the canvas using long-handled brushes to apply the paint.

PAL   A video playback and transmission standard used primarily in Europe and South America.

Pani projector   A high-powered film projector capable of creating very large images for onstage backdrops, architectural structures, or other applications. Created by Ludwig Pani, the optics make very little distortion of the original still image when enlarged many times. Movement, such as scrolling, and other visual effects can be added with special mechanisms. Often two Panis are used together to create stunning visuals. These units have typically been used at rock concerts, outdoor extravaganzas, and large opera productions. Large video projectors have replaced the Pani projector but don't always achieve the same affect.

panorama   A massive painting that contains a wide, all-encompassing view of a particular subject, such as a battle. These artworks became popular in the nineteenth century as an entertainment form. One of the most famous that can still be seen depicts the Battle of Gettysburg. **Moving panoramas** incorporated sections that moved. An amazing digital animated version created for the Shanghai Expo in 2010 of a famous Chinese panorama painted in 1085 was 130 meters (426 feet) long. Also see *diorama*.

Pantone Color System (PCS) or **Pantone Matching System (PMS)**
The Pantone Color System or Pantone Matching System is an index of standard colors used by both artists and printers to ensure accurate selection, specification, and matching of colors throughout the entire design and production process. Whether it is graphics, scenery, text, computer visuals, or other elements requiring color specification, this is an accepted system.

PAR Short for a parabolic reflector spotlight. A type of lighting instrument. Also, a spotlight-style bulb that can be used in standard household light fixtures.

parade A moving show. Like any show it should have a beginning, middle, and climactic end. Parades can be held for a lot of different reasons and be of different types, including military, celebratory, religious, or purely entertaining. During the Renaissance parades told complete stories with each scene portrayed on a wagon complete with scenery and actors. As the wagons rolled in sequence, the story was told.

🖊 Tips on correcting common mistakes made when staging a parade:

✓ Queue the entries tightly in the dispatch area in such a way that they can be fed into the parade lineup quickly.

✓ Avoid gaps. Keep the units tight, one behind the other. At the dispatch point, set the distance desired and order the lead element of that unit to maintain that same distance throughout the entire parade route. All parades have the accordion effect with the space between units enlarging and shrinking, causing participants to stop in place or run to catch up. Keeping the units tight eliminates most of this effect.

✓ Add music on as many units as possible to keep the excitement level up for the audience.

✓ Put the most exciting at the front and the best at the end, while mixing the other units to keep the *pacing* exciting.

✓ Place television coverage at the beginning of the parade to capture the participants in their best spirit.

✓ Make sure everyone knows what to do if a unit breaks down—whether they should go around, or whatever they should do. Large breaks in the sequence deflate the audience.

✓ If the viewing crowd is expected to be large, understand that those in front block the view of the many behind. Therefore, the units should be designed to have much of what is being presented higher than 6 feet above the ground.

✓ Encourage the parade participants to go close to the audience, on both sides, bringing action closer to the viewer.

P

At a Tournament of Roses parade, when my unit came to the dispatch point suddenly there was a large gap left by the previous unit. The dispatcher ordered me to race the unit forward, running everyone to catch up. But this was the television coverage area and we had a cast of one hundred beautifully costumed dancers and performers brought over expressly from China to be around the float in a highly structured and rehearsed dance routine. To run forward would have completely destroyed our performance on television and for the VIPs in this area. So I stood my ground and refused, and we moved out performing as planned, thrilling the audience, bringing roars of applause, and winning a top award. Sometimes one must just do what is right!

parallel Using one wire (or a pair of wires) for each *bit* or signal controlled so that the operator has separate control of each, such as each individual light in a row of lights.

parallel platform A collapsible frame support that, along with wooden tops, makes portable risers and stage platforms. The size and height can vary as required. Parallels and tops are inexpensive methods of creating portable platforms that are easy to set up and store.

See diagram in "Tables and Techniques" (page 440).

parcan A lighting instrument featuring a parabolic aluminized reflector lamp used extensively in stage lighting, particularly when a substantial amount of flat lighting is required for the scene. The sealed beam *lamp* produces an intense oval of light with unfocused edges. The instruments come in various sizes and can be fitted with an *LED*. Coloring can also be done with a *gel*. Also see *Leko* and *floorcan*.

party bus A large passenger vehicle designed to give a group of people a fun experience as they are transported. Some come complete with bars, surround sound systems, dance poles, karaoke equipment, and many other unusual elements. Some, such as converted London buses, offer open-air experiences.

passerelle An extension of the stage that is a narrow walkway around either the orchestra pit area or a group of audience seats. Typically it extends from one end of the stage to the other. This walkway allows for the performers to walk between the orchestra and the audience, bringing the performer closer to the audience or actually into it.

patchbay A series of *jacks* arranged to allow various changeable routings of audio, lighting, or video signals as selected by the operator.

patron One who supports—primarily financially, even if just by buying tickets—the arts or an event. A regular ticket holder.

pedestal Supporting system for video or film cameras that allows the operator to periscope the camera up and down, or turn all the wheels together to push the camera in the desired direction, or do both at the same time, creating flowing camera movements.

pegged candle holder A glass device designed with rubber-collard pegs that fit into the socket of the candlestick to hold a safer candle, such as a *votive*, instead of tall *tapers* that can fall out of the sockets.

Pepper's Ghost An illusion effect used in magic and theater that makes objects seem to disappear and reappear or morph into something else. This *special effect* is utilized in Disney theme parks and other attractions. The illusion can also be used to make an actor reflected in a mirror appear to change into an actor behind the mirror. It is named after John Pepper, who first demonstrated the technique in the 1860s.

performance An artistic presentation.

permanent set A solidly built, often generic set that must stay in place for all presentations. Usually only minor modifications, such as paint or attachments, can be made to the set. Furnishings, props, and other elements can be placed in front, and sometimes background elements can be added.

P

permit Government entities and their life safety representatives such as police and fire safety offices grant permission for most types of public assembly, such as an event, and before doing so have basic requirements that must be met. Once these requirements are met, and typically a fee is paid, then a document, or permit, is issued to the organizers permitting the event to go forward.

   Always check the local codes in the municipality in which the event will take place well in advance to gain an understanding of that location's regulations and permit process.

PERT Project Evaluation Review Technique. A management tool whereby a network of events and activities is established and then sequenced through a logical set of ground rules to determine critical paths.

pew card Small cards used at weddings and funerals with a pew number indicating where the cardholder is designated to sit. For weddings it may say, *Within the Ribbon*. The cards are either mailed with the invitations or sent just prior to the event.

pewter A type of tableware that is composed of an alloy of tin and lead and was originally used as an inexpensive substitute for silver. When polished and finished, it looks almost identical. Often pewter is manufactured to have its own look. It is grayish in color, does not tarnish, is very traditional in appearance, and goes well with earthenware. This type of pewter can be used effectively for barbecues and other rustic types of food events.

photo caption A brief written description of a photo or *video clip*. Every photograph or digital image sent to the press should be accompanied by a brief description of the picture itself.

📖 **See publicity photo sample in "Tables and Techniques" (page 409).**

✎ **A photo caption should list, clearly and factually, the following pertinent details:**

✓ Identification of all persons in the photo or video, reading from left to right.

✓ Brief description of the action being depicted.

✓ Brief summary of the event to which the photo pertains.

✓ Name, address, phone number, and e-mail address of the sponsoring organization and the sender's name and contact information.

photography At an event, it is the capturing of the event in pictures for historical purposes or future promotion. The problem is that good photography, other than snapshots, takes time, proper lighting, and the right background. If excellent photography is required, the challenge is to accomplish it without disturbing the timing of the event.

> *At a wedding I attended, photos of the bride and groom were taken after the ceremony while the guests went to a reception holding area. At this reception area no refreshments were provided until the bride and groom were present. The time taken for photography extended so long that finally many of the guests left and went to a nearby bar to continue the party. Many never returned to the wedding. Even if refreshments had been provided, the guest wait time for photography was much too much!*

pica A unit of measure in printing. Also called an **em**.

photo release A document signed by those in the photo that grants legal permission to use, display, air, or publish a photograph or video of a person for advertising, publicity, public relations, or educational purposes. Whatever the source of your photograph, if it portrays an individual person or group of people, be sure to safeguard yourself against a legal suit by obtaining a release before you use the photograph. A properly worded release will relieve you of any obligation to pay additional compensation or damages for the use of the photograph or video. If the photograph is of a minor, a release must be obtained from the minor's parents or guardian. Ideally a release is signed *before* the photos are taken. Speakers, celebrities, performers, etc., hired for an event usually have a clause in their contract specifying usage of the photos taken. *Stock photos* or video clips typically come with a release included in the fee, but that should be confirmed from the source.

See sample release form in "Tables and Techniques" (page 413).

Pigi projector   High-intensity, large-format projector that utilizes 70 mm film as the image source to project moving images (not motion picture) onto very large surfaces and architectural structures for special events. The images can be created on the film so that the visual or pattern keeps moving continuously without a repeat.

pin rail   Lines that hang the scenery on stages go up to pulleys under the *grid* and then back down to this steel rail that is firmly mounted on a side wall backstage, running the full length of the performing area. The ends of the lines, if rope, are tied to removable crosspieces or **pins** that can be placed into positions anywhere along the rail. Scenery can be raised by pulling the ropes and retying them when the scenery is in the raised position. Modern theaters use steel cables instead of rope and have replaced the traditional pin rail with various configurations of automated electric winches.

pipe and drape   The term used to create standard booths provided at a trade show that consist of fabric hanging in back and on the sides suspended from portable aluminum pipes.

pipe batten   See *batten*.

P

pit   The sunken area in front of the stage in which the orchestra plays or from which actors make entrances or exits. The pit is usually accessible from under the stage. Many stages have lifts in the bottom of the pit that can be raised to stage height, creating an *apron* to extend the playing area in front of the stage.

pizzazz   What every event should have! Excitement, thrills, the unexpected, enthusiasm, anticipation, animation, pleasure, liveliness, and the compelling are all elements of pizzazz. Even a small speech at a dinner can, and should, be given this element in a way to make the audience glad they attended.

place card   A small card set on the table with each *place setting* to identify where each guest is to sit. For formal dinners it is a white card about 2 inches long by .75 inch high after being folded in half so that it stands on the table. It has a thin gold border often with a family crest, monogram, or corporate logo top center. The name is hand lettered large enough to be readable, and at formal dinners titles are always used, for example, "Mrs. Walton" or "Judge Powers." For twenty-fifth anniversaries the border may appropriately be silver. Place cards for informal dinners can be colorful or sit in decorative holders. It is incredibly bad manners for guests to relocate their place card, but it happens all the time! See *menu card*, *seating chart*, and *escort card*.

See forms of address chart in "Tables and Techniques" (page 372).

place setting The arrangement of the *tableware* on the table for each person attending a meal event. The place setting varies depending on the type, purpose, and style of the dinner. A formal dinner has explicit rules as to how each dish, glass, fork, and other items must be placed. Less formal, themed, and casual meal events, as well as different food serving styles such as buffet, create opportunities for many different and unusual place settings.

P

Tips for a formal place setting:

✓ Only white linens are acceptable. Tablecloths must be full length. No fancy folded napkins.

✓ Dinner plates are set *exactly* the same distance from the plate on either side, and *exactly* 1.5 inches (3.8 centimeters) from the edge of the table.

✓ A charger may be set under the dinner plate. The charger is removed before serving the entrée.

✓ Flatware is placed in the order of its use, from the outside in. The forks are on the left. If the salad is to be served before the entrée, the salad fork is outside of the meat fork, but inside the fish fork.

If the salad is served after the entrée, the salad fork is next to the plate. The knives are placed on the right, the one to be used first farthest from the plate, all with their sharp edge towards the plate. The soup spoon is furthest to the right.

✓ Never more than three knives or three forks are set. An exception is the oyster fork. When used, it is placed next to the soup spoon. Salad knives are set closest to the plate when salad is served after the entrée, but omitted when not needed.

✓ Traditionally dessert forks and spoons are brought in with the dessert, but it is also acceptable to place them above the plate with the fork lower facing right and the spoon above facing left.

✓ If an individual sweet is served for dessert, a teaspoon is brought with the sweet.

✓ Stemware vary depending on the menu, but always start by placing the tallest, the water goblet, directly over the knives and working the wine glasses to the right.

✓ Keep all table decorations simple. Candles are required, as are flowers.

📙 **A layout of a formal dinner place setting can be found in "Tables and Techniques" (page 397).**

Attending a complete multicourse formal dinner is a rare experience for most guests. Therefore, it will make a strong impact on most attendees. This impact can be enhanced even more by adding a formal cocktail reception beforehand and a live string quartet, or harpist, performing during dinner.

✏ **Tips for an informal place setting:**

✓ Unlike a formal place setting, there are no rules, so make it fun!

✓ If the event has a theme, incorporate the theme into the place setting. For example, if the party is a youthful dance party, use old 33 rpm records as *chargers* under the *dinner plates*.

✓ The selection of style and color of napkins and tablecloths adds great visual effect to the place setting.

✓ Be clever with the placement of the flatware.

✓ Sprinkling the setting with flower petals or edible materials can be visually interesting.

✓ Photographs of an honoree can be effective if cut to fit on the plate or as a stand-up card. If it is a birthday celebration, mix different photos of the person from various years, or from high points of their life, at the various place settings, encouraging the table guests to share the photos and their comments.

Examples of informal dinner place settings can be found in "Tables and Techniques" (page 403).

plan   A written sequenced set of future tasks aimed at producing a desired result.

plan or **plan view**   A sketch or scaled diagram that is an imaginary *bird's eye view* or *floor plan* indicating all elements and their respective positions and size. Also see *elevation*, *scale*, *section*, and *bird's-eye view*.

planning   The invaluable process of listing, organizing, scheduling, arranging, and developing all elements that will compose the event, presentation, or function. The more planning, the better the event.

planometer   An electronic or mechanical measuring device to determine size on scaled drawings.

plant   An actor placed in the audience to create the illusion that an audience member is taking part in the production.

platform A structural unit that adds different levels to a stage or meeting room. Platforms are usually portable and collapsible, come in a variety of sizes and heights, and can be locked together in multiples to create an even larger variation of heights and sizes. Also see *portable stages* and *parallel platform.*

📖 **See diagrams of platforms in "Tables and Techniques" (page 440).**

playback The playing or replaying of a recording.

playbill The magazine of the theater and performing arts center. Originated for Broadway shows, it features details of the specific performance along with advertisements and general theater articles and is given free to those attending. On opening nights these are stamped as such to add to their keepsake value. While Playbill is a brand name, the name is often applied to any type of program provided at a theatrical performance.

playlist An approved list of recordings, typically musical, for a radio station, event, *DJ*, or other situation where control of the type of music utilized is important to management or others. For example, a wedding organizer may want to specify the type of music to be played by a disc jockey at the reception based on the preference of the bride. Control of music used may be determined by the theme, ethnicity of the attendees, restrictions of the venue management, etc. Also see *background music.*

play-on, play-off Music played to add excitement or interest to the time it takes for a speaker, performer, award recipient, etc., to walk onto or off of the stage.

✏️ **Tips for play-ons and play-offs:**

✓ Orchestral music without lyrics works best.

✓ *Hit it hard* in volume at the beginning and let it fade out as the person reaches the microphone onstage. The same with play-offs, hit it hard as the applause starts and fade it down as the person returns to the audience or exits offstage.

✓ Using play-ons is an ideal way to break the monotony of a series of speakers.

✓ An appropriate choice of song for each person helps set the tone of their presence onstage or their message.

✓ These can be achieved with either a live band or orchestra or recordings.

 "Hail to the Chief" preceded by "Ruffles and Flourishes" is reserved as a play-on for only the president of the United States.

Pledge of Allegiance to the Flag An oath of loyalty to the United States recited while facing the national flag at the beginning of many public events. Many countries have oaths of allegiance to their flags and some states (such as Texas) have pledges to their state flags. If a pledge is made to a state flag at an event, the pledge to the national flag is recited first. Only citizens of the country are required to take the oath. Francis Bellamy authored the original U.S. pledge in 1892. Those taking the pledge would begin with a military salute, and after reciting the words "to the flag," they would extend the arm toward the flag, palm-upward. Shortly thereafter it was changed to holding the hand over the heart and extending the arm palm-downward. During World War II it was decided that this gesture was too much like the Nazi salute, so it was changed to keep the right hand over the heart throughout.

 The proper wording of the pledge to the American flag is

I pledge allegiance to the flag of the United States of America, and to the republic for which it stands, one nation, under God, indivisible, with liberty and justice for all.

 The pledge should be recited while standing at attention with right hand over heart. For complete details see *flag protocol*.

plot The story line or sequence of events in a play, movie, or novel. Also, a layout and schedule of sequence of particular objects, occurrences, or specifications in connection with a performance—for example, scene plot, light plot, and sound plot.

plug A publicity term meaning a mention in a newspaper, radio or television broadcast, or Internet blog. Also, the half of a connector that mates with a jack.

plus Generally expressive word for adding something more to anything. When something you have planned is not enough for the desired audience effect, you plus it with more lighting, more music, and so on.

PO Abbreviation for Purchase Order. A legal document used by companies to sell or secure products or services. Once signed it is legally binding. The PO clearly defines price, quantity, services included, warrantees, delivery information, and vendor and buyer information.

podium Same as a *lectern*. Also, a small raised platform or pedestal for a speaker. Also, the wall around the *arena* of an amphitheater.

polish To clean up, sparkle, refine, or otherwise improve a presentation, speech, musical performance, show, or whatever after it has actually been completed.

POP Pay One Price. An admission system where the visitor pays for the entire experience at one time. Also, Point of Purchase, the location in a store or concession where purchases are actually paid for.

portable floors See *dance floors*.

portable stages These unitized structures are collapsible platforms that can be used in a wide variety of ways to create raised performing areas, dais, speaker platforms, and bandstands.

portal set A stage setting that has the same downstage flats throughout all the scenes of the production, changing only the rear wall flats and the two upstage side-wall flats to give the scene a whole new appearance.

 For suggested layouts of portable stages see "Tables and Techniques" (pages 428 and 441).

porta potty   A temporary toilet facility rented and placed for the duration of the event. All styles are available, including fancy, simple, handicapped, and those with sinks and other amenities. Also see *honey wagon*.

position   A person's assigned place on the stage, rostrum, or *head table*. Assigned positions are extremely important at a press event so that the camerapersons can accurately identify the individuals as they photograph each.

postproduction   Any production activities that take place after the event, including *striking*, thank-you letters, equipment return, and bill paying. In film or video production it is the editing, *foley*, prints, and other processes required after actual principal photography.

power   The electricity available and required for all of the elements of the event. There are three basic power options: 1) using the venue's existing wall plugs; 2) dropping a temporary subbreaker panel off the existing utility power (providing more power in different configurations); and 3) bringing in a portable *generator*. Generators are available in all sizes, and proper specification guarantees enough power for the event. Since power is a basic element of every event, it is critical to have the required amount. Electricity is measured primarily in amps (or *amperes*), but *voltage* and *wattage* are other necessary measurements. Electricity can also be made available in single phase or three-phase (for large usage). Different countries use different electrical systems, which affects power specifications. The big users of electricity are theatrical lighting, kitchen equipment (specifying gas cooking helps) and food warmers, and heating and air conditioning. Since providing power can be expensive, specifying the amount required as well as the distribution and *power runs* necessary is key to planning.

🖉 Tips on planning power requirements:

✓ Determine and list all of the equipment that will require power.

✓ Know how much power (amps and volts) each piece of equipment requires.

✓ Know where the equipment will be placed around the event site. Distribution and the length of power runs is critical knowledge for planning power requirements since long runs reduce voltage.

✓ Know when the power will first be required and how long it must remain in place.

✓ Determine whether a backup generator is required. For big-time events and live telecasts, it is critical.

✓ Contract a qualified event electrician to specify the amount of electricity required.

✓ Call generator companies as early as possibly to ensure that the equipment required will be available.

✓ Plan some overage for last-minute additions that may require power.

PowerPoint A type of visual presentation program developed by Microsoft that is prepared on and presented with a computer. Apple sells a similar program called Keynote.

power runs The electrical *cables* that connect the power source to the equipment requiring the power, such as a generator or transformer. In a large event, a substantial number and size of cables can be required, so their placement must be carefully planned for multiple reasons, but primarily for safety.

 Tips on planning power runs:

✓ Keep the high *voltage* lines completely away from the public. Have the higher voltage lines come in from behind the staging area and split to lower voltage lines going into public areas.

✓ Avoid crossing any aisle ways with cables on the ground to avoid tripping or damage to the lines.

✓ Where necessary to cross aisles or service corridors, various types of cable covers are available to provide a safe housing for the cables while eliminating guest tripping.

✓ At outdoor venues, cables are often placed in temporary trenches and covered over with dirt.

✓ Whenever possible, *fly* the cables overhead above personnel and moving equipment.

P

practical   Refers to scenery, props, or other items onstage that are really usable. For example, there may be a door in the set, but only if it opens and allows one to walk through is it practical. The reverse is **unpractical**, which includes items that may look practical, like a tree stump, but may not be constructed to be strong enough to hold a person's weight. A stage scene will combine items that are practical and unpractical.

preferred position   An advertising term for a specifically requested page in a newspaper or magazine, or time slot on the radio or TV, for an ad to be placed. A **preferred rate** is a lower rate for that advertisement given for any number of reasons but usually because of the number of appearances purchased or because the event is a charity.

prerehearsal preparation Rehearsals are expensive and typically too short on time. Therefore, they need to be well planned and efficient.

🖊 Tips on planning successful rehearsals:

✓ Ensure there are enough copies for all cast and crew of the latest version of the script.

✓ Ensure that all participants have previously received the rehearsal *schedule* and confirmed their attendance.

✓ Designate and have it understood by all as to who is in charge at the rehearsal, be it the director, stage manager, or company representative.

✓ Celebrities and major performers are historically late for rehearsals. Therefore plan what can be accomplished during the wait time.

✓ Ensure that all *tech*, including sound and projection, are ready at the start of the rehearsal. Nothing is worse than finding out the microphones don't work when it is time to start the rehearsal.

✓ If it is a series of rehearsals, ensure that all participants are given the specifics of the next rehearsal, as well as script and other changes, before departing.

P

preset To position items, people, or other elements prior to the start of an event, or section of the event, so that they are in place and ready to go when needed. For example, to preset the script for a speech is to place it on the lectern just before the event begins. A person about to be introduced is placed into a close **preset position**, enabling that person to enter immediately when announced so as to eliminate a long wait.

preshow An introduction to the main show. The preshow can be music, video, a small performance, reciting the *Pledge of Allegiance*, or any other type of activity that builds audience interest and anticipation or provides *backstory* leading to the main presentation.

President's Salute   See *gun salute*.

press   The general term used to describe journalists, reporters, correspondents, photographers, videographers, and others who work for media companies such as radio and television stations, newspapers, and online outlets, and the result of their work such as the articles they write. The people that tell the world about your event. Also see *fourth estate* and *press corps*.

press alert or **advisory**   See *media alert* and *media advisory*.

> An example of the standard form is in "Tables and Techniques" (page 412).

press conference   An event held exclusively for the purpose of making announcements of great importance to the media. If it is part of a *publicity campaign*, it should be used sparingly and for maximum effect. Typically it is smaller than a *media event*.

> See setup for a press conference in "Tables and Techniques" (page 410).

P

> Tips on staging a successful press conference:

✓ Select an appropriate location for the announcement.

✓ Ensure that the space is large enough to accommodate the anticipated crowd.

✓ If it is outside, consider the weather and have a backup location.

✓ Light the speaker with theatrical lights for excellent video and photos without flash.

✓ Be sure that the background to the speaker benefits the occasion.

✓ Provide a logo or seal of the sponsoring organization for the front of the lectern.

✓ Ensure that the rostrum is high enough for all to see.

✓ Ensure a more than adequate sound system and a *multbox* or other method for the press to attach their recorders, cameras, etc., directly into the sound system.

✓ Provide a lectern appropriate to the occasion and the size of the speaker.

✓ Provide an adequate press area for the media and cameras.

✓ Provide a holding room for the speakers and other guests.

press corps A group of correspondents or reporters representing newspapers, television, radio, Internet, and other media companies and agencies. Also, photo and filming crews are part of this corps.

press function Any event designed for the dissemination of information to the press or media. These events can be anything from a simple announcement to a cocktail reception (a press party) to an elaborate press conference. A press function can take place before (to announce what is going to happen), during (to allow the press the opportunity to experience the event firsthand), or after the event (to explain what has happened).

P

An example of a press kit is in "Tables and Techniques" (page 410).

Tips for media attendance at press functions:

✓ Promise and provide an announcement that is truly newsworthy and important to the community.

✓ Have a celebrity make the announcement.

✓ Plan a food or cocktail reception for those press who attend. They love free food and drink, and it encourages them to write a good article.

✓ Create a special "hook" to capture their interest.

✓ Hold the function at a time of day when the press can attend and get their story, photos, and video back to the office in time for their deadlines. Most press don't want to work on a weekend.

press invitation Inviting the press is essential to their attendance at a press function. The traditional way to do so is by an invitation in the form of a memo. It is also referred to as a **press memo**. It should contain the basic information, such as when and where the event will take place and what will be happening. It is also important to list information that will attract attention and make them want to attend, such as the list of important speakers and of guests, information about the press party, as well as other pertinent information. Add any notes about dress requirements or say that "SEATS HAVE BEEN SET ASIDE FOR THE PRESS" or that a platform will be provided for cameras. It is not a secret that getting the media to an event, particularly in large cities where so much is happening, might mean that you have to go to extremes to get them there. Some examples are sending a limo to pick them up; having costumed individuals, celebrities, etc., personally deliver the invitation; or including candy, flowers, or a keepsake (nothing of real value) along with the invitation.

 Make sure the invitation gets to the correct editor. Often there are many, including a fashion editor, social editor, city editor, and photo editor.

press kit More elaborate than a press release, the press kit is a complete collection of one or more press releases, other pertinent information, statistics, photographs, videos, biographies, and other appropriate materials, usually packaged in a simple or elaborate folder for convenience and impact and/or on a CD or DVD. It is designed to provide media representatives with enough material about the event and its elements from which they can create and write a comprehensive story. Usually it is handed to members of the media when they arrive at the *press conference*. In many cases, it is also mailed or electronically distributed to the media, primarily to those who don't attend the press conference.

📋 **Example of a press kit is in "Tables and Techniques" (page 410).**

🖊 **Tips for suggested materials to include in a press kit:**

✓ Copies of all previously sent press releases.

✓ New press releases—highlighting different aspects of the event.

✓ A brief history of the sponsoring organization.

✓ A guest list.

✓ Biographies of key speakers or guests.

✓ Photos, with captions, of speakers, products, entertainers, etc.

✓ CD or DVD with visuals, logos, commercials, video interviews, etc.

✓ Copy of the menu.

✓ Description of the decorations.

✓ Agenda, or schedule, for the event.

✓ Copy of speeches.

✓ Schedule of other media events planned.

✓ Event contact information for those who request additional materials or want to do interviews.

press platform A raised space, typically as high as the stage, to provide the press representatives and photographers an unobstructed view of a major event. Also see *platform*.

📋 **See setup for platforms in a rally in "Tables and Techniques" (page 411).**

🖉 **Tips on planning the press platform:**

✓ The platform is often multitiered, offering a clear view of the stage from all levels and enough space for the anticipated press, including cameras on tripods.

✓ The platform is located either center and parallel with the stage, extending into the audience 40–50 feet, or off to the side at about a 45° angle from *center stage*. If the anticipated audience is to be very large, then off to the side generally works best. The distance is critical because of the camera lenses typically used by the press.

✓ Provide power with multiple outlets so that the press can plug in their cameras and other equipment. While they carry batteries, if the event is to be lengthy, then electrical power is preferred.

✓ Mark preferred space on the platform for the large news companies such as CNN, ABC, etc., in the best positions. Typically a 4-foot box of space is adequate for each.

✓ Provide theatrical lighting to brighten the faces of those onstage for the cameras.

✓ Place the *multbox* in the center of the platform, allowing for easy access by all.

✓ Place security at the steps to the platform to keep the general audience from utilizing the space.

press release The best and most accepted way to get the details of an event to the media. Its purpose is to clearly outline the facts of your event or story, either before, during, or after the event. It also reflects an organization's position on an issue. Like all press stories, it should answer the questions of "who, where, what, when, and why." The information should be stated on 8½ × 11" size paper (or the electronic equivalent) and not exceed two typed pages double-spaced. Typically press releases are accompanied by appropriate photos that have been approved for release.

🖊 **Tips on writing a good press release:**

✓ Include all the basic name and contact information for the person or organization making the release.

✓ List the person to contact for more information along with their phone numbers.

✓ Indicate the date of release in the upper-right-hand side, such as "FOR IMMEDIATE RELEASE" or the requested date of release.

✓ Don't editorialize; keep it simple and factual.

✓ Don't use a headline, just tell the story.

✓ Provide background that could make for a good story or interview.

✓ When completed, reread it to ensure accuracy, grammar, and spelling.

✓ A press release should answer five basic questions:

1. Who is doing it?

2. What is being done?

3. Where is it being done?

4. When is it taking place?

5. Why is it taking place?

✓ A release should not exceed two pages in length.

🖊 **Getting news services to use, or even read, the release sent to them is a challenge that needs creative, energetic effort. Take it to them** in costume appropriate to the event along with a pie or other inexpensive gift item that also relates. Find a gimmick.

press room A gathering place for members of the invited *press corps* away from the general audience prior to, during, and after the event. It should be well lighted and contain tables and chairs for working on laptop computers, and refreshments should be present. Have a Wi-Fi or wireless Internet connection available for all. A host greets the press members, records their contact information, and provides each with *press releases*, *press kits*, photos, copies of speeches, and other pertinent information.

principals Key people of the event or the sponsoring organization, or people whose presence is important. Also, the primary actors in a play or presentation.

procession See *parade*.

procession of waiters The staging of waiters to make a grand entrance into the dining room all at the same time carrying all the same meal course. This is sometimes done to serve a flaming dessert at a banquet, such as bananas *flambé*.

A client of mine in the Middle East prided himself by serving each course of the formal dinner with a procession of waiters, one for each guest, carrying in silver plates with silver domes. Upon entering with each course the waiters stood behind the guests' chairs until all were in place, then, on cue, they would lean around the guest, place the domed plate on the table, and then on another cue, remove the domes to reveal the food. Quite impressive, even after five or six courses!

producer The individual responsible for the overall production.

Typically this person hires the production team, negotiates the contracts with entertainers and speakers, oversees the budget and schedule, and knows the answers to everyone's questions.

production team Those responsible for building, *striking*, and sometimes managing the event. In essence they set the stage and make it happen, coordinating all elements including food, beverage, entertainment, and all technical aspects.

product launches A show or presentation designed for a company to announce a new product or product line. These corporate events can be quite extravagant and combine multiple events, including shows, dinners, cocktail parties, seminars, and displays.

profile A scenic piece that is cut the shape of the object it represents. For example, a profile of a Greek column would be the shape of the column cut out of a flat board and painted to look three-dimensional.

program A brochure about the show or event prepared for the audience that lists such items as the order of scenes or musical numbers, activities or shows within an event, names of cast and production team, sponsors, and other important information. Also, the running order of the show or sequence of event elements as planned.

progressive dinner A multicourse dinner function in which each course is taken in a different situation, location, or restaurant. An innovative way to entertain a group.

project Work assigned to one or more people for a limited period of time to accomplish objectives within a defined scope.

projector One of many different types of machines that converts small visuals into images on screens. Typical projectors are video, film, slide, and overhead.

Complete details of projection setup techniques are in "Tables and Techniques" (page 432).

promotion A part of the mix of activities that make up marketing or the selling of an event to the targeted audience. Other elements of the mix are advertising, publicity (press), social media, and personal selling. For corporate or personal events the main promotion may be distribution of *invitations*. Promotion typically is finding creative ways to extend a marketing budget through free or inexpensive exposure. Included are such activities as celebrity endorsements, ticket giveaways, contests, sponsor tie-ins, price reductions, and online activities through various social media.

Tips for online promotion:

✓ Facebook and other social sites are an opportunity to share and advertise event details with your entire network, plus many others. Facebook ads also generate leads, including e-mail addresses.

✓ Twitter affords opportunities to motivate viral sharing with discount-for-a-tweet tactics and event-specific hashtags (markers). It can also be used to leverage the networks of other local event promoters.

✓ E-mail allows bombardment of your list with *press releases*, newsletters, and ads. Focusing on certain demographic traits can increase the effectiveness of an e-mail campaign.

✓ Online event calendars are an effective way to bring attention to events. Regions, cities, associations, venues, clubs, civic organizations, and many others maintain event calendars. For example, a Kiwanis Club day at the event will, through their calendar and other internal communication, spread the word.

prompter Traditionally a person who stands out of view in a low box *center stage* to help actors with lines and cues. But today it is a device that assists a speaker by projecting a written copy of the presentation or speech in a manner such that the speaker can see it but the audience cannot. Two popular methods are used. One uses the words on a television or computer monitor placed in the audience, another projects the words onto clear glass panels that are placed just in front center or to each side of the lectern. Also see *teleprompter*.

proof   The first look at a fully composed advertisement, collateral material, sign, or other visual arrangement. **To proof** or **proofread** is the process of reviewing such material to judge its appropriateness, details, grammar, or impact. In alcoholic spirits, such as **86 proof *whiskey***, it defines the amount of alcohol. In the United States, the percentage of alcohol is exactly half the proof.

props or **properties**   Any article used by an actor, performer, or speaker while onstage. A hand prop is an article carried onstage such as a sword or clipboard.

proscenium   The open area in a solid wall between the audience and stage area that provides a frame for the picture created onstage by the scenery and the actors, while hiding all of the side areas, flies, and equipment of the stage. The proscenium is in front of the main curtain, and in older theaters it is often highly architecturally sculpted and decorated. Also referred to as the **proscenium arch**, it is typically rectangular, but can be of any shape. The proscenium width is the horizontal distance of the opening from sidewall to sidewall, and the proscenium height is the vertical distance of this opening from stage floor to the uppermost part of the bottom side of the arch. The **inner proscenium** is constructed inside of the proscenium to adjust the size or shape of the opening. This modification may be permanent or semipermanent for a particular show, or sometimes it is composed of a *teaser* and *tormentors* that are adjustable to provide options in size and shape. The **false proscenium** is inside the inner proscenium and further adjusts, shapes, or decorates the opening so that it complements the scenery of the current production or a scene within the production.

protagonist   The main character or hero of a story who typically carries the action. The person around whom the narrative plot revolves and with whom the audience is intended to share the most empathy. Also see *antagonist*.

protocol The etiquette or rule of how an activity should be performed, such as showing proper respect for heads of state, ranking officials, and even the nation's flag. Protocol also exists within some corporations, churches, and other entities. At events these guidelines are important for seating arrangements, *introductions*, *invitations*, and various activities. Also see *dais* and *flag protocol*.

See forms of address in "Tables and Techniques" (page 372).

public address system or **PA** The audio system used to disseminate speech or music over an entire event area. The equipment used in PA systems is purposed to penetrate over large areas with volume and intelligibility rather than the quality of a performance sound system. Typically the PA system's operation is simple and does not require an audio engineer or one with other specialized skills. It is utilized for small speeches, announcements, and nonperformance music. Small- to medium-size meeting rooms typically have this type system, with the loudspeakers built into the ceiling of the space. Also see *sound system* and *background music*.

publicist a person doing or managing *publicity*. Their main function is to plan for and secure as much attention for the event as possible through media sources.

publicity Any activity designed to increase public awareness or interest in something or somebody. Publicity is primarily free exposure made up of any combination of elements, including press releases, media coverage, public speeches, blogs, Internet sites, or other activities that are paid for with energy, ingenuity, hard work, and very little money. *Advertising* is the opposite. Publicity can be more effective in attracting attention and motivating attendance because it is presented more like news or community awareness. Events seeking attendance from the public require an organized *publicity campaign* to complement advertising and other marketing activities. Publicity also works effectively after an event with news of the event's success, important people who attended or were awarded, and special activities that were part of the event.

publicity campaign Generally considered to be the entire organized promotional plan and effort to attract attention to an event or person. A well-orchestrated publicity campaign begins with early announcements of what is going to happen, followed by the well-timed release of specific information just prior to the event, followed by information releases of specific highlights and happenings during the event, and concluding with post-event information releases about what happened during the event.

✐ **Tips on organizing and executing an effective publicity campaign:**

✓ Determine the exact need for the publicity. Is it to raise awareness of a cause or product or to drive attendance to an event or just to expand the public knowledge of the planned activity?

✓ Evaluate the abilities of staff, volunteers, hired publicists, or others and how they can be best utilized to maximize the impact.

✓ Evaluate contacts in business, political and government organizations, sponsors, or others who can be approached to assist.

✓ Make a specific plan of what needs to be done, when it needs to get done, who is going to do it, and how best to get it done.

✓ Create or select an identifying image in the form of a *logo*, trademark, or design pattern, etc., that all elements can be tagged with for continuity. A logo design contest early in the process creates opportunity for early press.

✓ Consider printed publicity materials, including letterhead, invitations, programs, posters, invitations, displays flyers, street banners, buttons, stickers, signs, etc.

✓ Determine which elements of the event are most newsworthy and create press releases, photos, and blogs for each.

✓ Approach radio and television stations to make appearances, or get mentions, on local community activity shows, newscasts, talk radio, or local DJ shows. Newspapers have different editors for news, fashion, sports, etc., so create different newsworthy stories as appropriate.

✓ Tie in with a sponsor, like a supermarket chain that places printed materials in every bag of groceries.

✓ Create a *press conference* to announce the event or important elements of the event.

✓ Create an unusual happening or stunt to attract the media. This can range from a groundbreaking event to a performance by a major entertainer to a parade of pachyderms down Main Street. The press claims to have "seen it all," so be creative.

publicity photo   A photograph either taken or secured for the purpose of placement in the media to promote your event. Most media prefer that the pictures be in electronic form (high resolution only) but will usually accept standard prints. Publicity photos are also typically used in press kits. Videos are also used for distribution to television stations and websites. Good photos have the best chance of getting used by the media.

🖉 **Tips for good publicity photos:**

✓ Hire a professional photographer/videographer.

✓ Stage the pictures.

✓ Include action, such as people kissing, shaking hands, raising a trophy, etc.

✓ Eliminate backgrounds that distract the eye.

✓ Include an image, seal, or logo of your organization within the action.

✓ Do not "plaster" people against a flat background.

✓ The subject and actions must be timely and appropriate to the event.

public liability Part of general insurance designed to protect the purchaser (insured) from third party insurance claims, typically where payment is not made to the insured but rather to someone suffering loss who is not a party to the insurance contract. Liability insurers have three duties: 1) to defend the insured, 2) to indemnify, and 3) to settle a reasonably clear claim.

public relations (PR) An action program to earn public understanding and acceptance of a product, organization, idea, or individual. This action is based on established goals and is accomplished through various means, including *advertising*, *publicity*, speechmaking, and lobbying.

public service announcement (PSA) Promotional announcements by the media outlets for local charitable events. Radio and over-the-air television stations are required by law to support the community in which they are located by providing media exposure for local current affairs, and they do so by providing such announcements. Many local television or cable companies also have "calendar" type shows designed to inform the community of worthwhile events. All are a great source of promotion for an event.

pulldown   A style of flag *bunting* that is tall and thin, with the star field on top and the red and white strips running vertically. It can be used where use of an actual flag is not practical or where space is limited. Ideas for uses can include as the framing of a large entryway, business lobby, convention hall, or banquet hall; on a speaker's lectern; or on street lampposts.

 An illustration of bunting is in "Tables and Techniques" (page 343).

pulley   An indispensable device in stage *rigging* that when positioned as necessary allows a rope to move through it smoothly and efficiently. A pulley has two parts—the wheel and the block, which holds the wheel and allows for fastening.

punch   A popular beverage for many occasions that is typically made of fruit juices. Thousands of recipes exist, both alcoholic and nonalcoholic. It is served in wide bowls, known as **punch bowls**, allowing guests to fill their glasses using some sort of dipper. The word "punch" comes from a Hindi word meaning five. Originally there were five ingredients: alcohol, sugar, lemon, water, and tea or spices. The drink was brought from India to England in the seventeenth century by sailors and spread from there. Many countries have their own traditional blend.

punch list   A list of tasks yet to be completed; a to-do list. This list should be compiled at intervals before the opening of an event and distributed to all staff to limit the number of items forgotten or lost in the rush to opening. Also, a list compiled by a client that must be completed per the contract before final payment is made.

punch up   To make bigger and more exciting; to give more impact.

puppet   An inanimate figure or object manipulated by a **puppeteer** to tell a story or entertain. While most associated with children's entertainment, such as Punch and Judy hand puppet shows, puppets of all sizes have been used for centuries in many cultures to communicate to, educate, and entertain all ages. Sock puppets, such as those made famous as Muppets, appeal to all. Blacklight puppets like those used in performances in leading cities of Europe, and the interpretive style used in Disney's Broadway show *The Lion King*, are extremely popular with adults.

pyrotechnics Fire and other explosive devices used as a special effect. Also see *fireworks*.

"Q" The written abbreviation for a *cue*, often handwritten in scripts at the appropriate point by the individual stage technician and sometimes followed with the number of the cue, such as "Q 22." This may be followed by a note as to what activity that technician performs on that cue, such as "close middrape" and other specifics, such as "on a four count" (the duration of the time established to close the drape).

quick-change room If an actor or performer will need to change their costume very quickly, this small room is created by flats immediately offstage, saving the time it would take for the person to go all the way to a dressing room and back. The room is just large enough to hold the person, a costumer to assist, and a rack for the costumes.

quinceañera In Hispanic society, the coming-out celebration for a young girl on the occasion of her fifteenth birthday. Traditionally it includes a Mass and large reception with a court of honor consisting of fourteen couples and her **chambelan de honor** or escort, the person she will dance with.

rags Theatrical slang for *costumes*.

rail See *pin rail*.

rain card A card enclosed with the invitation to an outdoor event stating what happens, whom to call, and where to go if rain occurs. Since people have different definitions of inclement weather, someone should be positioned at the site not being used with instructions for those who may show up.

rake The traditional slanting of the stage floor from low in front to high in back to increase the audience's perception of depth. Because of the difficulty of walking on a raked floor, the technique is usually limited to professional theater.

rally An event, either indoor or outdoor, with the purpose of raising support and enthusiasm for a cause or an individual, such as for a political candidate. Typically a rally features speakers on a stage supported by entertainment addressing a large crowd, but it could also be a **march** or *parade*.

  See setup for a rally in "Tables and Techniques" (page 411).

Rallies for political purposes and candidates for office have been extremely common events. For tips, see the following: *press conference*, *press platforms*, *sound system*, and *multbox*.

ramp Any inclined platform or the sloping part of a platform. Also see *ADA*.

read through A rehearsal where the entire script for the presentation or show is read by all members of the cast with the production team present. This process gives an opportunity for all to discuss accompanying elements such as visuals and various cues for lighting, sound,

music, etc. It is an extremely valuable process to familiarize and organize all concerned with the production prior to an actual full rehearsal
in the venue.

real time An event happening in the actual time it takes to happen as
planned. The time is not edited or changed for the sake of effect. A
real-time rehearsal means that an element, such as a speech, is given
its full anticipated time during the rehearsal, including the transitions
into and out of the speech. This allows the operators to practice their
timings to make events happen (a light change for example) as they will
during the actual show.

rear projection The use of the projector on the backside of a trans-
lucent screen. The image is projected on the rear of the screen material,
properly diffused, and transmitted through the screen to the eyes of the
audience. The big advantage is that the projector is located out-of-sight
of the audience behind the staging area. It also allows actors or presenters to perform with the screen image as a background. Disadvantages are 1) that space is required behind the screen, often taking
audience space from the room, and 2) a bothersome "hot spot" can be
seen by the audience if a quality screen is not utilized or if the projector's angle is not correct.

receiving line A method for the host to receive or meet the guests at
a party or other function, such as a wedding reception. The host and
other selected individuals, who may include other business executives,
family, or *VIP*s, stand in a line in order of precedence to greet every
guest in turn. Each guest greets the first person (lowest precedent) and
if necessary introduces oneself. The first person then introduces the
guest to the next person in line and then turns to greet the next guest.
It is not a time for extended conversations, but rather each guest says
little more than a conventional greeting or congratulations to facilitate
the progress of the line. In very large functions, the process is facili-
tated by an announcer at the head of the host's line who boldly states

each guest's name, with just brief greetings then exchanged between each down the line. At very, very large functions, only certain individuals are invited to attend the receiving line.

 A wedding receiving line should be as follows:

1. Mother of the bride.

2. Father of the groom.

3. Mother of the groom.

4. Father of the bride.

5. Bride.

6. Groom.

7. Maid or matron of honor.

8. Bridesmaids.

Ushers and the best man—unless he is also the father—do not stand in the receiving line.

 The receiving line order for other affairs, such as a business dinner or retirement dinner, can vary greatly. Those receiving the guests are always organized by rank from the least important to the most. However, always have at least one individual after the most important, such as an assistant or close relative, whose responsibility is to pull the guests along and away after they have greeted the most important person.

 Typically, if there are fewer than fifty to sixty guests, a receiving line is unnecessary. In this case, often a couple of staff or family members are assigned to see that every person who arrives is introduced to the host, who is placed in a set position.

reception A formal function held to celebrate an event, make an

R

announcement, or welcome somebody. A reception can be large or small and typically has food and beverages. As the term implies, the event is less than a party or dinner. A cocktail reception is a predinner gathering. In the case of a wedding, the party after the ceremony is called a reception, even though it may be a gala event with the works, because the couple "receives" society for the first time as a couple.

red carpet   Traditionally the red carpet marks the route taken by heads-of-state on ceremonial occasions and *VIP*s and *celebrities* at gala formal events. Often on either side are red ropes extending from golden stanchions to further isolate the pathway. The red carpet tradition in literature is in the play *Agamemnon*, written by Aeschylus in 458 BC. Any special effort in hospitality is often referred to as "rolling out the red carpet" or "red carpet treatment."

regelling   The process of replacing the color media, the *gel*, in theatrical lighting instruments. This is done for two reasons. Either the color effect was not satisfactory, and all of the colors need to be changed, or the lights have been operating at high levels for a long period of time and the color has washed or burned out. In this case, regelling refreshes the intensity of the colored light.

registration   The process of aligning multiple images into one. It can involve using different images, such as when matting a building against a sky, or aligning two projectors so that one image can easily dissolve into another. Sometimes two video projectors are registered together with the same image so that the combined image on the screen is twice as bright in intensity.

Registration also refers to the process of officially recording something, such as guests attending an event. At many dinners, meetings, conferences, or other such events, attending guests report to a **registration table** to report their attendance, show their invitation, receive a table assignment, receive admission tickets, or pick up necessary materials.

🖉 **Tips for a successful registration table process:**

✓ Prominently locate the registration table so that it is the guest's first encounter.

✓ Avoid long lines. Break the process up alphabetically by the guests' names, prominently displaying the breakdown so that it is easy for the guests to find their position.

✓ If payments need to be made by some, use separate lines for this purpose.

✓ Don't overburden the workers at these tables by giving them too much information to collect or materials to hand out. If materials such as a list of attendees, maps, program materials, etc., are being distributed, have them assembled in one envelope for each registrant.

✓ Have name badges prepared so that they just need to be handed out.

✓ Select people to operate these tables who are smart and personable and who create a good image for the event. This is the guest's first impression of the event, so make it good.

✓ Have those manning the table be groomed and dressed appropriately.

✓ Have one supervisor present, a person who knows well what must happen and can handle any problem.

✓ Keep one person on the desk throughout the event to handle latecomers.

✓ There are many *apps* available that ease the guest registration process.

rehearsal The process of practicing a speech, show, or other activity in preparation for a performance or presentation to an audience. If rehearsal time is limited, it is best to rehearse all the way through the show or program so that everyone gets a feeling for the flow, and then go back to spend more time on problem or individual segments. Ideally, another full run of the show, with these changes, would then be executed. Also see *dress rehearsal*.

rehearsal dinner A celebration dinner of the two families about to be united through marriage. Typically it is held immediately after the wedding rehearsal and on the eve of the wedding day. Generally it is the responsibility of the groom's family to provide. It can be as simple or elaborate as they wish. Only the families and official wedding participants attend.

> For seating arrangements, see diagram in "Tables and Techniques" (page 407).

rehearsal schedule Efficiency is extremely important in rehearsals, so this well-thought-out list of who does what and when they do it is extremely important. Typically *VIP*s, speakers, and celebrities do not want to rehearse, so schedule them closest to the event and be sure all is ready for them when they arrive. Be sure that the schedule gets into the hands of the person who is to rehearse and isn't stopped by the agent, secretary, or assistant who "forgets" to pass on the information.

release A legal document that permits one party to use the property of another. Typical releases at events include a photo release for pictures, a model release for fashion models, a music release for the use of a particular piece of music, etc. The release document is signed by both parties. When in doubt as to whether a release is needed—do one!

> A sample release is in "Tables and Techniques" (page 413), but a lawyer should write one specific to your event or company.

remote pickup or **remotes** Video accumulated from a location such as at an event and then transferred via microwave back to the news department's studio or home base. Often news crews will perform a remote pickup at the actual site, or sites, for newsworthy events. Controlling the site, what is seen in the background, and personnel interviewed, is essential for good media coverage. Always provide something of special interest to ensure the video is ultimately selected for the newscast over other options the editors may have available.

rentals Equipment obtained for a short period of time and returned to the owner for a fee. Typical events have hundreds of rentals of all types, including tents, dinnerware, lighting, costumes, and heavy equipment.

repertoire A collection or selection of material such as songs, plays, or speeches within a person's or group's prepared portfolio. **Repertoire theater** is a resident company of actors who know and present a selection of the same plays in rotation, such as one per week. Sometimes a different celebrity performer is added to the cast for each selection performed. Also called **rep** or **stock theater**.

reprise The repeat of a passage or complete musical number, sometimes at a faster *tempo* or in a different key. This may be used during the applause after an entertainer as a *chaser* or at the end of a presentation.

repro Short for reproduction or the duplicate copy or copies of printed material, videos, photos, or CDs.

reshipping After the run of an exhibition, trade show, or show, the materials need to be repacked and returned or forwarded to the next show location. This is also referred to as the reverse drayage process. Plan repacking prior to move-in and identify your crates for easy, quick retrieval. Have packing instructions, new shipping labels, and extra packing materials available on site to expedite the process.

response card See *invitation*.

retention A percentage of the total fees of a contract withheld (retained) until final buy-off by the client.

retouching A process of correcting a photograph, either electronically or by hand, to remove imperfections or to eliminate unnecessary or confusing detail.

return A flat, or a drapery, placed between the tormentors or inner proscenium and the downstage end of the box set to mask the opening made when a set is narrower than the width of the performing area.

reveal The sudden disclosure of something that has been covered or hidden. Reveals are effective for the presentation of new products or to introduce a celebrity speaker. A quick reveal can be accomplished in several ways, including the use of a *drop curtain*, or a wall of balloons that are suddenly released or are *rigged* to explode. Often magical illusions are used for dramatic effect, or items can be lifted quickly onstage with an elevator or lowered from the *flies*.

reverb or **reverberation** Acoustical resonance or the persistence of sound in a particular space after the original sound is removed. Reverb is used to enhance voice and instrument sound and as a *special effect*. Originally it was created in echo chambers, but now it is accomplished digitally through signal processing.

R

reverse Artwork or copy featuring white lettering or images against a black background.

review An evaluation of an artistic work, be it theater, literature, a film, or an event. Good reviews can be valuable marketing tools, and every effort should be made to solicit qualified reviewers with a following.

revolving lights Very high intensity lights, mounted on a movable base such as a trailer, that shoot large beams of light into the night sky while turning. Typically these lights have a controller that can make the lights spin, move up and down, flash, and even beam color. All can be programmed to execute such commands on *cue*. Also see *moving lights*.

revolving stage A stage with a circular platform that can be rotated to either present a 360° view of an object or to *reveal* a second subject on the back half of the circle. It is often a practical method of presenting two different musical groups that require extensive equipment setups. If the stage is rotated, the second group comes into view already performing, which keeps the excitement of the event intact. A **revolving set** is multiple scenes mounted on a turntable, like slices of pie, enabling the scene to change rapidly. Sometimes the *act curtain* is lowered for the changes, sometimes the change takes place in full audience view. Also see *turntable*.

RF Synonym for wireless communication and acronym for Radio Frequency, which is a system of transmitting using the radio spectrum. Most often this system is used for two-way radios and wireless microphones, but it is also used to control *moving lights* and other theatrical equipment.

RFP Abbreviation for Request for Proposal. Many companies, government entities, organizing committees, and associations issue these documents outlining the specifics of the event and sometimes the total budget available (or budget range) to secure bids from event production companies for the execution of the project or parts of the project.

rider A document attached to a performer's contract defining what must be supplied by the buyer, at the buyer's cost, to support the performance. Requirements such as the size of the stage, dressing rooms, security, hotel rooms, power, etc., are typical, but some riders are quite extensive with many demands right down to the color of jelly beans in the *dressing rooms* or the *green room*. Many big-name performers have been known not to perform if all of the conditions of the rider are not met exactly.

rigger   The technician responsible for hanging drapes, *scenery*, lighting, and all other equipment both onstage or from ceilings of other venues. Most states require this person to be licensed. Be sure to check their license. They are responsible both for their own safety as they hang from often very high positions and the safety of the audience, or performers, who may be below the hung equipment.

rigging or **rigged** or **to rig**   The actual process of hanging equipment, lights, *drapes*, etc., from either the ceiling or grid system on a stage. It is also the term used to describe the actual systems used to raise, lower, or move the stage equipment overhead. The **rigging system** is traditionally composed of pulleys, ropes, counterweights, and a *pin rail* where the *rope lines* are tied at the appropriate length by wrapping them around wooden pins. Modern systems now control the ropes or steel cables with electric wenches controlled by an automated system. Also, the process of fastening items for theatrical presentation.

riser   A raised platform of any height, shape, or size. It can also have multiple levels such as those used for choirs. Also, the vertical part of a step.

📖 **See riser examples in "Tables and Techniques" (page 440).**

road show   A show production, exhibit, sales meeting, or other event that moves from one city or location to another.

roast   A comedy event in which the participants pay tribute to or honor someone or something through insults, jokes, outlandish true or untrue embarrassing stories, and heartwarming criticism. The **roastee** needs to be able to take the comments in good humor and not as serious criticism. The participants are good friends. The host is the **roastmaster**. Roasts started privately at the New York Frier's Club in the 1920s. Most consider it an honor to be roasted.

Also, the method of cooking meat in an open pan in the oven, making it well-browned on the outside while moist on the inside. **Roast beef** is the most commonly known menu item cooked in this manner.

roll The cue given to begin an action such as the start of videotaping or the playback of a video or audio cue.

roll curtain A curtain that rolls up, usually from the bottom. A **roll drop** is a painted scenic drop rather than a curtain rigged in similar fashion. Also see *olio*.

room charge A fee for the use of a function room exclusive of other services such as catering. While many hotels will exclude a charge for the room if a minimum is met for catering, most nonhotel venues require a room charge. Understand what is included in the charge and what will be extra. Some venues charge extra for everything, even the electricity used.

room setup The layout of the interior venue space in the best way to accommodate the audience, the presentation, and other activities of the event. Also see *seating plan* and *angle of view*.

 See samples and guidelines for room setups in "Tables and Techniques" (page 415).

R

rope line The divider between the audience and attendees at an event that attracts crowds because of the popularity of those attending. Often security or police control this line. Traditionally it was just rope strung between posts, but over the years, and depending on the event and the security required, it became, sometimes, a solid barrier. Politicians often want to **work the line** to shake hands with their supporters.

rope line rigging Unlike most rope lines on a stage that are rigged up to the block pulleys and then over to the side of the stage, these lines are rigged in a line from downstage to upstage. A stage can have several of these rigs. They are used for special needs of the production.

rostrum A raised place or platform for public speaking. The *lectern* would be placed on the rostrum. Also referred to as a *dais*.

rough cut The first assembly of an edited video, film, or digital presentation. Typically its purpose is for review before further editing.

roundels Circular *color media* that are made of heat-resistant glass and fit over a light fixture. Also see *gel*.

royalty A fee paid to the copyright owner of an *intellectual property* such as a *script* or *musical score*.

R.S.V.P. From the French "Rèpondez s'il vous plaît" (Respond if you please) and only correctly written with the periods as R.S.V.P. On formal invitations it always requires a *mandatory* and prompt response, be it positive or negative. Traditionally this response is written, but often it is communicated by other means. On formal invitations, the R.S.V.P. must always be in the lower left corner. If the address to which the reply is to be sent is different from the address given in the invitation, the new address is written below R.S.V.P.

R.S.V.P. Regrets Only Currently popular, this request requires a response *only* if the guest is *unable* to attend. This form is never used in a formal invitation. Traditionally the response is in writing.

See invitation responses and other illustrated invitations in "Tables and Techniques" (page 361).

"Ruffles and Flourishes" A musical fanfare for distinguished people. The ruffles are played on drums and the flourishes on bugles. Four of each is the highest honor and is reserved for only the president of the United States as he enters a public gathering. This short fanfare is followed immediately by the musical composition "Hail to the Chief." Also see *gun salute*.

rum An alcoholic spirit originating in the Caribbean. It is distilled from molasses, a residue of sugar-making. Made throughout the islands, rum varies greatly in style: it can be light or dark in color, light or heavy in body, and low, high, or really high in proof. While Puerto Rican rums tend to be light-bodied and great for sipping, Jamaican rums are pungent, darker, and heavier.

run The period of time, or number of performances, that a show or event will take place.

rundown or **show rundown** A brief outline of a show in sequential order listing key elements, performers, speakers, and other events. Rundowns are handy quick references for performers and crew and are often posted backstage, in the control room and other key locations, during rehearsals and performances.

runner A long, narrow strip of fabric used over a tablecloth to add color or visual impact to a *place setting*. Often runners are used in the center of a table when place mats are used under the place settings. Also see *linen*.

Also, a person on the crew whose job is to fetch or deliver whatever is needed for the production crew and staff, be it materials, scripts or memos, or lunch. Also see *gofer*.

running time The duration of a complete show or presentation or a segment of the presentation, such as the playback of a video or the length of a speech.

run of show The duration that the show or event performs in one location, be it a day, week, month, etc.

runway A long, narrow platform extension from the stage either thrusting directly into the audience or in an arch around the orchestra pit. A staging method to bringing the action into the house close to the audience. Typically used effectively for fashion shows because it permits multiple views of the fashions on the models.

rye A type of *whiskey*. American rye must be distilled with at least

51 percent rye grain mash, which gives it a fruity or spicy taste. Because of its distinctive flavor, rye is often used to bolster the flavor of whiskey sours, manhattans, and old-fashioned cocktails. Very popular in the 1700s and 1800s, the center of its production was Pittsburgh, Pennsylvania. After Prohibition its popularity never came back. Canadian whisky historically was made with rye, but there currently is no requirement to use rye; it need only possess the aroma, taste, and character of the traditional Canadian rye.

SAG The abbreviation of the labor union for actors in motion pictures, the Screen Actors Guild.

sake An alcoholic spirit originating in Japan that is actually classified as beer since it is made from rice grain and not from fruit as is typical of wine. However, in the United States, the *BATF* categorizes it as wine. Sake has low alcohol content (12 to 16 percent) and if tightly sealed in the refrigerator will last for two to three weeks.

sandbag Traditionally a canvas bag filled with sand or lead shot placed on the end of a line or line set to hold the line taut when not in use. Today sandbags come in all shapes and sizes and are an extremely handy item used to temporarily hold down just about anything. Also see *counterweight.*

satire A form of comedy that uses wit, sarcasm, and ridicule to attack an idea or individual. Often used in political or corporate presentations.

save the date A communication to alert people to an upcoming event long before it is customary to send invitations. This communication is particularly important if many of the expected guests are coming from distant locations. Notice can be a simple letter, printed card, or even an e-mail.

scaffold   A modular system of metal pipes, clamps, and platforms used for the temporary construction of stages, sound system towers, control towers, lighting, bleachers, and many other purposes required by events. The flexibility of the system, combined with the speed of assembly, makes **scaffolding** an ideal solution for many event challenges.

scale   The dimensions to which architectural plans are drawn at a specific ratio relative to the actual size. Also referred to as **scale drawings** or **architect's scale**. Various scales may be used for different drawings in a set. Typical large areas, such as venue sites, may be drawn at a scale of $1/16$ inch = 1 foot, while a structure would be $1/8$ inch = 1 foot and a single room may be drawn in the larger scale of ¼ inch = 1 foot. In the latter, ¼ inch on the paper drawing equals 1 foot of real construction. Typical metric scales are 1:5, 1:100, and 1:2,000. Most architectural drawings have a scale indicator on the drawing. Only if the drawing has been printed to the proper scale can a ruler be used accurately. Also see *technical drawing.*

scene   A short section of a play or writing that represents a single event. Also, a visual or picture presented on a stage or in a photograph.

scene dock   An area for the storage and/or the loading of scenic elements. In a theater it is typically located either in the *wing* area or behind the *backdrop.* Adjacent are usually very tall *elephant doors* for accessing large scenic pieces from outside the theater into the scene dock.

scenery   All of the visual elements that make up the background for a presentation such as a drape, a full theatrical set, a company logo, or even the natural view at an outdoor venue.

scene shift   The moment in time when the scenery changes onstage.

It happens on a cue in the script. It can refer to one piece of scenery or an entire set, completely changing the appearance onstage.

schedule   The backbone of any event. A timetable of all elements, from planning and ordering through setup, operation, and final strike. A good schedule must be a complete and accurate timeline yet be flexible enough to accommodate last-minute problems and changes. A schedule is not an event *script*, nor an *order of events*, but it is the backbone for both. Also see *milestones* and *sequence*.

✎ **Tips on creating a powerful, workable schedule:**

✓ The following important elements should be included on every schedule spreadsheet:

   1. The task, such as "buy flowers."

   2. The date and/or time the task must be completed, such as "buy flowers on xx date" and "flowers delivered on xx date." Or, "9:55 p.m. Speaker #1 is introduced."

   3. The person responsible to accomplish the task and that *one* person's contact information.

   4. A line in the budget that is associated with the cost of this task.

✓ Start it at the very beginning of the project so that it can grow appropriately.

✓ Usually the day and time of the event are the first entries in the schedule. Working back from this entry is the easiest way to begin.

✓ List everything that comes to mind. Items can be dropped later if not appropriate.

✓ Distribute the schedule to all key individuals, certainly those listed on the schedule as being responsible for items, so that everyone understands what must be done, when, and by whom.

✓ Date the schedule each time it is revised and redistributed. Some like to change the color of the paper with each distribution so that it is easy to see who is working with an outdated schedule.

✓ Develop a distribution system that ensures that everyone who is designated to receive the schedule receives the updated version each time one is released.

✓ When talking with vendors, be specific about exact delivery days or times and enter these in the schedule immediately so they are not forgotten. If the vendor argues that the date of delivery must be determined later, enter on the schedule a date to call the vendor back to get the delivery date.

✓ Follow-up calls are necessary with most vendors, unfortunately, so list these in the schedule.

✓ Drop or mark off accomplished items on the schedule as they happen so as to keep it visually uncluttered.

📖 See sample schedule in "Tables and Techniques" (page 330).

schematic A technical drawing or diagram that shows the layout of parts for a particular item in a set pattern.

schoolroom seating The layout of tables in rows parallel to the presenter's position with the attendees' chairs on one side facing the presentation like desks in a schoolroom. Often these tables are narrow, allowing just enough space for writing.

 See layout examples in "Tables and Techniques" (page 430).

Sciopticon A lighting instrument used to create moving visual effects such as rain, flames, or clouds.

scope or **scope of work** The equipment and materials to be provided, and the work to be done, as defined by a contract for an entire project or part of the project.

score Simply defined as **sheet music**, or the notes of a musical composition handwritten or printed on paper to be read by a musician or the musicians in an orchestra. The musical process is that a *composer* will transfer his/her creative thoughts onto a sheet of musical paper as one line of music notes (and sometimes lyrics) representing the basic melody, chord changes, and notations. This is a *leadsheet*. The composer and/or assisting *arranger* will then break down and expand this leadsheet into parts for individual instruments, or in pop music, for various members of the band. This arrangement in its many sheets of music for each instrument (or part of the orchestra) becomes the score. A **conductor's score** contains all of the parts in the arrangement. A musical piece can be arranged in various ways, making each a new score of the original melody or song. Sometimes the word "score" is also used to describe any completed piece of music.

screen A surface and support system used for displaying a projected image. Screens fall into three categories. **Front projection screens** have a reflective coating to increase the gain of the reflected light projected to enhance the image. A **rear projection screen** is made of a fabric that enhances the luminous power of the projected light as it passes through the screen. An electric or **video screen** creates its own image based on impulses fed to them by either tuners or computers. Each of these is only as effective as the existing ambient light level of the space. A fourth type is the **water screen**, which is rear projection, used as a *special effect*. Each of the screens has its advantages and disadvantages and all come in a variety of sizes. All screens have different *angles of view*, which needs to be carefully considered in selecting the right screen for the *venue* and *room setup*.

See screen selection plans in "Tables and Techniques" (page 436).

screening room A space set up for ultimate viewing of a film or computer presentation. Typically these rooms have high-definition (HD) film or video screens and projectors, luxurious seating, and surround-sound audio. Usually presentations are accompanied by snacks and beverages.

scrim A large, seamless piece of bobbinet-style fabric or sharkstooth that is painted with one scene and positioned in front of another, allowing the visual to *cross fade* from one to another by changing the lights. It is opaque when lighted from the front and transparent when lighted from the rear. A scrim is sometimes used in front of a *cyc* to eliminate the possibility of seeing wrinkles.

script The written version of the show, play, or speech, often containing other information important to the execution of the event, including a description of visuals, action to take place, and *cues*. Scripts should be distributed to all members of the production team, key stage crew, and all others concerned with the execution of the production. Updates to the script are distributed to all of the same with the changes clearly marked. A list of all those who receive a script is kept and maintained, indicating that each person with a script received the changed pages. When a script contains confidential information, it is numbered and signed for by the appropriate individual given a copy, and then it is collected at the end of the production. A **shooting script** is the final version of a script that has been approved for videotaping or filming and complete production.

seating plan or **seating chart** Defines who sits where at a function. While it seems simple to compile, often it proves to be an extremely difficult task. While it is important that people have the ability to meet and mingle, certain people must be together, and a table of one group often needs to be next to a certain other table. Placing the final seating chart outside the dining room makes it easy for guests to find their seats and use *escort cards*. Have a waiter, or host, available in the dining room with a copy of the plan to help those lost or confused. If seats are assigned at each table, use *place cards* to identify each. Also see *head table*.

🖉 **Helpful tips for forming a seating plan:**

✓ Start with *VIP*s and place them together as necessary, or spread them out so that there is one at each table.

✓ Keep couples together, which is sometimes hard to do because of singles and threesomes. Depending on the event, consider mixing couples at a table or even over different tables. VIP couples are often split, and are used to being so, particularly if one is a speaker or plays another key role in the event.

✓ If it is a family affair, know the current relations between family members. An ex-wife probably doesn't want to be at a table with her ex-husband and his lady friend.

✓ Should foreigners be attending, their customs must be considered, particularly at weddings or political events. Place a foreigner who speaks no English next to someone who can communicate.

✓ If the event is a fund-raiser, certain prospective donors need to be positioned with key influencers.

✓ Mix conversationalists with the more silent types.

✓ Mix the old and young.

✓ Know exactly who is attending. For example, a celebrity may arrive with security guards who must sit within a certain distance of the celebrity.

✓ Anticipate how adjustments can be made for unanticipated problems or no-shows.

✓ The easiest way to accomplish the layout is to start with a table layout and write the guests' names on sticky notes. This enables the guests' names to be placed and then repositioned as often as necessary.

See wedding seating plans in "Tables and Techniques" (page 407).

See seating plans by rank in "Tables and Techniques" (page 402).

See how to establish a seating plan in "Tables and Techniques" (page 405).

> *At a motion picture premiere dinner I did at New York's 21 Club, the leading lady was seated next to a popular television gossip show host, and within five minutes the sparks flew between them. Her husband stood up and, in a loud voice all could hear, declared that his wife would not sit next to this person. Obviously it made all the guests very uneasy and required the two to be separated.*

SECAM A video playback and transmission standard used primarily in France.

second generation A copy of a video or audiotape from the original master. Unlike digital recordings, *analogue* recordings lose quality, known as a **generation of sound**, when copied, even when the best rerecording equipment is used.

section or **section view** or **cross section** A scaled drawing that slices through the elevation of an entire building, set, or other structure in a single view either from the front or a side. Also see *plan*, *elevation*, and *scale*.

security The safekeeping of people, equipment, and the venue of an event. Unfortunately in today's world, this task has increased substantially, adding greatly to the cost and complexity of planning and executing most events.

🖉 **Tips for event security:**

✓ Don't consider yourself an expert. Plan or review all plans with local professional safekeepers, such as police, firefighters, or private security firms.

✓ Volunteer security personnel are rarely adequate.

✓ Consider event security firms that provide people trained to handle crowds in a manner different from police.

✓ Utilize existing resources such as miscellaneous gates and doors. Know who has all the keys or provide locks where necessary.

✓ Consider who your *VIPs*, celebrities, or *headline talent* are and their special security requirements.

✓ Keep excellent notes of meetings with safekeepers and recheck the notes to ensure their requests are provided for.

✓ Check the event insurance policies to understand what requirements are stated.

sell To make it work and be acceptable to the audience.

sequence The arrangement of a series of elements in a production or presentation, such as video shots, speakers, or entertainers, that happen one after another. Also, the order in which these elements are carried out. This order, or **sequence of events**, is extremely important in structuring an effective program. Also see *schedule*. Also see *order of events*.

🖉 **Tips for structuring an effective sequence of events:**

✓ Start with something that will catch the audience's attention and imagination.

✓ Vary the different types of elements, mixing speeches with entertainment with computer-generated visual presentations, etc.

✓ Keep the sequences short, or at least tolerable.

✓ Mix the emotional value. Two or three testimonials, one after the other, is not as effective as if these same testimonials are separated by other production elements.

✓ Add *audience involvement* whenever possible.

✓ Consider the overall flow of the sequence of events. Are there highs and lows? Does the tempo of the various elements change throughout?

✓ End with an impact. End with what you want the audience to remember or the feeling you want them to leave with.

set The complete arrangement of scenery with props and lights that combine to make an entire *scene*. For example, a kitchen set, or setting, would have all the look of a real kitchen and be used for a cooking presentation. To "set" is to place scenery or items on the stage. When finished, the stage is "set." Also, a number of songs performed by a band, or acts by an entertainer, on a single occasion is called a "set." For example, a band could play a certain number of sets a night, each of a defined duration and each with different songs.

set dressing Props and other materials, such as window curtains, arranged to decorate a set.

set height In theater and cinema, the average height of a set, such as a living room, is 12–14 feet.

set line The outline of the entire set in relation to the stage floor. Traditionally the set is placed onstage so that the front set line, the line across from the most downstage ends of the set, coincides with the *tormentors* of the inner *proscenium*.

set of lines See *line set*.

set piece An individual item of a set, such as a chair in a living room set.

setup To erect or install all the elements of an event. A **setup plan** is necessary when the situation is complicated or needs to be accomplished in a very short period of time. Also, the **camera position** at the beginning of a scene. Also, a specific **display** of certain products or materials. Also, a *table setting* for one person. Also see *strike*.

setup fee A cost levied by hotels, restaurants, and other venues for preparation of the room prior to an event. Typically the fee covers staffing to set tables and a cleanup after the event, but the cost varies depending on the requirements of the event.

SFX An abbreviation for special effects.

shared vans When several companies exhibiting in the same show consolidate their shipments together in a single van for cost savings. Van lines per se cannot consolidate shipments.

shear A visual distortion where one axis is at an angle while the other is correctly straight. The resulting image is slanted. For example, horizontal shear causes normal text to look like italic type.

sherry A traditionally dry, but occasionally sweet, wine made only from Palomino white grapes grown in the area around the town of Jerez de la Frontera near Cádiz in Andalusia, Spain. The name "sherry" is an Anglicization of Jerez. Sherry is unique in that sherrys from different years are blended before bottling so that every year's vintage contains a small amount of very old wine.

shot The particular view of a camera or the view as recorded by a still camera. On a motion camera it is the continuous action that appears from a single, uninterrupted operation of the camera. A series of shots makes up a *sequence*.

show Any public presentation, including but not limited to theater performances, exhibitions, concerts, demonstrations, and events. **Showable** is when something is ready to be presented to the public.

show action equipment A mechanical or electrical unit that moves, drives, or affects show *props* or *sets*. For example, a treadmill built into the floor of a stage that allows an actor to walk or run in the same spot.

show curtain A curtain or drop that portrays the theme of the show or play. It is located either immediately behind the *main curtain* or behind a musical performing act.

showmanship A knack for dramatically effective presentation; a flair for visual effectiveness.

show rotation A method of controlling the flow and dispersion of attendees at an event or project by the manipulation of various show performance times in different areas of the event site. For example, having a show performance at the far end of the site just before closing holds the audience, extends their time on site, and lessens the number exiting just prior to closing.

shtick Slang for an entertainer's or comedian's act, gimmick, or routine.

shutter Metal flippers, irises, mats, or other means of cutting off part or all of the light emanating from a lighting instrument. Sometimes the shutter is mounted on the front of the fixture; other types of light instruments have it inside the fixture.

side light The light emanating from theatrical instruments placed along the sides of the stage that strike the sides of the performers. Also called cross light.

sight lines An imagined line on each side of the audience area that divides the area where the audience can see all of what is being presented from the area where the view is restricted or totally blocked. The audience wants to see everything, so understanding the limits of the sight lines in a performance environment is extremely important to the success of a production.

See diagrams and layout examples to better understand sight lines in "Tables and Techniques" (page 445).

signal Information that has been transposed into electronic impulses, passed along wires or circuits to receivers, and interpreted to lead to an action, such as making a lighting instrument turn on.

signal-to-noise ratio The ratio of the recorded signal level to the noise level induced by the recording equipment. A better-quality recording has the lowest amount of noise.

silent auction A type of auction that does not utilize an auctioneer, but rather a bidding system whereby individuals write their bids on a card adjoining each item to be sold. This popular method of fund-raising may be used as part of a cocktail party or other function. The guests enjoy circulating around the items displayed and placing bids. The bid cards usually have a minimum bid indicated and a number of spaces for bidders to indicate the value they are willing to pay. At a certain time in the event, the bidding is closed and whoever submitted the card with the highest amount on it acquires the item. What makes silent auctions interesting is that the items offered are items not typically available, such as personal mementos that have been donated for the cause. The more unique the items, the more enjoyable and successful the auction.

silverplate A less expensive alternative to sterling silver *flatware* and *hollowware*. Manufactured with only a plating of thin silver on the base metal instead of solid silver. Commonly used in many homes and at the more expensive venues for banquet, restaurant, and other food events.

simulator An attraction, usually enclosed, which uses advanced hydraulic/mechanical or electrically powered motion reproduction coupled with film or video, often 3D, to realistically convey motion-based situations, such as piloting a jet fighter.

site See *venue*.

site acts Entertainment that must be watched to be enjoyed, such as magicians, jugglers, and strolling costumed characters such as Mickey Mouse.

sitting on their hands A phrase to describe an unresponsive audience.

sizing The process of applying a shrinking agent to the canvas stretched over the frame of a *flat* or other set piece to tighten the fabric, making the whole unit rigid. Sizing liquid is water-based and composed of mainly modified starches. It fills the fabric fibers and creates a finish on the fabric that can be easily painted.

skirt See *table skirt*.

skirt clips A variety of differently designed spring clips used along the edge of a banquet table to hold the tablecloth and table skirt in place. Also used for modular platforms to attach the fabric skirt.

skit A short comical sketch visualizing a satirical writing. The *Saturday Night Live* television show is the best example. Skits can be used effectively to make a point in a speech, add a laugh to a part of a presentation, or serve as an introduction.

sky drop A *drop* or *cyc* painted blue to represent the sky. Typically it is used upstage to provide a background for other scenic elements.

slapstick A style of comedy that relies on farcical situations and fast physical action. Slapstick was used extensively in the silent movies because the obvious jokes require no language.

smoke pot   A *special effect* device that, when loaded with a *pyro* mixture and electronically sparked, creates a burst of smoke. The amount of smoke is controlled by the amount of mixture.

SMPTE   Society of Motion Picture and Television Engineers.

SMPTE time code   A standard code developed to identify specific *frames* by hour:minute:second of audio, video, or motion picture film, making electronic editing possible. It is also used to synchronize multiple recorders or players being used at the same time.

sneak   The very gradual introduction of sound, lighting, or another element done so that its presence isn't immediately known to the audience. Also, a slow *fade* in.

snow machine   A *special effect* machine that creates snow. Traditionally this was accomplished using a **snow bag** or silted canvas attached along two overhead battens, which was filled with shredded polyethylene snowflakes mixed with some *glitter*. By shaking one batten up and down, while the other remained fixed, the flakes gently fell through the slits onto the stage. New equipment actually blows simulated snowflakes made of water.

soliloquy   A theatrical device in a play when the actor speaks alone, sometimes directly to the audience, allowing a character's thoughts and ideas to be conveyed to the audience. Also, a section of a drama in which a soliloquy is spoken.

sorbet   A tart-tasting frozen dessert typically made from fruit, similar to sherbet but without any milk. It is often used to clear the palate between courses of a dinner.

soubrette   In a comedy, a minor female part whose characterization is pretty, coy, and flirtatious.

sound check   The procedure of making the final adjustments and balancing the audio system to ensure that all of the elements, including microphones, are working properly and are tuned for maximum sound quality and audience coverage. In events with musical performance, this process can be quite lengthy (and loud) but very necessary, and it needs to be accounted for in the production setup schedule.

sound effects   Sounds, either recorded or performed live, that enhance or accent the action being presented. In comedic presentations the sound effects are a part of the visual comedy, such as the sound of a man's pants tearing as he bends over.

sound engineer   The production person responsible to specify, design, install, and test the proper sound system appropriate to the type of presentation. This includes the loudspeakers and their placement, power supply, monitors, cabling, mixing consoles, and microphone types and placement.

sound level   See *decibel.*

sound mixer   The member of the stage crew responsible for balancing the volume levels of all of the audio sources to achieve the correct level for the audience. The mixer also activates the various sound sources such as microphones, audio playbacks, projector sound, etc., as necessary on cues given by the director.

sound reinforcement   See *sound system.*

soundscaping   The process of covering a large area with music or sound effects to create background atmospheres, often with the intent of subtle motivation. Stores use soundscaping to encourage longer stays and more purchases. Theme parks, casinos, and other attractions use it to establish a mood or to enhance a theme. Also see *background music.*

sound stage   A large structure with very tall ceilings designed to accommodate scenery, actors, and crew for the purpose of filming a motion picture. The name derives from the fact that the walls, doors, and ceiling are thickly padded with insulation, making the interior space soundproof by eliminating all outside noise.

sound system The audio system used to enhance and disseminate the performance sound, be it speech or music, to the assembled audience or entire event area. It includes microphones, *amplifiers*, a mixing console, and *loudspeakers*. Such sound systems vary greatly, so the right equipment needs to be specified and utilized for the specific purpose. Quality and understandability of the sound is as important as volume. Nothing can ruin an event quicker than the person, or whatever is being staged, not being comfortably heard and understood by the audience. Yet it is the mistake most often made by event planners.

🖉 **Always plan for too much sound. It can always be turned down.**

sous chef Assistant chef.

souvenir dinner program A printed keepsake of a dinner event of extreme importance. The event may be a retirement, anniversary, good-bye, or religious occasion. The program may include a logo, picture, seal, or other important visuals of the person or organization. It must be on quality paper stock with embossed lettering, perhaps a ribbon, or other elements to make it special and worth keeping.

🖉 **A souvenir program should contain:**

✓ The logistics (time, date, place).

✓ The reason for the event and a written tribute.

✓ Names and titles of key guests.

✓ The menu.

✓ A blessing, quote, or thoughtful phrase.

✓ If the event is a charity, or a project of one, some information about the cause.

spacing stick A wooden dowel exactly 5 feet long (1.5 meters) used by those setting banquet tables to set them with exactly enough space between tables to allow for the chairs and serving space. This distance is established by local fire codes, and while fairly standard it may vary from one area to another.

 See room setup diagram in "Tables and Techniques" (page 421).

speaker An orator, lecturer, or anyone who makes a verbal presentation at an event. He or she is often referred to as a **program speaker** or an **after**-**dinner speaker**, but depending on the type of event, there could be thousands of reasons for who the speaker is and when and why he or she is speaking. Also see *keynote speaker*. Also, the part of a sound system that turns the electronic pulses into audible sound. See *loudspeaker*.

🖊 Tips on presenting a program speaker at an event:

✓ Select the speaker carefully.

✓ Clearly define the reason for selecting each speaker. Perhaps he or she is an expert in the same industry, or inspires or motivates, or entertains, or provides fascinating or helpful information on associated topics.

✓ Determine the speaker's appropriateness to the event and audience. I once watched a celebrity football champion give a locker room–style speech to a large group of executives who were all totally embarrassed by the presentation. Not good. The group president immediately apologized to the audience as the speaker stormed out of the room.

✓ Always get prior approval from the client or key event organizers before booking a speaker.

✓ Always tell all speakers they have less time than what has been scheduled. They will always exceed the time limit.

✓ Make sure the speaker knows the reason for the event, who the audience is, the company business, key executives, etc., long before the date of the presentation. Work with them to integrate the information into their standard speech.

✓ Nothing is worse than too many speakers. The audience moans after two.

speaker stacks A series of sound loudspeakers placed on top of one another, usually with the low frequency bass cabinets on the bottom and the treble horns on top. Most often these stacks are placed on either side of the stage, but the placement and the types of speakers within the stack are determined by the sound engineer to get the best quality sound spread evenly over the entire audience. In very large venues, additional speaker stacks are located either within the audience area or along the sides of the audience and put on a delay system so that the sound coming from these speakers reaches the audience at the same time as the sound from the primary stacks located next to the stage. Also see *loudspeaker*.

special A lighting instrument placed for a specific purpose, such as to illuminate one individual item, or an individual, on a stage or dais.

special effect See *effect*.

special format Films designed to be shown on a very large screen, usually in 70 mm.

special needs Guests who are handicapped, elderly, ill, or disabled in other ways require special planning and attention. Not only does the law require it, but meeting these needs ensures all guests a good time. Keep in mind that the disabled never come alone but are always accompanied by escorts who are not disabled and who want to enjoy the event. So taking some of the burden away allows a more enjoyable experience for all. Be especially gracious and helpful. Seat them in a place of honor and provide someone to help them. If the event is outdoors, or at a nonstandard venue, such as a beach, there are strict rules for wheelchair access in sand, *porta potties*, and at tables. All stages, regardless of how temporary, must also provide wheelchair access. Insurance coverage demands adherence to the rules. See *ADA*.

spectacle An event memorable for its appearance. Often it shows things rarely seen. Dating back to the Roman circuses, spectacles have been staged continually throughout history right up to recent opening ceremonies at the Olympics and other major events. Also see *spectacular*.

spectacular A lavish artistic production or celebration that is grand, stunning, amazing, fabulous, and different from what is expected, leaving lasting impressions on the viewer.

> I include in the definition that a spectacular must include something not seen before. For example, I was the first to have everyone in the Super Bowl stadium add dazzle to the show by using flashlights with different colors and the first to turn out the stadium lights for the show. I was also the first to create an entire parade out of lights with the Main Street Electrical Parade at Disneyland. So while a spectacular must be magnificent and dramatic, it must also provide a new audience experience.

Spelvin, George The fictitious name traditionally used by a real actor who "doubles" or plays a second part and whose name already appears in the program. George Spelvin was a real actor who in 1907 doubled in the cast of *Brewster's Millions*, and because the play was so successful, the author, Winchell Smith, continued to list Spelvin in his programs for luck.

spike To mark the location onstage of a person's position, or the placement of something such as a standing microphone.

spill Unwanted light from a lighting instrument or projector. Spill is eliminated by refocusing the light or by using a *mask*. Also, something unfortunate that can happen with a liquid when being served.

spirit or **spirits** A term used for alcoholic beverages. See *liquor.*

splice The putting together of two pieces of film or recording tape with a butt-joint. A splice can also be accomplished electronically with a computer editing program.

split screen When two or more images, either still or moving or both, appear side by side on a single screen. Very effective, high-impact presentations can be achieved by using this technique of multiple imagery.

S.P.O.C. Abbreviation for Selected Person of Contact. The designation given to the key person with the client, a vendor, other resource, or the production team. It is the person with authority to answer all questions, give and take advice, negotiate terms, and make final decisions. Often a contract between a client and event company will specify this person so that it is understood by both parties that this S.P.O.C. is the only one authorized to speak for the client.

spotlight Any lighting instrument that is designed to produce a concentrated intense beam of light on a defined area. Also see *followspot*, *parcan*, and *Leko.*

spouse program Activities for those accompanying attendees at meetings, conferences, conventions, and other such events. The activities are carefully planned to occupy a large percentage of the available time and need to meet the interest of both sexes, their age group, and special interests. Typically the program is in addition to amenities offered by the venue, such as golf, tennis, pool, etc. Most common are sightseeing tours, shopping at an interesting part of the city, or special theatrical performances. Also popular is an entertaining and informational lecture concerning the hosting company or organization's field of business.

> *While we were attending a multiple-day meeting is Seoul, South
> Korea, the spouse program took my wife and other spouses on a
> tour of the royal palace, followed by a session at the royal cooking
> school where they learned to make artful Korean hors d'oeuvre,
> followed by a traditional lunch, then all, women and men, donned
> costumes to watch and participate in folk dances. Upon returning
> home these were the first pictures my wife showed everyone.*

S.R.O. Abbreviation for Standing Room Only. Use when all of the
seats are reserved or full for the performance but tickets (usually dis-
counted) are available to watch the show by standing in the *back of the
house.*

stadium A venue for (mostly) outdoor sports, concerts, or other large
events that consists of a field entirely, or mostly, surrounded by a structure designed to hold seats for spectators to view the event. Also see
grandstands.

stage In a theater it is any floor space behind the proscenium used for
performance. In events it can be any floor space, usually elevated, used
for presentation or performance, indoor or outdoor, in any size and
shape. Also see *mobile stage.*

stage areas The stage floor is divided into six basic sections, each
referred to as an area. These areas are up stage right (or *up right*), *up
center*, *up left*, downstage right (or *down right*), *down center*, and
down left. All direction references are from the performer's point of
view facing the audience. Also see *stage mood.*

📖 See diagram specifics of stage areas in "Tables and Techniques"
   (page 447).

stage brace To support and strengthen flats, this wooden brace of
adjustable length has a metal hook in the top end that slips into a

special *stage brace cleat* and a flat iron piece with a hole on the bottom end that can be screwed into the stage floor with a *stage screw*. These braces are often used behind a door flat so that the scenery doesn't shake when the door is opened or closed.

stage brace cleat A specially designed strong metal fastener with an eye on one side in which the hook on the top end of a *stage brace* can be caught for a strong connection. The cleat is attached to the frame of the scenic flat just above middle.

stage crew All of the individuals who represent and carry out the duties of the various crafts required for the production or event on a stage. This includes the lead individuals, such as the *lighting director* and *stage manager*, as well as those working under each of the department heads.

stage directions Instructions concerning placement, movement, or other arrangements on the stage. Often these are given by the *director.*

stage floor The best stage floors are made of soft wood so that screws and fasteners of different types can be easily driven into them. Stage floors have sections, or *traps*, that can be removed to allow for access through the floor. Sometimes stage floors integrate a turntable and lifts of various types. A stage floor for a dance presentation *must* be of wood, and professional dancers have strict requirements as to how the wood surface is supported. The stage floor can be covered with various materials and painted as required by the production.

stage floor pockets Metal electrical receptacles sunk just below the level of the stage floor to provide power to various areas of the stage. The power to these pockets is usually controlled by the switchboard so that the lighting director has control.

stagehand The common reference for any member of the stage crew.

stage house The portion of the theater containing the stage area, including the fly loft and grid. Typically it refers to the area behind the proscenium.

stage left   That side of the stage on the actors' left when facing the audience.

stage manager   The person responsible for the smooth and safe operation of the stage and overall production, including rehearsals, stage crew, actors, and all other personnel and equipment related to the performance.

stage manager's desk   Traditionally a small shelf located offstage just behind the proscenium arch on the side of the stage with the pin rail and other controls from which the stage manager cues and operates the overall production. In different types of productions and venues, this key position is located in various places in the facility or site, but it is always the seat of the project operation.

stage mood   Each area of the stage has its own inherent value of weakness and strength and denotes a definite feeling to the audience. For example, action *down center* is hard, intense, and harsh, the proper area to stage fights and crises, while the *up right* area is warm and intimate, ideal for love scenes or confessions.

See a diagram illustrating stage areas and moods in "Tables and Techniques" (page 447).

stage orientation   The process of positioning, or the position of, all the elements on the stage, including the actors, performers, speakers, or others and their movements on the stage. Also see *stage mood*.

stage right   The area of the stage to the actors' right while facing the audience.

stage screw   A specially designed large screw with a handle used to easily fasten various elements, such as a *stage brace*, securely to the *stage floor*.

stage wait An undesirable moment in a show or presentation when nothing is happening. It can be caused by a late entrance, late music cue, or any of many other unfortunate occurrences.

stainless steel The most common type of *flatware* and *hollowware* used for banquet and restaurant service. Stainless steel is the ideal metal since it is an alloy of many metals. It never requires polishing and is durable, stain-resistant, and inexpensive.

stakeholder Any person, inside or outside an organization, who has an invested interest in the project. Stakeholders may have a positive or negative influence upon the project or stand to gain or lose by its success. They can be financial investors, sponsors, clients, municipalities, various team decision makers, or disgruntled neighbors. Understand each person's relationship to the project before meeting.

stanchion An upright, self-standing pole about 30 inches high (12 centimeters) to which rope, garland, chain, or fabric bands are attached and then placed in sequence with others to direct or control the flow of people. Typically referred to as **ropes and stanchions**.

stand by The warning cue indicating something, often the *cue* itself, is about to happen. A stand-by warning should always be given just prior to a cue or action both as a reminder to all concerned and to ensure that the cue will be executed simultaneously by all concerned. For example, if there are multiple actions on a cue, such as the lights fade, the music starts, the performer goes out onto the stage, etc., then the stand-by cue will be followed by a countdown, such as "Stand by for cue 21, in 5, 4, 3, 2, 1, Cue!" allowing everyone to perform the cue together.

standing ovation A great honor for any performance, when the audience is so pleased that it stands while applauding at the completion. Also see *curtain call*.

standing set Interior and exterior scenery that is used on a regular basis over and over again for continuing episodes of a series of films or for different films, commercials, photo shoots, etc. Typical standing sets are jail, courtroom, kitchen, operating room, airline interior, etc. Exteriors are frontier towns, neighborhood streets, and a European village.

stands Any metal device used to support lights, microphones, speakers, or other pieces of equipment. Also, lines of seats for an audience. See *grandstands*.

star The leading performer, actor, or speaker of a show or event.

stemware See *glassware*.

stencil Thin paper, plastic, or metal sheets cut with patterns that can be used repeatedly to easily paint detail or lettering on scenery, signs, or visuals. The art of stenciling is **pochoir**. Sections of material within a cutout area, like the center of an O, are called **islands**, and the tabs holding the islands in place are **bridges**. Also see *trompe l'oeil*.

step and repeat A background wall used for publicity photos that is covered with a staggered pattern of *logos* or other identifying marks associated with the event. Often these are placed on one side of a red carpet entrance so that all the photos taken of those attending include the event and sponsor logos. Also see *red carpet*.

stiffener To strengthen a line of scenic flats, this wooden batten is fastened to the back of the flats before they are hung or placed into position.

stile The vertical support boards of a scenic flat that join to the bottom and top horizontal rails. Also see *flat*.

 Complete diagrams of flat construction are in "Tables and Techniques" (page 449).

sting or **stinger** The loud and sudden introduction of music for shock value or emphasis.

stock or **in stock**   Disposable goods or possessions currently owned or in house. For example, a supply of liquor or a number of party chairs.

stock music   Libraries of music and songs of all different types that can be purchased or licensed for use. Similar to *stock photos*, below.

stock photos or **stock footage**   Any photos, either film or electronic, used in a presentation or publicity package that are preexisting. Often the usage of these photos is purchased or *licensed* from commercial photo libraries on the Internet that maintain a large number of photos all categorized by subject. Moving images either on film or video are also available for use, and these are typically referred to as **stock shots**.

street performers   Entertainers or actors who perform on sidewalks and street corners to audiences casually passing by. In theme parks and festivals, these performers are well planned to attract audiences to specific areas and to enhance the audience's enjoyment during their visit. An endless variety exists, including mimes, jugglers, clowns, dancers, magicians, and musicians of all types. Select those most appropriate to the *theme* of the event.

street theater   Performances by costumed actors utilizing simple props to interpret short and usually funny stories designed to stimulate the audience's imagination and wit.

stretch   To make longer. Often a cue given to the speaker or presenter to extend the time being taken for the presentation. The visible cue is a two-handed motion that resembles stretching a piece of fabric or elastic. The word is also used by caterers to put less food on each plate when too many people unexpectedly show up.

strike   To remove the entire show or event, or to remove a single item, or to clear a stage of its props or scenery.

strike plan A written document outlining the procedure, manpower, and sequence of events for the safe and efficient removal and loading of all the show equipment after the completion of an event or performance. Most often the venue has strict requirements as to the amount of time available after the event for striking. Sometimes another show or event is standing by to load-in immediately after the strike, so the strike plan is often reviewed and approved beforehand by the *venue*.

strip light A long, thin lighting instrument that has a row of lamps along its length. Usually these lamps are wired in series of three so that the colors can be blended or used independently. Strip lights are typically used behind *ground rows* and for lighting a *cyc*.

stunt Any physical action performed by an actor, which includes everything from simply falling down to driving a car through a ball of flame. In filmed performances, and sometimes onstage, stunt people double for the actor in the performance of these actions.

subtext An underlying message or meaning in the lines.

subtitles Lettering and graphics below an image that describe the image, such as the person's name, title, or location. Typically these are in the lower 25 percent of the screen viewing area. Also, a printed translation of the dialogue in a foreign motion picture or other presentation. It is common at events for a speaker who cannot speak the common language to have a translation of the speech appear simultaneously as spoken on a projected screen, preferably along with the speaker's image.

subvendors or **subs** Sometimes a contracted vendor will not be able to provide complete services or materials and will contract another vendor to provide all or some of the primary vendor's contract. This second vendor is a subvendor, also referred to as a **subcontractor**. This can be difficult in that the sub is often unknown and the contractual relationship between the two may not be legally binding. If something negative happens, there may be no recourse. Insist on no subvendors. If it is absolutely necessary to have subs, than the written agreement with the primary contractor must state their performance and financial responsibility for the total contract. Also insist that the primary contractor secures a release from each sub stating that the sub has no recourse for payment, additional payments, and so on from the entity hiring the primary contractor.

superimpose In video it is to overlap one image over another, such as titles over a person speaking. The abbreviated command for this action is to "super."

Super Trouper The brand name for a large, high-powered *followspot* manufactured by the Strong lighting company, which has become synonymous with all follow spots.

surround sound A range of techniques used to enrich audio sound reproduction characterized by a *sweet spot* where the audio effects work best. Typically it involves a range of different *loudspeaker* types placed in strategic positions. A **multichannel surround** application encircles the audience with channels of either the same or complementary sound.

swag Drapery, curtain, festive fabric, flowers, or fruit that is festooned between two points. A common method of decorating events, especially with patriotic *bunting* or holiday colors.

sweet spot The focal point in a room or space where the audio sound and effects work best. This location is determined by factors such as *loudspeaker* location, room *acoustics*, number of people in the room, and direction of the listener. It is the spot to place the most important guest.

symmetry Design elements that are balanced and create harmony, order, and aesthetically pleasing results. There are three types: the first, reflection, is bilateral or mirrorlike. The human body is the same, but reflected on both sides of the vertical central axis. A logo placed on each side of the stage is reflection symmetry. Second is rotational symmetry, like petals on a flower or numbers on a watch. It can be used effectively to portray motion. Transitional symmetry is the third, in which objects are placed in a repeated pattern such as back to front. Symmetry is great for general layout, patterns, and anything meant to be generally passive. **Asymmetry** is great for breaking monotony and grabbing attention. See *asymmetric design*.

sync The abbreviation for synchronization, the process of aligning sound with picture or dialogue with music. This process may take place during the making of the film or video or during the actual event. An example of the latter is when a live orchestra accompanies a speaker or visual presentation.

syntax The system of ordinary arrangement of words, sentences, or phrases and the rules that govern the arrangement in language. In computers it is the rules and structural patterns governing the use of words and symbols for writing codes in a software program.

tab The curtain that extends forward to back (downstage to upstage) next to the leg drops on either side of a stage to prevent the audience from seeing into the side backstage area. See *leg drop*.

📑 See entire stage curtain plan in "Tables and Techniques" (page 446).

to tab See *paging the curtain*.

tableau or **tableaux** A large, striking, dramatic visual scene often used in the finale of a presentation, such as when all performers and key participants join together onstage. Adding a *ballyhoo*, *confetti* falling, and the orchestra playing excitedly, it's the perfect visual end to a great event.

tableau curtain A curtain that is gathered in a decorative arch. Also see *main curtain.*

table clips See *skirt clips.*

table host A guest designated at each table whose responsibility it is to introduce all other guests to each other, keep the conversation going, answer questions about the event and its schedule, brief all on the menu, and, if the event includes buffet-style food service, lead those at the table to the food table at the appointed time, thus avoiding long lines. Those selected to serve as a table host need to be briefed in advance on the details of the event and the procedures.

table layout The placement of all tables at a dinner event or meeting. Different types of functions require different table arrangements. Also see *seating plan.*

See table considerations, guidelines, and suggestions in "Tables and Techniques" (page 422).

table linens Generally all coverings, napkins, tablecloths, table skirts, tablecloth toppers, runners, napkins, place mats, pillows, chair covers, and chair cushions or other cloth items used on or for decorating tables, bars, or food service counters. Traditionally made of linen fabric, now available in many different fabrics and designs, either reusable or disposable. Table linens greatly enhance the style of a dinner, be it formal (classically all white) or themed, and should be selected accordingly. Also see *linen.*

T

Tips on effectively using table linens:

✓ While formal dinners have rigid rules, be creative with informal dinners by using colors and fabric patterns to add visual interest and effect to the look of the table settings.

✓ Monogrammed linens add a personal touch. Corporate logos also create an impression.

✓ Layer the table coverings with a long cloth below a shorter topper in accenting colors.

✓ Use pleated linens as table skirts.

✓ When using rectangular or square tables, fold the corners of the tablecloth.

✓ Add to the look by folding napkins into interesting patterns.

🛍 Some examples of classic, easy-to-do napkin folds are in "Tables and Techniques" (page 387).

✓ An entire variety of contour covers for tables and chairs is available to drastically change the look of the dinner.

🛍 Examples of linen usage and styles are in "Tables and Techniques" (page 380).

table number Cards placed on a table with the number assigned to that table prominently displayed so that guests can easily find the table to which they are assigned. Often these cards are on a tall stand. Once the table is totally seated, the waiter removes the number and stand.

table setting See *place setting.*

table skirt Fabric or other material that hangs around a table to both add decoration and to hide materials or the legs of people sitting at the table, especially when the table is on a *dais*. Various materials are used besides just colored fabric, including fabric with logos or designs and even palm thatch to enhance the theme of Luau-type events. If the table has a special purpose, such as for a wedding cake, get away from the standard hotel prefabricated pleated skirting and make the skirting special.

🛍 Examples of special pleats and sways are in "Tables and Techniques" (page 384).

tabletop The total design of the top of the tables for an event including its theme, dinnerware, linens, and floral and other decorations, all artfully combined for striking visual effect. Great tabletops can change even the simplest dinner into a memorable event. Also see *linen*, *flatware*, and *place setting*.

tableware A general term for all dishes, glasses, cups, and other articles used in a table setting for a meal. Also see *flatware*.

tag line A line of speech at the close that succinctly points up or comments on the preceding speech or situation.

take a call When the actor, performer, speaker, or other presenter goes before the audience to take a bow.

takeaway A gift or souvenir that each person takes with them as they leave an event. The best takeaway is a *lasting impression*. Also see *favors*.

takedown The process of removing a show or event. Also see *strike*. Also, to *dim* a light or music cue.

take off An area on a *plan* drawing or area calculation achieved by measurement. On paper plans this is accomplished with a *planometer*; on computer plans it is done as part of the *CAD* program.

T

talent The general term for the people who make the presentation. These can be entertainers, actors, speakers, politicians, corporate executives, or other performers or members of the event *cast*.

talent manager A person hired by talent to handle all of their logistics and business affairs. In some cases talent managers are also agents, but typically with big name performers they are different individuals. The State of California forbids one person or company from being both. Usually the agent is responsible for sales while the manager is responsible for many other aspects of the performer's work and career.

taper   Traditional tall, thin, elegant candles used in candelabras on tables and other decorative locations. Tapered candles come in a multitude of colors. Tapers can be dangerous, because often the base fits poorly into the candle-holder socket, allowing the candle to fall out and creating a possible fire hazard. If the candle is too large for the socket, it can be shaved with a razor to fit. If it is too small, traditionally the base is wrapped in tin foil to make it fit snuggly. Using tapers requires attention throughout the evening for wax dripping and for replacement when they are burned down. Also available is **faux taper**, which are much easier to use. Also see *bobeche*.

   🖋 Always check the local fire code before using tapers. Many municipalities forbid their use.

team-building activities   Techniques involving a wide range of activities and games intended to enhance bonding, group dynamics, and organizational development. Utilized by companies, schools, churches, sports teams, and many other groups, they are designed to improve performance.

teamster   A member of the International Brotherhood of Teamsters labor union, which has jurisdiction over many event-related occupations, including warehouse workers, truck drivers, chauffeurs, and many other such services.

tea party or **afternoon tea**   An afternoon social event in which tea, small sandwiches, and sweets are served, with the purpose being good conversation. Originated by Catherine (wife of King Charles II of England, who found it difficult to wait for the late dinners), who ordered tea, bread, butter, and cake to be brought to her and invited friends late every afternoon. In the 1880s this tradition spread widely and often included a dance, or **tea dance**. The appropriate starting time is 2:00 to 4:00 pm.

See tea party menu in "Tables and Techniques" (page 355).

tear sheets Copies of an advertisement, review, or article torn out of a publication after it has appeared.

teaser A short curtain or piece of fabric or scenery hung across and above the stage to mask from the audience's view light instruments or the bottoms of other *scenery* and equipment hanging from the *flies*. If the teaser is hung close to a batten of lights, it is often made of, or lined with, a nonflammable material, traditionally asbestos.

tech Slang for all things technical, including the person operating technical equipment.

technical director The member of the production team responsible for the installation, integration, and operation of all technical aspects of the production, including power, projection, lights, video, and sound.

technical drawing The process of producing scaled *plans* and the plans themselves. Typically these plans are for architects, engineers, set designers, or others involved in the specific planning of structural elements. A *venue* may ask for a technical drawing of the stage, showing the power runs that lead to it and the scenery upon it for the purpose of having it reviewed by the *fire marshal* or other authority. Also see *scale* and *elevation*.

technical rehearsal A rehearsal of the performance's or event's technical elements, or the integration of these elements into the overall production, including lighting, sound cues, special effects, projection, scene changes, curtain closings, and stage crew actions. Depending on how complicated the technical components of the performance are, often several technical rehearsals will be conducted prior to integrating the actors or performers into a rehearsal.

technician An individual who installs, repairs, and operates the technical equipment required for the production, including sound, lights, and special effects.

teleconference The live exchange of information among several persons in different distant locations linked by a telecommunications system or the Internet.

teleprompter A device to prompt the speaker that fits directly over the lens of a television camera and utilizes a piece of clear glass to display the words. By positioning the words directly in front of the lens, it allows the speaker to look directly into the lens while reading. This system is workable only when the camera can be positioned close to the speaker, as in a television studio. Also see *prompt*er and *cue cards*.

tempo The pace or rate of an event, music, speech, or a performance, and a critical part of planning and reviewing a project. The tempo should not be too slow—putting the audience to sleep—nor too fast so that they can't mentally keep up with it. There are many options for planning the tempo, including varying it through the event, starting slow and building it toward the end, or even starting fast and slowing down at the end while being careful not to let the audience doze.

tent A flexible, movable, usually temporary structure able to be adapted to a multitude of event purposes. Tents can be elegant, dramatic, and open or closed with side walls or windows. They are easily available for purchase or rental; can come in different sizes, shapes, colors, and patterns; and can be either *clear-span* or high-span, hi-tech or low, clear or opaque, simple or complete with flooring, air conditioning, or heat. Many event organizers find that tents as temporary venues are the most versatile and cost-efficient. They are also called fabric structures. Traditional tents are referred to as **pole tents**.

📝 **Tips regarding tents:**

✓ Fire codes for occupancy are often different for tents, so it is critical to check with the fire department early in the planning process.

✓ Not all tent rental companies are the same, and many are better than others at visually hiding, or covering, the ropes, poles, and other support equipment to create a better visual presentation.

✓ Check the tent before renting to ensure that the fabric is in good, clean condition.

📝 **Terms to help you sound like a tent expert:**

✓ Eave—The lower edge of the top at the sides that determines height of the side walls.

✓ Valance—The trim fabric that hangs off the eave to decorate the edge.

✓ Blackout—The vinyl liner on the inside of the tent that does not allow sunlight to come through so that the inside light can be controlled for theatrical presentations or projections.

✓ Opacity—The degree to which the light is blocked.

✓ Oz—The weight, or thickness, of each square yard of vinyl used in making the tent. The thickness determines the durability and look of the tent.

✓ Bailrings—The cast steel rings used at the top of large tents of 50 or more feet wide. The tent fabric is attached to the rings, which attach to the top of center poles to hold the tent fabric in position.

✓ Ratchets—These replace staking ropes to allow for quick tightening of the tent to the stakes or hold-down weights.

tent flooring system Innovative platform systems that are easy to configure to make a floor for a tent of any size over just about any terrain. This allows for a tent to be placed over uneven ground or even over a swimming pool. These systems can be rented, allowing for a cost-effective solution that is easily installed by a small crew, in a fraction of the time required for other types of floor construction.

tequila A twice-distilled alcoholic spirit from Mexico. Tequila must contain 51 percent of its distilled alcohol from blue agave, a plant grown in specified areas. The best distillers go beyond these minimum amounts, some reaching 100 percent. Most tequila is briefly aged, but some is "fresh." Longer aging gives it "snifter-quality." Another Mexican spirit is **mescal**.

thank-yous What everyone appreciates. After an event, thank-you letters or notes need to be sent to virtually everyone except those in the audience. Vendors, speakers, key participants, volunteers, donors, and staff all are pleased to have been part of the event upon receiving a pleasant acknowledgment of their efforts. Brides must certainly send thank-you notes for gifts. Event producers give thanks to their clients.

theater or **theatre** (Take one's pick on the spelling.) A place of performances, whether live stage productions, musical concerts, dance, or film showings. A theater consists of four parts: lobby; audience seating, usually tiered; stage; and *backstage* areas. Also see *back of house*.

T

theme A dominant or unifying concept or idea for a speech, gathering, party, or other event. See *theme party*.

theme park An amusement park designed with a particular focus or unifying quality or idea reflected in the park's décor, rides, and special characters.

theme party A great way to turn a typical function into a fun and memorable event. By selecting and utilizing a unifying concept or concepts, you can quickly bring into play several important ingredients for a good event, such as audience participation, decoration, the food and beverage menus, entertainment, location, special effects, favors, and the opportunity to surprise the guests with something different.

✐ **Tips on planning a theme party:**

✓ Choose a theme that has potential for exploitation. Using "accounting" as a theme doesn't go far, while "Halloween" can be over-the-top.

✓ Choose a theme appropriate to the audience. While "accounting" doesn't conjure fun, "numbers" could be a fun theme with such things as "dressing to the nines," "the ten best," "pieces of eight," "sub zero," "seventh heaven," etc.

✓ Consider the age and other special characteristics of those attending. Those over fifty do not want to sit in the sand at the beach for a "luau."

✓ Choose a theme that is new and different, not typical like "Western" or a "luau."

✓ Start the theme at the beginning, with invitation design, and carry it all the way through to a special dessert and good-bye musical number.

✓ The venue can add greatly to a good themed event: a planetarium for a space or futuristic party, a clearing in a forest for a Merry Ol' England affair, a high school stadium for a Super Bowl party, or an old barn rigged with chandeliers for a glamorous barbecue. Many different and sometimes unusual facilities have generated additional income as party venues.

✓ Theme parties are a great opportunity for audience involvement, from wearing costumes to participating in the entertainment.

✓ Grand openings can be very effective when the actual facility or business becomes the theme. For example, a new auto dealership grand opening theme could be a rally or fifties carhop party.

thickness piece   That portion of a window, door, or arch frame that recedes into a set piece, thereby visually becoming the thickness of the wall or arch. Also referred to as **architectural thickness**.

three-**fold**   Three flats hooked together that unfold and stand free to make a quick background for a press photo, display, or other immediate need.

thrill ride   A high-speed or otherwise exhilarating amusement attraction.

throw   The distance between a projector and the projection surface or between a lighting instrument and what it is lighting.

thrust stage   The stage floor extended into the audience area. While this extension can have many different shapes, typically it allows for audience seating on three sides.

ticket   A device used to gain admission to or to control who is given admission privileges to an event. Tickets come in many different forms, from simple paper printed with information to electronic mechanisms of various sorts that can be read quickly by electronic scanners.

T   **Well-designed tickets have the following basic information stored on them whether they are printed, electronic, or in some other form:**

✓ The title of the event.

✓ The date for which the ticket is valid.

✓ An identifying number that can be used to track the source of sale and other such information.

✓ The ticket price. Some municipalities legally require this information.

✓ The audience area or seat designated for the ticket holder.

✓ The venue and its location.

Tickets can originate on the Internet, where the individual buyer prints a bar code that can be scanned at the gate. This system gives the event management many helpful details about the purchaser, such as their e-mail address, payment type, and credit card information. All tickets can carry other information, such as future events or sponsor identification.

tie-in The cooperative efforts of two or more groups, sponsors, or companies in one promotion.

tie off To secure a decoration of a piece of equipment, sometimes as a secondary safety line.

timed move-in Prior to the opening of an exhibition, many trucks arrive at the same time with the exhibit materials. Therefore, a procedure is established whereby those trucks arriving first are allowed to unload first. If your truck arrives late, there is a chance that it will not get unloaded in time to move in. Or, the exhibitor can be subject to additional labor costs to unload it under special circumstances. Schedule enough time for the truck to arrive for adequate move-in, including for breakdowns or unexpected delays.

time-sensitive A term applied to those elements of cost that will be incurred or expended on a time-unit basis (monthly, weekly, hourly, etc.). The salary of a secretary on a project is a time-sensitive cost.

timing The duration of an event or a sequence in the event. Timing is critical when executing a function or event. First, ensure that it starts at the prescribed time. Second, timing aids in tempo. By varying the segment lengths, overall event tempo can be varied as well. Third, control of timing keeps the function from going on too long—a deadly curse. Remember the old phrase, "Leave 'em wanting more!" Finally, **perfect timing** is when it all happens how and when it should.

tipping A well-known expense that many forget to include in budgets. See *gratuity*.

title See *form of address*.

toast The act of proposing a sentiment or honor to a person, accompanied by a drink. The toast itself can be any variety of well wishes, thank-yous, or traditional expressions. The expression "to toast" comes from the Anglo-Saxon tradition of wassailing. A piece of bread toast was thrown into the wassail bowl, and whoever got the toast in their drink would have good fortune the next year. Although wassail is usually associated with the old English Christmas tradition of drinking spirits from the "wassail bowl," the ritual of wassail was actually a Danish import to England. "Ves heil" in Old Norse meant "be healthy" and was routinely offered as a salutation to one's drinking buddies, who would then reply, "drinc hail," which meant "drink to good luck."

At a wedding reception, **wedding toasts** begin right after all are seated for dinner and the champagne is poured, with the best man offering the first toast. The groom offers the next toast to the bride, followed by the bride toasting the groom. The fathers and mothers of the bride and groom each toast next, followed by any family and friends. If necessary, the best man ends the toasting.

toastmaster A person who introduces the guests or speakers and proposes the *toast* at a banquet.

toggle The wooden structural part of a scenic *flat* that runs horizontally between the *stile* on each side, giving the sides strength. It is held in place by a keystone or triangle on each side. Also see *flat*.

Complete diagrams of flat construction are in "Tables and Techniques" (page 449).

tormentor Tall narrow flats, or curtains, used on both sides of the stage playing area to mask the side *offstage* areas. Using tormentors directly behind the act curtain creates another frame to reduce the size of the proscenium opening to the desired size. Tormentors are tall enough to reach behind the *teaser* trim height and can be adjusted onstage or off to perfectly frame the scene.

tormentor lights A stack of lighting fixtures, usually mounted on a rack hanging from a line but sometimes on a tall stand, placed directly behind a *tormentor* and providing side light to the acting or performing area.

tower A high platform used for sound speakers, lighting instruments, video monitors, projectors, or other such equipment as required by the production. Often towers have multiple levels with different equipment on each and dimmers or other related equipment positioned below.

tracking control In most shipping situations the shipper provides a method whereby the shipment can be tracked to determine its exact location at any moment either online or through the shipper's own special systems. Knowing precisely where the shipment is and when it will arrive aids in planning your materials move-in schedule.

trades Magazines and newspapers of the industry trade, originally in theater and show business.

trade show A gathering of companies within a given industry to display, demonstrate, and market their products or services to other companies within the industry. Unlike *consumer shows*, most trade shows are not open to the public but rather only to those within an industry or group of related industries or professional association. Typically each company creates an *exhibit* within an assigned space within a hall or group of halls. Also see *exhibition*.

tragedy The *genre* of drama or other literary works in which the protagonist loses or is overcome by a disastrous circumstance.

transfer To record from one medium to another such as from a video player to a computer. When a transfer is made between two similar media such as from one tape to another, it is typically referred to as a *dub*.

transportation The manner by which guests are brought to an event and returned from the event location. Transportation is often overlooked as an important element of the event. It can be provided by stretch limousines, double-decked British buses, or covered wagons. In New York City it may be by horse-drawn Hansom cabs.

> *For an awards show and party, all guests were instructed to park in a nearby garage and were taken from there by a shuttle of limos to a red carpet entrance lined with press photographers (fake) and cheering crowds (also fake). Everyone felt very important!*

For conferences, meetings, and other business events, you must carefully establish and monitor air, train, and bus shuttle travel arrangements to ensure as pleasant a journey as possible for participants. This may include a hot line for last-minute ticket changes, greeters at the airport and hotel lobby (with refreshments), or other amenities.

Transportation also includes the trucking of the materials required for the event—show equipment, food supplies, or exhibit equipment. Also see *drayage*.

trap or **trap door** An area of the stage or apron that can be removed to provide access under the stage for a variety of reasons, such as allowing an actor to make an entrance up through the floor or to sink into the ground. Often traps are used by magicians to make themselves, or elements, appear or disappear.

traveler curtain A curtain that opens and closes by moving along a track above either by hand or with lines to a motor. The curtain can consist of two halves that open in the center or a solid piece that opens from either side and moves to the opposite side. This is sometimes utilized with a painted curtain that keeps moving and thereby simulates the effect of a person walking down the street. This may be combined with a *treadmill stage* for added effect. Also see *main curtain*.

treadmill stage A mechanical device built into the floor of a stage that moves scenery or actors onto or off of the stage. It can also be used by actors to give the illusion that they are walking a long distance or for a long duration. Sometimes it is used in conjunction with a roll drop, or projection, with images moving the opposite direction behind the walking actor.

trendsetter A person who starts a trend, or prevailing style, or one who is critical in making a trend more popular before most other people adopt it. Setting or being aware of new trends is critical in the event world because everyone is constantly finding new and better ways to present events, whether meetings, festivals, presentations, dinner parties, or shows, to provide new audience experiences. Be a trendsetter!

tribute artist or **bands** Musical groups or vocalists that only play the music of a single very famous recording artist or band. A Beatles tribute band only plays Beatles hits.

trim The determined height of maskings, curtains, light battens, signs, or decorations. **To trim** is the process of adjusting the height of a sign, batten, or decoration or to level it to make it parallel to the floor.

tripod A three-legged device designed to hold a camera steady at a certain height, providing easy access by the cameraperson, yet also designed to collapse for easy transportation and storage. Also see *press platform*.

trompe l'oeil A magnificent variation of painting or stenciling to create painted effects that appear to have three dimensions. In French it means "deceive the eye." Used extensively in decorating and scenery painting to make the flat painting seem to have depth. The simplest example is the cartoon Roadrunner painting a tunnel on a wall for Coyote to run through.

truck A camera movement when the camera is mounted to a dolly that is to the left or right. For example, a television director's command to move the camera and dolly to the right would be "truck right."

truss Lightweight yet strong aluminum load-bearing linear structures, used extensively by those rigging a show from which to hang lighting instruments. A truss is composed of two, three, or four load-bearing aluminum tubes connected by small braces at regular intervals along the length of the tubes. Many different-sized sections are available along with various corner sections so that the truss can be assembled in many different configurations simply by pinning the units together. Running the power and control cables within the truss structure provides a well-dressed appearance.

tryout See *audition.*

turkey A show or presentation or cast member that is bad or a failure. The term originated in theater when bad shows were opened on Thanksgiving Day to make quick money over the holiday period.

turnstile A mechanical device, traditionally with spokes that were turned by each visitor as they entered or left an event, designed to count attendance.

turntable A portion of the stage floor, or a platform on the stage, that can rotate to change the scene or as part of the action. Small turntables are often used to give motion and added interest to displays. Also see *revolving stage.*

twisted pair A pair of individually insulated wires wrapped together.

twist lock The type of electrical connector that must be inserted and turned, making it difficult to accidentally pull apart.

typestyle See *fonts*.

typo Typographical error in any written document or printed materials.

UL Underwriters Laboratories. A nonprofit, independent organization that operates a listing service for electrical materials and equipment. "UL-approved" indicates a product has met strictly defined safety criteria.

ultraviolet light See *blacklight*.

understudies Actors and performers hired to substitute for the lead actors or performers in a theatrical production in case of illness or other emergencies. The understudy learns all of the lines, music, movements, and other required duties, just as the lead does, and typically attends all performances.

up center (UC) The area of the stage furthest from the audience and in the center of the stage. It is the ideal area to use for grand entrances, royalty, and scenes of domination. Also see *stage areas* and *stage mood*.

up left (UL) The area of the stage furthest from the audience on the right side of the stage as viewed by the audience. It is the ideal area to use for staging supernatural scenes. Also see *stage areas* and *stage mood*.

up right (UR) The area of the stage furthest from the audience on the left side of the stage as viewed by the audience. It is the ideal area to use for romantic scenes. Also see *stage areas* and *stage mood*.

upstage The area of the stage furthest from the audience. Also, the method of one actor who steals the attention from another by positioning himself behind the other so that the first actor must turn away from the audience. This technique is often used by politicians, speakers, executives, and others seeking the most attention from the audience.

up-tempo A rhythm that is bright and quick, be it in music, a speech, dance, or another presentation.

USDA United States Department of Agriculture. The federal government's agency responsible for setting and overseeing food safety regulations and nutritional guidelines. Food safety is key to many events, and the rules and regulations must be adhered to.

 See "Tables and Techniques" for cooking guidelines (page 355) and serving portions (page 351).

usher A person who escorts the audience to seats in a theater, wedding, or other event. Ushers also serve as doorkeepers, provide information, distribute programs, and provide security and *crowd control*. At a wedding, plan for one usher per fifty guests. At other events, the quantity is determined by the type of event, the size and makeup of the audience, and the duration. All ushers must be well trained in their duties, emergency procedures, and crowd management techniques.

U

VAC Abbreviation for volts, alternating current.

vamp A short piece of music that is played over and over during a planned performance pause, or while a singer is speaking to the audience, perhaps at the beginning of a song. Also, in drama it is the female sexual and glamorous counterpoint to a naïve, wholesome character.

variable cost An expense that is determined by multiplying a cost rate over time, such as an hourly rental fee. See *budget*.

VCR Abbreviation for any device that uses a videotape cassette to record, store, and play back video information.

VDC Abbreviation for volts, direct current.

velour A style of curtain, made from velour fabric, that is often used to dress a stage. The fabric hangs nicely and absorbs unwanted light, particularly black-colored velour. Velour fabric is a heavy, long-life fabric with a fuzzy finish or nap. It is also referred to as *blacks*.

venue Any site where an event, or part of an event, is held. A venue can be more typical, such as a concert hall, meeting room, convention center, hotel ballroom, or theater, or more unconventional, such as a field, beach, park, swimming pool deck, patio, aircraft carrier, studio back lot, warehouse, or "field of dreams." Many unusual structures and locations have recently found the value in hosting events, providing planners previously unimaginable and exceptional venues. That said, a dinner, for example, on the beach with fire pits and entertainers on a floating stage creates both a wonderful evening and lasting memories, but it may be much more difficult (and expensive) to accomplish than holding the function in a standard venue such as a hotel ballroom. Also, a **multiple site venue** within one event can provide a unique experience. For example, a wedding where guests move through six environments such as a garden area for preceremony beverages, and then through an arched hedge to a lawn area with a gazebo for the ceremony, to a small tent decorated with vintage photos of the couple for hors d'oeuvre, to a large festively decorated tent for the dinner, to an interior space like a sleek lounge for dancing, and finally to an exterior area lighted with votives hanging in the trees for dessert and coffee.

Tips on selecting the appropriate venue:

✓ Decide if the event should be inside or outside.

✓ Be creative. Decide if this is an opportunity to do something different and unique. The venue selection can add to the color of the event. People get bored attending the same, typical events at the same types of venues.

✓ Consider your requirements for A/V and other technological, entertainment, and presentation facets of your event.

✓ Know the dates, including alternate dates, of the event and what flexibility there is should the venue you want not be available on the date that is your first choice.

✓ Know the potential number of attendees.

✓ Know the source of the attendees. Are they local or traveling in for the event?

✓ Does the event have a theme, and if so, how can you expand the theme by venue choice?

✓ Consider the typical age of the attendees.

✓ Consider the budget and what fees can be paid for the use and preparation of venues.

✓ If the overall event has more than one subevent, decide how many venues are needed and what their proximity to one another needs to be.

✓ Ask the venue about their policy for *cancellation fees.*

✓ Consider other amenities required, or nice to have available, such as spa, gym, resort area, golf course, local nightlife, etc.

With this information in hand, proceed to select a venue.

✐ **Tips on selecting an *indoor* venue:**

✓ Determine the general type of facility needed for the type of functions and presentations planned.

✓ Check the history of other events at the selected potential sites. How did others utilize the venue and what was the success of their events?

✓ Ask for references from previous groups.

✓ Determine if a sufficient number of meeting or function rooms are available.

✓ Determine the size and capacity of the potential rooms or site and how this compares with your event's requirements for space and technical capabilities.

✓ Check to see if the meeting rooms are soundproof.

✓ Review the food and beverage capabilities. If they are not adequate, what restrictions exist on the use of outside caterers and other service providers?

✓ Check on the rules for decorating, signage, and other materials that may need to be displayed.

✓ Is the potential venue in compliance with the *ADA*?

✓ Is adequate parking available, and what does it cost?

✓ Is there a stage of adequate size, or is *platforming* available?

✓ Ask to review sample contracts for the rental of the space.

✓ Ask about the payment schedule for the space.

✓ If it is a venue not typically used for events, what additional obstacles does it present?

✓ Determine the amount of power available and how that matches the requirement for the presentation. How does the venue bill for power usage?

✓ Determine how large materials like scenery, or the company's product, can get into the function space.

✓ If registration, tickets, or checking invitations are necessary, check how and where that can take place.

✓ Check to see if the space is available for move-in and move-out days.

✓ How are the waiters, ushers, etc., dressed?

✓ If an outside caterer is being used, have them check the space for their needs.

✓ Are specific vendors required?

✓ What are the hidden extra costs (like charges for broken glassware)?

✓ Is there a piano available? What kind, and is it tuned?

🖉 **Tips on selecting an *outdoor* venue:**

✓ Determine if the location is appropriate for the event.

✓ Consider possible weather problems and what needs to be done as a backup plan in case of bad weather.

✓ Check the surface of the ground and determine if it is appropriate for safe walking, including for women in high heels, and for wheelchairs.

✓ Consider the time of day for the event and how the sun may or may not affect the event.

✓ Determine the physical limitations of the site.

✓ Determine the physical advantages of the site.

✓ If tents are required, how large will they need to be, what style is required, and will sidewalls be necessary?

✓ Determine if adequate power is available or if generators are necessary.

✓ Determine if portable heating or air conditioning will be required.

✓ Determine how the event can best be staged to take maximum advantage of the site.

✓ Determine if backstage or kitchen space needs to be created.

✓ Check restrictions that may be put on the site by police or the fire department.

✓ Determine what could become damaged on the site and what the consequences of that will be.

✓ Check noise levels, both sounds that may be distractions to the event, such as the noise of a nearby highway, as well as residents or other situations nearby that may be bothered by the sound created by the event.

✓ Determine what the plan would be if there were an emergency.

✓ Determine how restrooms will be handled and whether portable toilets will be needed.

✓ Consider the *ADA* rules and how they need to be met.

✓ Determine how trash will be handled.

✓ Have the caterer review the site.

✓ What kind of insurance will be required?

✓ How much time is available before and after the event for move-in, *rehearsals*, *strike*, etc?

Whether the venue is inside or out, make the best of it and utilize all the space, even if you are just filling blank spaces with greenery, having a lounge area for networking, or just making comfortable quiet space. Even the floor of the entranceway can be utilized as a giant welcome sign painted with chalk.

📑 **Venue aspects and conditions are diagrammed in "Tables and Techniques" (page 422).**

vermouth A wine flavored with herbs, flowers, spices, and seeds. There are basically two types of vermouth, sweet vermouth (red in color) and dry vermouth, also called French vermouth (white) since it was originally made in France, whereas sweet vermouth was created in Italy. The flavor of vermouth dissipates in a couple of months, even when refrigerated after opening.

Vichy water A natural sparkling water bottled from springs in Vichy, France.

video In general, it is the picture portion of the television signal. The broader usage is any type of visual program (usually accompanied by audio) recorded with an electronic camera, or any type of visual and audio program played back on any electronic medium, whether it is a VCR, MP3, DVD, or computer.

video clip A short sequence of video often used for event promotion or played back to illustrate a point in a speech. Also see *press kit*.

videoconference An electronic meeting between two or more participants at various different locations via simultaneous two-way video and audio transmissions. New computer services constantly improve the capabilities while reducing the cost.

video feed The playing of video either into the event, such as live coverage of a happening elsewhere that supports a speech or other presentation, or from the event, to be aired on a newscast or other program.

videotape An audio and video recording and storing medium utilizing spools of plastic tape with a magnetic coating. Made obsolete by digital storage methods. See *DVD*.

video wall The combination of several video screens placed closely together both horizontally and vertically to create one large picture. The size and shape of the completed screen varies depending on how the individual units are placed. A computer program allows different video information on individual screens, on all the screens, or on selected screens to make individual pictures, one large picture, or anything in between. *LED* screens can also be utilized to form almost any screen shape and size.

vintage In the wine industry, the vintage is both the year of the grape harvest and the wine made from those grapes. If the label indicates 1999, it means the wine was made that year and at least 95 percent of the grapes used were harvested that season. Wines made from multiple year growths, or made not in the same year as the harvest, are **non-vintage** and sometimes signified with NV on the label.

VIP or **Very Important Person** Any person extremely important to the event. Some examples are the keynote speaker, celebrities, presidents of a company, political figures such as a mayor or president, headline entertainers, special guests, etc.

🖉 **Tips on hand-holding VIPs:**

✓ Have a space where they can rest comfortably and ready themselves after arrival but prior to their appearance. This space is often referred to as a *green room* and typically it is set up with refreshments, flowers, and other amenities. If necessary, makeup can be applied there as well.

✓ Assign a personable escort or *usher* to be with them from arrival to departure. This escort must have a cell phone or radio so that constant contact can be maintained by the event staff or stage manager.

✓ From the green room, move them to a prestage position close to their entrance location. Do this well ahead of their cue to enter. This may be backstage, outside a kitchen door, or wherever they are not visible to the audience. This spot should make them visible to the audience in just a few steps. A long wait for them to arrive onstage is unacceptable.

✓ Before being announced, check the VIP for upturned collars, possession of script, clinging skirt, etc. If they are fitted with a wireless *mic*, have the sound *technician* check it. Also, last-minute instructions can be given, such as which steps to use to get onstage, what lectern to go to if there is more than one, etc.

✓ When they are introduced, the escort should give them a polite but strong push forward, open the door if necessary, and follow them out a few feet before disappearing.

✓ After the performance, the same usher should greet them as they come offstage and escort them back to the green room or the next location.

visual effects (visual FX) or **photographic effects** A wide variety of image manipulations that can be accomplished with the aid of various computer, optical, or mechanical systems. Building a model of a ship and then matting it over a background is a visual effect. Many visual effects can also be created in real time onstage through various special effects equipment or projectors.

vocalist A singer or one who uses the human voice to produce musical sounds.

voice-over A performer offstage or off camera, unseen by the audience, who describes action, gives an account, or makes announcements. An offstage *narrator*.

voltage or **volts** In an electrical circuit it is, in simple terms, the unit of measure for the pressure pushing the electrons through any given point. In a 12-volt hair dryer, the voltage pushes the current through the motor at the rate of 12 *amps* per second. Think of it as the water pressure in a faucet.

volunteer A person who works hard for no or very little financial remuneration. Many events from simple fund-raising dinners to the Olympic Games require a number of volunteers for all sorts of tasks. Often people volunteer because they are interested in and want to support the cause, or because they find it fun and exciting, or just because it is different from their ordinary daily routine. Treat volunteers well and they will go to the end of the earth to make it happen.

🖊 Tips for working with volunteers:

✓ Make sure they are well trained in their duties and understand the overall plan.

✓ Keep them busy. If they feel they are wasting their time, they will leave or won't volunteer again.

✓ Treat them with respect and kindness.

✓ Teach them something new in the process of working with them.

✓ Lavish them with appreciation for their efforts on the project when completed. Letters are a must. Certificates are very important. A thank-you reception or party is always appreciated.

When I produced the opening ceremonies for the Xth Pan American Games in Indianapolis, the event took place in August. It was very hot and humid. I had 10,000 performers as our cast of the show, all volunteers, and another 10,000 athletes who would march in during the ceremony. The event took place on the straightaway of the Indy 500 racetrack. During one of the planning sessions I asked for a volunteer to take on the responsibility of ensuring there was plenty of drinking water for everyone. This was to be a really big, tough, and thankless job. The large jugs would need to be moved from the trucks to the more than twenty water stations and each loaded into the top of the dispensers. There would be hundreds of jugs. To my initial chagrin, an older, slight lady volunteered for the duty. When I asked where we would get all the people to assist her she replied that she had lots of retired friends. She seemed so confident I gave her the assignment but asked one of my assistants to keep close watch on her progress. Both during the sweltering days of rehearsals and on performance day, I was amazed to see all the water stations fully manned, with retirees, and fully loaded with the large bottles of water and plenty of paper cups. No one complained that they didn't have water. I believed it a small miracle! Immediately after the event she was one of the first of the volunteers that I went to thank. I found her surrounded by her "team." All were covered in sweat and exhausted. After giving her a big hug and praising all for a job well done, her response was, "When can we do it again?"

votive A short, stubby candle whose size makes it very workable in many decorative applications and relatively safe from fire risk because it is hard to make it fall over. Also called a **tea light**. A large variety of holders are designed for votives.

VTR A video recorder and playback machine that uses videotape on reels rather than a cassette.

WAG Wild-Ass Guess. A gross estimate of cost loosely based on prior experience. Also called a *ballpark estimate* (see *order-of-magnitude estimates*).

wagon A platform on casters that moves onstage to carry actors, scenery, or both.

wagon set A set built on low platforms, or wagons, that run on tracks all the way across the playing area and offstage into the *wings*. Often there are two or more wagons so that when one is onstage the other is offstage being changed and prepared to be rolled back onstage with a new set as the first comes offstage. Sometimes another wagon rolls on from the rear of the stage. When the changes appear as the audience watches, it makes for a fascinating, fast-paced show.

walkie-talkies Portable communication devices. Two-way radios. Also see *intercom*.

walking the curtain To hold the leading edge of a traveler curtain and walk behind it as it closes to ensure that it closes completely.

walk-on A very small part in a presentation, usually without lines.

walk-through A rehearsal in which all participants move through the show or presentation so that each gets familiar with their movements, the stage, the lectern, the lighting, etc., and so that the stage crew and technicians can rehearse their cues. This style of rehearsal is often substituted for a full rehearsal, particularly when time is limited.

wall-**to**-**wall**   Continuous or seamless. Wall-to-wall music means the music goes from the beginning to the end of a speech, video presentation, or whatever it may be without a break. This might also refer to speeches that fill an entire afternoon. In most situations, it is less effective than something varied or effectively sectioned, because the audience tires of it.

wardrobe   All articles of clothing, uniforms, and costumes required for an event or show. Also, the room or area in which these are stored, fitted, and distributed.

wardrobe mistress   The traditional name for the crew person, when this was always a woman, responsible for all wardrobe functions, including repairs, storage, and cleaning.

warm-up   Entertainment prior to the main attraction designed to get the audience in the mood of the event. This can be anything from a sleight-of-hand *magician* performing to small groups as the audience waits to enter, to a secondary musical act performing onstage before the headliner. **Warm-up hosts** are used in television shows that have a studio audience. Before the show begins they teach the crowd how to applaud, use humor to get them laughing, and do silly things to "bring the audience alive."

warning   The command given a short time before a verbal *cue* is given to alert all that the cue is about to be executed.

wash   To spread over a large area. For example, to "wash" a wall with a light pattern is to spread the pattern over a large area of the wall or the entire wall.

water cannon A special effects device that shoots one large burst of water into the air on cue. It can be placed on land or under water. If underwater it can be fired repeatedly as quickly as the water chamber refills.

water screen or **mist screen** A surface for projection created by spraying water droplets under high pressure into the air. Each droplet functions as a small bead to hold and magnify light being projected through it, similar to what the tiny glass beads do on a standard projections screen, except that in order for a water screen to work the light must pass through the droplets from the rear. These screens have been used very effectively in spectacular presentations on lakes and other bodies of water. They can be quite large, creating a fan shape of water mist. The water can be sprayed either from the center, falling to each side, or from one side.

WBS Work Breakdown Structure. A dissection of a project into various levels—phases, activities, and tasks—developed in a checklist fashion.

well drinks Cocktails made from the cheapest, less popular, or generic spirits. The name derives from the location behind the bar in the speed rail for easy access by the bartender.

whiskey or **whisky** A distilled alcoholic spirit obtained from fermenting mash of grains, including primarily barley or rye. There are many common types of whiskey, including Canadian, Bourbon, Tennessee, Irish, Scotch, and even Hooch. But regardless of where they are made, they basically fall into four categories. **Straight whiskey** must be made from at least 51 percent of a particular grain, aged in oak barrels for two years, and not exceed 160 *proof*. **Blended whiskey** combines two or more straight whiskeys with neutral or grain spirits. Often used for blending, **light whiskey** is distilled to a higher alcohol level, stored in charred oak containers, and diluted with water to the specified proof. Single-malt whiskey is made from only malted barley and from a single distillery. **Irish whiskey** is distilled in Ireland from straight malts, or malts lightened with grain spirits. All are triple-distilled to make them very smooth-tasting. Scotch whisky, or **scotch**, is blended whiskey that is about one-third flavorful malt plus two-thirds nearly flavorless grain spirits. Single-malt scotch is still blended, but is the individual, undiluted product of a single distillery, some aged up to thirty years.

whiteboard Also known as **dry-erase** or **dry-wipe**, this white surface has replaced chalkboards as an easy way to write or draw information using nonpermanent colored markers and then to easily erase the information. Typically found in meeting rooms. An **interactive white board (IWB)** is a system that projects a computer-generated graphic unto the board's surface, allowing the presenter to use a stylus to control the computer as one would with a mouse device. Using a handwriting recognition program, the presenter can write over the projected image.

white chocolate Not really chocolate (sorry!) but rather a mixture of primarily milk solids, sugar, and vanilla with cocoa butter.

white noise A sound composed of a combination of all the different frequencies of sound that is fed through an audio system by technicians to balance the tonal qualities of the system prior to use.

wind machine A large circular fan with a powerful motor used to create wind blowing across the stage or scene.

wind up To finish or complete. Also a hand cue or signal given to a presenter or performer indicating to finish the presentation. The signal is made by rotating a hand in front of one's body in a circular motion. The faster the rotation, the quicker the presenter should finish.

wine Alcoholic beverages created from the natural fermentation of primarily the juice of grapes, but also from other fruits, spices, and even vegetables. The history of wine goes back thousands of years. Today excellent wine is made in most countries. Basic wine is either still or sparkling; red, white, or rosé; and either dry (not sweet), semi-sweet, or sweet. **Vintage** wine is made from grapes 95 percent of which are harvested within a given year (as indicated on the label). Rosé or blush wines are made from red grapes. **Aromatic** wines, such as vermouth, have been infused with herbs and spices. **Fortified** wines such as sherry or port have brandy or other spirits added. Brandy typically is made from grapes but also from other fruits. Cognac is considered the best brandy. Hundreds of different wine types are available.

See "Tables and Techniques" for a guide to wine types (page 314), serving temperatures (page 313), saving (page 321), and more.

wing or **wings** The backstage area immediately to the right and left sides of the acting or performing area.

winged set This is the oldest form of a set and includes the borders, backdrop, and *wing*s. While it emanates from classical theater, it is currently used for many outdoor shows or shows in large interior spaces such as arenas.

wipe A visual graphic effect whereby the image changes from one image to another with a movement from one side to the other.

wireless Equipment such as radios, microphones, lights, etc., that connect via radio waves instead of wires. Also see *RF*.

within the ribbon Pews or chairs, particularly at a wedding, that are located closest to the ceremony or presentation and are held for family or other selected individuals. Usually there is a ribbon across the entrance to these rows.

wives' program See *spouse program*.

woofer The part of an audio speaker system that reproduces the low frequencies of the audio spectrum. A **subwoofer** reproduces the very low frequencies.

working drawings The drawings, including both *elevations* and *plans* of the scenery, stage, platforms, or other areas of the event, with enough detail and scale to accurately represent the intentions of the designer. Sometimes they are direct copies of the designer's sketches or drawings used as reference before the final drawings are complete.

work light The general lighting available to illuminate the area for construction, setup, and rehearsals, usually controlled by a switch rather than the *dimmer board* so that the lighting technician is not required to operate it.

wow Distortion of the audio signals due to variations in the tape speed during recording or playback.

wow factor The special and most exciting elements in a show, presentation, or other type of event. It makes the audience say "wow!" Every project should have one.

to wrap Short for "**wrap it up**." To strike or put away the entire event, parts of it, or certain pieces of equipment. "**It's a wrap**" signifies the end of a film or video shooting day or scene.

wrap party The best part of an event, the celebration at the end of the show or event by all those who made it happen.

wreath A circular arrangement of natural materials such as flowers and greenery. Wreaths are hung up as a decoration, or placed as a memorial on a grave, or put on a person's head as a sign of honor.

wristband A plastic band worn around the wrist used for identification. Different colors, shapes, or styles can signify admission paid, assigned seating area, crew access, verification of age for drinking alcoholic beverages, or many other key things about the person wearing the band. Good quality bands are hard to remove so that they cannot be transferred easily. Some have embedded codes for easy electronic scanning.

xylophone Every "x" category must have this musical percussion instrument listed. The instrument originated in both Asia and Africa and consists of tuned lengths of wood or metal bars struck by mallets.

yoke The metal U-shaped bracket with a clamp that secures the light to a batten or other support.

Yorkshire pudding Not a pudding at all, but rather a puffy soufflé-like specialty of eggs, milk, and flour flavored with beef drippings that traditionally accompanies British roast beef.

Yule log Traditionally a small, decorated log presented as a gift during the Christmas holidays before being burned in a fireplace. It can also be used effectively as a prop, gift, or theme during a holiday presentation. Also, bûche de Noël (yule log), a French Christmas cake of chocolate buttercream rolled, baked, and decorated to look like a log.

Zamboni Wherever ice skating is enjoyed as a sport or entertainment around the world, the trade name of Frank Zamboni is present as the machine that shaves the ice, picks up all the snow, and applies fresh water to the ice while removing excess water. The end result is perfectly smooth ice.

X
Y
Z

zest Important ingredient in many event elements. A hearty, lively, exciting enjoyment. Also, the outer skin of a citrus fruit used to flavor food and some beverages.

Zinfandel A red, high-sugar wine grape believed to be grown originally in California (probably from vines brought from Italy). Makes excellent full-bodied fruity wine that rivals Cabernet Sauvignon. First became popular as white zinfandel, a light, blush wine, which still outsells the red six to one.

zoom A lens that can change from a wide angle to a telephoto position while remaining in focus. A **parfocal** lens. Or the process of changing the lens focal length, or angle of view, of a shot during actual shooting. **Zoom in** is to move closer to the subject while **zoom out** is to pull back from the subject, or widen the shot, making the subject smaller.

Z

Tables and Techniques

Beverage Guide

BAR MEASUREMENTS

1 Dash/Splash	$^1/_{32}$ oz	1 ml
1 Teaspoon/Bar Spoon	$^1/_8$ oz	3.7 ml
1 Tablespoon	$^3/_8$ oz	11 ml
1 Pony	1 oz	29.5 ml
1 Jigger/Bar Glass	1½ oz	44.3 ml
1 Shot Glass	1½ oz	44.3 ml
1 Wineglass	4 oz	118 ml
1 Split	6 oz	177 ml
1 Cup	8 oz	236.5 ml

STANDARD BAR TOOLS

BAR STRAINER   COCKTAIL SHAKER   CORK SCREW   JUICER

ICE BUCKET   BOTTLE OPENER   JIGGER   COASTERS

TONGS   LONG-HANDLED SPOON   MIXING PITCHER   MUDDLER

NAPKINS   KNIFE   SERVING TRAY   STIRRERS

A Bartender also needs: Cherries, olives, cocktail onions, lemon and lime slices, Angostura bitters, Worcestershire sauce, pitcher of water, sugar, and lots of hard frozen ice.

🖊 A jigger should always be used to measure liquor for each drink. Too much liquor spoils a good drink and sometimes a good party!

🖊 Use maraschino cherries with stems and pierce olives and other fruit with a toothpick. Guests appreciate the convenience.

🖊 A good bartender knows that if the recipe for the drink says shake . . . don't stir. If it says stir . . . don't shake.

📖 See *cocktail party* on page 48.

STANDARD BAR GLASSWARE

CHAMPAGNE
GLASS
5 - 6 OZ

COLLINS
OR BEER
GLASS
12 OZ

COCKTAIL
GLASS
3 - 4 OZ

OLD-FASHIONED
GLASS
4 - 6 OZ

LIQUEUR
GLASS
2 ¼ OZ

JIGGER OR
SHOT GLASS
1 - 1 ½ OZ

MARTINI
GLASS
7 ⅜ OZ

HIGHBALL
GLASS
6 - 8 OZ

STANDARD
WINE GLASS
6 OZ

SOUR
GLASS
5 OZ

✎ Choose styles that suit the drinks being served. Plan a total of four glasses per guest in proportion to the type of drinks being served. Have plastic glasses as a backup.

✎ *Glassware* must sparkle! Wash in warm water, dry with a towel, and polish with a fresh dry towel.

STANDARD BOTTLE SIZES

Fluid Ounces	Type	Metric Measure
1.7 oz	Miniature—spirits	50 ml
3.4 oz	Miniature—wine	100 ml
6 oz	Split	177 ml
6.3 oz	Split—wine	187 ml
6.5 oz	Split—champagne	200 ml
8 oz	Half-pint	237 ml
12 oz	Beer or soft drink can or bottle	355 ml
12.7 oz	Half bottle—wine	375 ml
13 oz	Half bottle—champagne	400 ml
12.8 oz	Tenth	379 ml
16 oz	Pint (U.S.)	473 ml
33.8 oz	Half liter	500 ml
1.05 pints	Half liter	500 ml
.52 quart	Half liter	500 ml
25.4 oz	Standard bottle—wine, spirits, etc.	750 ml
26.5 oz	Fifth	783.5 ml
32 oz	Quart (U.S.)	946 ml
2 pints	Quart (U.S.)	946 ml
33.8 oz	Liter	1000 ml
2.11 pints	Liter	1000 ml
1.05 quarts	Liter	1000 ml
50 oz	Magnum—wine (2 btls)	1.5 liters
54 oz	Magnum—champagne	1.6 liters
59.2 oz	Large standard bottle	1.75 liters
64 oz	Half gallon (U.S.)	1.9 liters
2 quarts	Half gallon (U.S.)	1.9 liters
76 oz	Tappit hen—wine (3 btls)	2.5 liters
108.2 oz	Jeroboam or Double Magnum—champagne (4 btls)	3.2 liters
128 oz	Gallon (U.S.)	3.8 liters
4 quarts	Gallon (U.S.)	3.8 liters
1 gallon	Demijohn	3.8 liters
152.2 oz	Rehoboam—champagne (6 btls)	4.5 liters
202.9 oz	Methuselah—champagne (8 btls)	6 liters
202.9 oz	Imperial—wine	6 liters
304.4 oz	Salmanazar—champagne (12 btls)	9 liters
405.8 oz	Balthazar—champagne (16 btls)	12 liters
507.3 oz	Nebuchadnezzar (20 btls)	15 liters

Standard bottle sizes have changed over the years in the United States. The standard *spirit* and wine size is 750 milliliters (ml) or approximately 25.4 ounces—almost exactly equivalent to the old American fifth (four-fifths of a quart) measure. Since the fifth is so close in size, the term is still used. Sizes vary by country.

DRINKS PER CONTAINER SIZE

Beverage Type	Container Size	Serving Size	Number of Drinks
Liquor/Spirits	750 ml bottle	1 oz (29.6 ml)	25
	750 ml bottle	1.5 oz (44.3 ml)	16
	1 liter (L)	1 oz (29.6 ml)	33
	1 L	1.5 oz (44.3 ml)	22
	1.75 L bottle	1 oz (29.6 ml)	59
	1.75 L bottle	1.5 oz (44.3 ml)	39
Wine	750 ml bottle	5 oz (147 ml)	5
	1.5 L bottle	5 oz (147 ml)	10
Champagne	750 ml bottle	4 oz (118 ml)	6
	Magnum (1.5 L)	4 oz (118 ml)	12
Beer	Can or bottle	12 oz (354 ml)	1
	Full keg (15.5 gal / 58 L)	12 oz (354 ml)	160
	Pony keg (7.75 gal / 29 L)	12 oz (354 ml)	80
	Mini keg (1.32 gal / 5 L)	12 oz (354 ml)	14

The above chart is "by the measure." Often bartenders pour by experience and the pour is heavier than measures, thus using more of the beverages. Some venues and caterers intentionally do this because they charge by the bottle opened.

LIQUID CONVERSIONS

Amount	Alternative	Cups	Fluid Ounces	Liters
Gallon (U.S.)	4 Quarts	16	128	3.8
Imperial Gallon	1.2 Gallon	19.2	153.7	4.5
Quart (U.S.)	2 Pints	4	32	0.95
Pint (U.S.)	½ Quart	2	16	0.5
1.75 Liter	1.6 Quarts	7½	59	1.75
Liter	1.06 Quarts	1¼	34	1
750 ml	0.8 Quarts	3¼	25	0.75
Cup	16 Tablespoons	1	8	0.24
6 lemons Juiced		1½	12	0.35
4 Tablespoons	¼ Cup	¼	2	0.06
3 Teaspoons	1 Tablespoon	$\frac{1}{16}$	2	0.06

Some conversions rounded.

A cup on the above chart is a standard measure as in cooking, unlike a 6-ounce coffee or teacup or 4-ounce punch cup.

 Be careful not to confuse fluid measurements with dry weight measurements. For example, 8 ounces of potatoes is not 1 cup.

CALCULATING BEVERAGE CONSUMPTION

Planning for the amount of alcoholic beverages that will be consumed at an event is often a combination of careful calculation and understanding the guests. Different amounts of different beverages will be consumed depending on the type of event, the purpose of the event, those attending, and the liveliness of the event. For example, a formal dinner is quite different from a Hawaiian luau party, and different amounts of liquor will be consumed per person. A party for younger adults will demand more beer, wine, and popular or "trendy" drinks than a retirement event. All factors must be considered when planning.

AVERAGE PER PERSON CONSUMPTION PER TYPE OF BEVERAGE

Type of Beverage	1st Hour	2nd and Additional Hours	Total for 2-Hour Event	Total for 4-Hour Event
Cocktails (1.5 oz / 44.3 ml)	2 Drinks	1 Drink per Hour	3 Cocktails	5 Cocktails
Wine (5 oz / 147 ml)	$\frac{2}{5}$ Bottle	$\frac{1}{5}$ Bottle	$\frac{3}{5}$ Bottle	1 Bottle
Beer (12 oz / 354 ml)	2 Bottles	1 Bottle	3 Beers	5 Beers

🖋 The stock required to provide a full bar with a full selection of spirits to cover all preferences can be very expensive. A bar with standard drinks such as scotch and water, vodka and tonic, etc., is usually very acceptable.

🖋 Some venues and caterers tend to pour more liquor per drink, and more drinks per hour, because they charge by the bottle. Dictate beforehand the amount that should be poured and served.

🖋 Never skimp on ice. A rule of thumb is to plan half a pound per person when it is cool and two pounds per person in warm weather.

🖋 A typical melted ice cube adds 2–2.5 ounces (59–74 milliliters) of water to a drink, diluting the alcohol by $\frac{2}{3}$ when totally melted. Use hard frozen ice and never reuse cubes—it will spoil the drink.

🖋 If an event with cocktails goes longer than 1½ hours, be sure there is plenty to eat!

🛍 See *cocktail party* on page 48.

BEVERAGE CONSUMPTION

100 Person, 2-hour Cocktail Party

Type of Drink	Serving Size	% of Guests	Drinks 1st Hour	Drinks 2nd Hour	Total Drinks	Required	Order
Cocktails	1.5 oz / 44.3 ml	50	100	50	150	225 oz / 6.6 L	14 Bottles
White Wine	5 oz / 147 ml	15	30	15	45	225 oz / 6.6 L	9 Bottles
Red Wine	5 oz / 147 ml	10	20	10	30	150 oz / 4.4 L	6 Bottles
Beer	12 oz / 354 ml	20	40	20	60	720 oz / 21.2 L	60 Bottles
Soft Drinks	12 oz / 354 ml	5	10	5	15	180 oz / 5.3 L	15 Cans

Note: This chart assumes all cocktails are the same. If a variety of different cocktails are being offered, such as a full bar, more bottles of different types would be necessary.

🖉 Always order extra. It is embarrassing to run out of liquor. Typically unopened bottles can be returned.

🖉 A practical and economical approach is to offer one or two signature cocktails, along with beer, wine, and some nonalcoholic choices.

BEVERAGE CONSUMPTION

100 Person, 3-hour Dinner Party with Specialty Drinks

Type of Drink	Serving Size	% of Guests	Drinks 1st Hour	Drinks 2nd Hour	Drinks 3rd Hour*	Total Drinks	Required	Order
Margarita	1.5 oz / 44.4 ml	85	170	85	85	340	510 oz / 15 L	25 Bottles
Beer	12 oz / 354 ml	10	20	10	10	40	480 oz / 14.2 L	40 Bottles
Soft Drinks	12 oz / 354 ml	5	10	5	5	20	240 oz / 7 L	20 Cans

*Depends on the atmosphere of the party—many may not consume another drink or change to a soft drink.

Note: Specialty drinks require 1.5 ounces (44.3 milliliters) of liquor per serving.

🖉 A standard glass of wine (5 ounces) and a bottle of beer (12 ounces) have the same amount of alcohol as a specialty cocktail (1.5 ounces or 29.6 milliliters).

🖉 **Be Aware:** Liquor laws in many states hold the host liable if a person leaves your party drunk and has an auto accident. Blood alcohol rises above the legal limit if a person drinks more than one drink per hour. To control consumption, cocktail hour is typically that—one hour long.

BEVERAGE CONSUMPTION

100 Person Formal Dinner

Type of Drink	No. of Guests	% of Guests	No. of Drinks	Required	Order
Predinner Cocktails	80	80	80	120 oz / 3.5 L	5 bottles
Beer	10	10	10	120 oz / 3.5 L	10 bottles
Champagne	90	90	90	450 oz / 13.3 L	18 bottles
Sherry	90	90	90	450 oz / 13.3 L	18 bottles
White Wine	90	90	90	451 oz / 13.3 L	19 bottles
Red Wine	90	90	135	675 oz / 20 L	27 bottles
Dessert Wine	90	90	90	720 oz / 21.3 L	29 bottles
Soft Drinks	10	10	30	360 oz / 10.7 L	30 cans

The above example is for a formal dinner with multiple courses of food and beverage. While the consumption may appear high, the predinner and dinner may last for hours, spreading the beverage consumption over an extended time.

🖊 When serving drinks to persons at a table, serve to the right side of each person, using the right hand.

🖊 Wine is served to all women at a table first, starting with the eldest, then to men, always moving clockwise around the table.

📋 See *place settings* on page 198.

WINES

Wine-Serving Temperature Guidelines

Wine Type	Degrees F	Degrees C
Sherry	67	20
Vintage Port	66	19
Bordeaux, Shiraz	64	18
Burgundy, Cabernet	63	17
Rioja, Pinot Noir, Brandy	61	16
Chianti, Zinfandel	59	15
Tawny Port, Madeira	57	14
Ideal Storage—All Wines	55	13
Beaujolais, Rosé	54	12
Sauternes	52	11
Chardonnay	48	9
Riesling	47	8
Champagne	45	7
Retsina	45	7
Asti Spumanti	41	5

All *wine* should be served at the temperature that best shows off its personal characteristics. Too warm and one tastes the alcohol, but too cold hides the flavors.

 Selecting the right type of wine is important not only for taste, but also for the style of the event and its budget. Rather than the old standards, surprise guests by offering something different. Always sample the selection before purchasing or serving.

 Stemware should always be held by the stem when drinking.

Guide to Wine Types

Wine	Red	White	Rosé	Dry	Sweet	U.S.	French
Anjou		X	X		X		X
Barbera	X			X		X	
Barberesco	X			X			
Barberone	X			X			
Bardolino	X			X			
Barolo	X						
Barsac		X			X		X
Beaujolais	X			X			X
Bordeaux	X				X		X
Burgandy	X			X			X
Cabernet Sauvignon	X			X		X	X
Catawba		X			X	X	
Chablis		X		X		X	X
Chamertin		X		X		X	X
Chardonnay		X		X		X	X
Chassagne-Montrachet		X		X			X
Châteauneuf-du-Pape	X			X			X
Chenin Blanc		X		X		X	
Chianti	X			X			
Claret (Clairet)			X	X		X	X
Est-Est-Est		X		X			
Franconian		X		X	X		
Frascati		X		X			
Gamay	X			X			X
Gamay Beaujolais	X		X	X			
Gewürztraminer		X		X	X	X	X
Graves	X	X		X	X		X
Grenache Rosé			X		X	X	X
Grignolino	X			X			
Hermitage	X			X			X
Kosher Wine	X				X	X	
Lacrima Christi	X	X		X			

Italian	German	Other	Comments
			Medium sweet
X			Full body
X			Full body
X			Full body
X			Medium body
X			Full body
			Rich, full body, sweet Sauternes
			Light body, fresh
			Deep, full body
			Full body
		X	Sturdy, full body
			Medium dry to sweet, full body
			Light body, fresh
		X	Generally full body
			Crisp fruitiness, oaky
			Full flavored (also Puligny-Montrachet)
			Full flavored
			Light
X			Fruity, full body
			Medium body
X			Medium flavor and body
	X		Dry to medium sweet
X			Medium body
			Fresh, light body
			Fresh, fruity
			Rich, medium sweet
			Both red and white, medium sweet
			Distinctive bouquet
			Medium body
			Full body
			Fruity (Concord, Cherry, etc.)
X			Both red and white, medium body

Guide to Wine Types (*continued*)

Wine	Red	White	Rosé	Dry	Sweet	U.S.	French
Liebfraumilch		X		X	X		
Mâcon	X	X		X			X
May Wine		X		X	X		
Médoc	X			X			X
Merlot	X			X		X	X
Meursault		X		X			X
Moselle		X		X			
Neibbiolo	X			X	X		
Nuits-Saint-Georges	X			X			X
Orvieto		X		X	X		
Pinot Blanc		X		X		X	
Pinot Noir	X			X		X	
Pomerol	X			X			X
Pommard	X			X			X
Pouilly-Fuissé		X		X			X
Pouilly-Fumé		X		X	X		X
Retsina		Gold		X			
Rhine Wine		X		X			
Riesling		X		X		X	
Rioja	X			X			
Rosé			X	X	X	X	X
Saint Emilion	X			X			X
Saint Julien	X			X			X
Sauternes (Sauvignon)		X		X		X	
Sauternes		X					X
Sauvignon		X		X		X	
Sémillon		X		X		X	
Shiraz	X				X	X	
Soave		X		X			
Steinwein				X	X		
Sylvaner		X		X			X
Syrah	X				X	X	X
Tavel			X	X			X

Italian	German	Other	Comments
	X		Medium sweet, soft
			Fresh
	X		Medium sweet, aromatic
			Elegant Bordeaux, generally medium body
		Chile	Deep flavor, fruity
			Full flavor
	X		Light, delicate bouquet
X			Dry and semisweet, full body
			Very dry, very full body
X			Also semidry types
			Medium body
			Light, medium red
			Full body, strong bouquet
			Medium body
			Light body, crisp
			Semidry
		Greek	Pine resin flavor
	X		Full body, outstanding bouquet
	X		Pleasantly tart
		Spain	Sturdy, full body
			Fruity, tart, light, can be medium sweet
			Full flavor
			Medium body
			Full body, can be semidry
			Fragrant, rich and full body
			Another name for Sauternes
			Another name for Sauternes
		Aust.	Pungent, rich
X			Soft
	X		Another name for Franconian
			Medium body, fruity
			Deep red
			Very dry, light body

Guide to Wine Types (*continued*)

Wine	Red	White	Rosé	Dry	Sweet	U.S.	French
Traminer		X		X		X	X
Valpolicella	X			X			
Verdicchio		X		X			
Vouvray		X		X	X		X
Zinfandel	X		X	X	X	X	
Zinfandel—White			X	X	X	X	

Guide to Champagnes and Sparkling Wines

Wine	Red	White	Rosé	Dry	Sweet	U.S.	French
Champagne							
Typical		X		X	X	X	X
Brut		X		X		X	X
Extra Dry		X		X		X	X
Sec or Dry		X			X	X	X
Rosé or Pink			X	X	X	X	X
Demi-sec		X		X	X	X	X
Blanc de Blanc		X		X		X	X
Cava		X		X			
Asti Spumante		X			X		
Crackling Rosé			X	X	X		
Lacrima Christi	X			X	X		
Nebbiolo Spumante			X	X	X		
Recioto della Valpolicella	X				X		
Soave Spumante		X		X			
Sekt (Sparkling Liebfraumilch)		X		X			
Sparkling Burgundy	X			X	X	X	X
Sparkling Moselle		X		X			

 Champagne should always be poured by holding the bottle with the thumb inside the concave bottom. A napkin should be wrapped around the bottle to keep it from dripping condensation.

Italian	German	Other	Comments
			Tart, medium body
X			Soft, medium body
X			Crispy, medium
			Stilling and crackling
			Spicy
			Semisweet

Other	Comments
	"Champagne Method" when not French
	Light, delicate
	Very dry
	Medium dry
	Dry
	Refers to color only, may be dry or sweet
	"Demi-sec" is French for half-dry
	Very dry, elegant, very light-bodied
Spain	Very dry and light
Italy	Fragrant, medium sweet
Portugal	Sturdy, full body
Italy	Semisweet
Italy	Light body, fresh
Italy	Full body
Italy	Medium dry, medium body
Germany	Fruity, touch of sweetness
	Fuller-bodied than Champagne
Germany	Another name for Sekt

See *champagne* on page 43.

Guide to Sweet Wines

Wine	Dry	Sweet	Origin	Comments
Amontillado	X		Spain	Nutty
Angelica		X	U.S.	White, full-bodied
Ice Wine		X	Germany	Very refreshing, medium to full body
Madeira	X		Portugal	Medium dry, soft, fruity
Malaga		X	Spain	Rich, raisin-like sweetness
Manzanilla	X		Spain	Bone dry, austere
Marsala		X	Italy	Full flavor and body
Muscatel		X	Portugal	Mellow, sweet, pronounced grape flavor
Oloroso	X	X	Spain	Creamy, medium dry to very rich, nutty
Port		X	Portugal	Rich dessert wine
Sherry (in general)	X	X	Spain	Appetizer and dessert wine—very dry to very sweet
Cocktail Dry Sherry	X		Spain	Light
Cream Sherry		X	Spain	Nut-sweet, rich
Tino	X		Spain	Very dry, fruity
Tokay (California) or Tokaj		X	U.S.	Full body
Vermouth—Dry	X		Italy	Light, tart pale
Vermouth—Sweet	X		Italy	Medium dry, bittersweet undertone

Wine Saving Guide

Type of Wine	Storage Method	Freshness Duration
Red Wine	Properly corked	1 Week
White Wine	Recork promptly, in refrigerator	2 Weeks
Wine (over 14% alcohol)	Uncorked or corked	Indefinitely
Champagne	Finish immediately	0
Vermouth	In refrigerator	60 Days
Sparkling Wines	Finish immediately	0

🖊 Preventing wine from spoiling requires keeping wine from being overexposed to air. One way to accomplish this is to pour leftover wine into smaller decanters to reduce the amount of air to which the wine is exposed. Also, systems are available that displace the oxygen with argon gas to save the wine for longer periods of time.

🖊 While some wines benefit from "breathing" (letting the bottle stand open for a while before pouring), it is widely recognized and accepted that simply pouring wine into a glass is enough for it to breathe. Air quickly reacts with the critical components in wine that create its complex aroma and flavor.

🖊 A standard 750 ml bottle of wine contains five servings.

FAVORED ALCOHOLIC DRINKS BY NATION

Country	Most Favored (Ingredients)
Argentina	Wine (grapes)
Australia	Rum (sugarcane)
Austria	Schnapps (fruit)
Bali	Arrack (sugarcane)
Belgium	Jenever (malt and juniper) and Beer
Bermuda	Black Seal Rum and Dark 'N' Stormy
Bolivia	Singani (muscat grapes)
Brazil	Cachaça (sugarcane) and Caipirinha
Bulgaria	Rakia (fruit)
Canada	Canadian Whisky and Caesar Cocktail
Chile	Pisco (grapes)
China	Moutai (sorghum)
Colombia	Aguardiente (sugarcane)
Costa Rica	Guaro (sugarcane)
Croatia	Rakija (fruit)
Cuba	Mojito
Cyprus	Brandy Sour
Czech Republic	Becherovka (herbs) or Slivovice (plums)
Denmark	Akvavit (grain)
Ecuador	Aguardiente (sugarcane)
El Salvador	Tic Tack (sugarcane)
England	Gin (juniper berries)
Ethiopia	Tej (mead or honey)
Finland	Koskenkorva Viina (barley)
France	Brandy, Cognac, and Champagne
French West Indies	Rum (sugarcane)
Germany	Schnapps (fruit) and Beer
Greece	Ouzo (anise)
Haiti	Rhum Barbancourt (sugarcane)

Favored Alcoholic Drinks by Nation (*continued*)

Country	Most Favored (Ingredients)
Hungary	Unicum (herbs) and Pálinka (fruit)
Iceland	Brennivín (potatoes)
Indonesia	Arrack (sugarcane)
Ireland	Poitín (barley) and Guinness
Italy	Grappa (grapes) and Limoncello (lemon)
Jamaica	Rum (sugarcane)
Japan	Shochu (rice) and Sake
Korea	Soju (rice, barley, corn)
Lebanon	Arak (anise)
Mexico	Tequila (blue agave), pulque, and brandy
Netherlands	Jenever (malt and juniper)
Norway	Akvavit (grain)
Panama	Seco Herrerano (sugarcane)
Peru	Pisco (grapes)
Philippines	Palm Wine
Poland	Vodka and Mead (honey)
Romania	Tuica (plums) and Pálinka (fruit)
Russia	Vodka
Scotland	Scotch Whisky (grain)
Serbia	Slivovitz (plums)
Slovakia	Borovicka (juniper berries)
Spain	Sherry (grapes) and Sangria (wine punch)
Spain—Basque	Picon Punch
Spain—Catalonia	Cava (Spanish champagne)
Sri Lanka	Arrack (coconut)
Sweden	Akvavit or Snaps
Thailand	Mekhong Whiskey (sugarcane and rice)
Turkey	Raki (anise)

Business Affairs

BUSINESS CALCULATIONS

Calculating Personnel Costs

Days	Item
15	Personal Days
9	Holidays
5	Allowance for Illness
104	Weekends
133	Days Lost
232	Working Days
1,856	Working Hours

If paid $40,000/year, the actual rate is $21.55 per hour
(annual rate divided by working hours).

To determine a salaried employee's "actual hourly rate," you must determine the actual number of days worked per year after deducting personal days, holidays, etc. Take the working days and multiply by the hours worked each day (in most cases eight) to determine the total annual hours. By dividing the employee's annual salary by the total annual hours, you find the employee's actual rate per hour. This actual personnel cost rate can then be used in the following chart either as an individual cost or averaged with the hourly rate of all other employees assigned to the event to determine an average cost of labor.

Calculating Annual Gross Profit

Calculating Annual Net Profit

Calculating Overhead Percentage

🖉 Operating expenses include utilities, administrative salaries, office rent, phone, and anything else not charged to a project. (Example: $100,000 ÷ $350,000 = 28.6 percent overhead.)

Calculating Labor Charge-Out Rates

Item	%	$	Notes
Average cost of labor per hour per person		$15.00	May be necessary to do separate calculation for different employees
Employer contribution to FICA and Medicare	7.65	1.15	Determined by federal government
Employer-paid taxes	0	.00	State and federal taxes
Payroll handling charge	1	0.15	If outside company does payroll
Company overhead rate	28.6	4.29	See Overhead Calculation Chart
Employee downtime (2 hours out of 8)	25	3.75	2 hours is 25%
Employer's contribution to health insurance	12	1.8	Varies by company
Vacation and paid holidays	6.75	1.01	Unions have set rates
Company profit	100	15	Name your price
Total labor cost per hour		$42.15	
Company contingency rate	19.00	7.98	Determine your rate
Labor rate per hour		$50.13	Present this to client

Charge-out rates are what the client should be billed per hour for your employee.

✎ Don't forget to add a rate, if necessary, for overtime or late night work (sometimes a union requirement). If these work conditions are expected, it is sometimes easier to do a second chart including these rates and then use the appropriate chart as necessary to calculate the extra-charge hours.

Estimating Project Cost with Overhead and Profit

Item	Amount	Rate
Estimate of all project hard costs	$100,000	100%
Labor charge-out rate—10 people for 10 hours (see Labor Charge-Out Rate Chart)	$5,000	$50
Contingency	$10,000	10%
Total project cost	$115,000	
Overhead costs (see Calculating Overhead Costs Chart)	$32,890	28.60%
Total cost with overhead	$147,890	
Profit markup	$29,579	20%
Estimated total project cost	$177,468	

The above chart illustrates how to determine the total costs for the project. If the project is an in-house one, the profit markup may or may not be included. The contingency percentage may also change depending on the project's history or complexity. Anticipated overtime hours can be an additional "Labor Charge-Out Rate line" in the chart.

Percentage of Profit Table

Markup	(on $100)	Selling Price	Gross Profit
10%	$10	$110	9.10%
20%	$20	$120	16.70%
30%	$30	$130	23.10%
40%	$40	$140	26.60%
50%	$50	$150	33.30%
100%	$100	$200	50%
200%	$200	$300	67%

Expense Budget

As of: (Date Last Revised)   Event Date:

Category / Item	Description	Budgeted Amount	Actual Amount	Difference	Paid To Date	Next Pay	Due Date	Left To Pay
STAFF								
Event Director	10 wks @ $100	1,000	800	−200	500	100	14-Oct	300
Consultant	T Jones	5,000	5,000	0	2,500	2,500	Event Day	2,500
Ushers	6 @ $150	900	900	0	0	900	Event Day	900
CAST								
Keynote Speaker	James Smith	2,000	4,000	2,000	0	1,000	Signed Deal	4,000
Dance Band	The Aces	1,000	1,000	0	0	1,000	Event Date	1,000
PRODUCTION								
Music Track	Hosman Music	2,000	2,500	500	500	1,000	18-Oct	2,000
Lighting Rentals	DC Lighting	3,000	3,000	0	0	1,500	18-Oct	3,000
CATERING								
Dinner Menu	35 @ $60	2,000	2,100	100	500	1,600	Event Date	1,600
Cocktail Reception	35 @ $40	1,400	1,400	0	0	1,400	Event Date	1,400
Centerpieces	10 @ $100	1,000	1,000	0	0	1,000	Event Date	1,000

Expense Budget (*continued*)

Category / Item	Description	Budgeted Amount	Actual Amount	Difference	Paid To Date	Next Pay	Due Date	Left To Pay
LOGISTICS								
Limos	4 @ $100 w/ Tip	500	400	–100	0	400	Event Date	400
Shipping	UPS	150.00	85.99	–64.01	85.99	0	Charged	0
Subtotal		19,950	22,186	2,319.64	4,085.99			18,100
Contingency	5%	998						
Total		20,948	22,186	2,319.64	4,086			18,100

This budget form has many advantages: It is easy to see what was originally budgeted, what is currently budgeted, how much has been paid, when more payments are due, and the amount left to pay. Also notice that it is already over budget by $2,319.64. By seeing what payments are due and when, managing cash flow is a snap.

✎ Be sure to begin each update by entering the revision date.

📖 See *budget* on page 28.

THE EVENT SCHEDULE

Since every type of event has different schedule requirements, it is impossible to provide a comprehensive sample schedule that meets every requirement. The following is generic yet workable for most events.

Event Master Schedule

Schedule Issued: July 2 - 5:30 pm

Date	Time	Item	Relates to	Vendor	Staff Assigned	Budget Category	Status
3-Jul	9:00A	Barge For Fireworks Docked	Fireworks Load In	Jameston Barges	Susan	313	Done
3-Jul	11:00A	Work Lights & Generator Delivered	Fireworks Load In	United Rent Alls	Bobby	314	Done
3-Jul	11:15A	Police Meeting / City Hall Rm 10	Public Parking	NA	Frank	—	Delayed to 4pm
3-Jul	11:50A	Lock Gates 10 & 11	Fireworks Load In	Park Maintenance Office	Mazzy	—	
3-Jul	12:00N	City Newspaper Meeting	Event Promotion	City Inquirer	Twyla	210	
3-Jul	2:00P	Site Walk-Through	Site Review	Fire Chief / Meet at Flagpole	Susan	—	
3-Jul	2:30P	Record Narration	Show	Delux Studios / Announcer	Ryan	239	
		Etc.					
		Etc.					

The best schedules are simply created on a spreadsheet and contain all key functions from the start of the event process to its conclusion and strike. Always assign responsibility to each function and update and distribute the schedule on a regular basis, indicating work accomplished. Many different software programs are available for more complex scheduling.

See *schedule* on page 239.

Centerpieces

Creativity should not interrupt function. Centerpieces planned effectively enhance an event rather than interfering with the event's impact.

A centerpiece that is too tall blocks views.

The correct size for easy conversation.

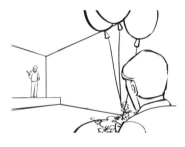

Some centerpieces look good in concept.

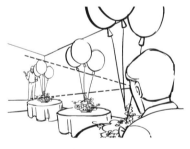

With multiple centerpieces, views are blocked.

 Centerpieces are the quickest and easiest way to enhance the event theme.

See *centerpiece* on page 40.

FLORAL TREATMENT VARIATIONS FOR A HEAD TABLE

FLOWERS FOR TRADITIONAL THEMES

Theme	Flower
Christmas	Holly (with berries)
	White Hydrangea
	Red and White Roses
	Various Ixia with star-shaped flowers
	Poinsettia and Pine Garland
Chanukah	Various blue flowers such as Cornflower, Iris, Lavender, and Lilac, mixed with white, including Roses and Carnations
Caribbean/Hawaiian	Hibiscus
	Birds of Paradise
	Orchids
	Halyconia
	Ginger and anything brightly colored
African	Protea of various types
English Garden	Roses
	Daisies
	Aster
	Geraniums
	Lavender
Western	Sunflowers
	Texas Bluebonnets
	Cactus
	Yucca
Thanksgiving	Corn, Gourds, Pumpkins, and other vegetables
	Marigold
	Chrysanthemum
	Pincushion Protea
	Safflowers
	Eucalyptus Seedpods
	Silver Brunia

Exhibitions

TRADE SHOW EXHIBIT BOOTH LAYOUT

Exhibit booths should be designed to visually attract and pull passing delegates into the booth. Once inside, multiple visuals, along with personal contact, should effectively present the sales message.

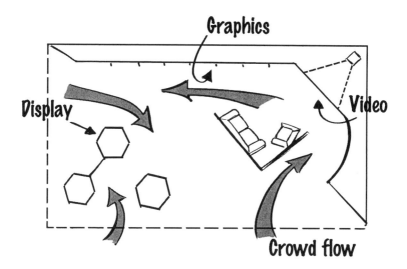

SIMPLE ART SHOW DISPLAY PANELS

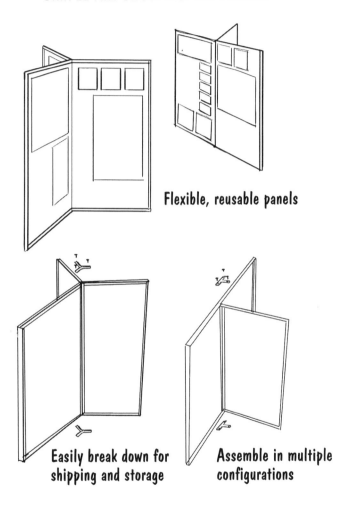

Flexible, reusable panels

Easily break down for shipping and storage

Assemble in multiple configurations

🖋 Easy to construct. Each of the three panels is separate and fits together with cleats quickly and easily.

DISPLAY PANEL SHAPES

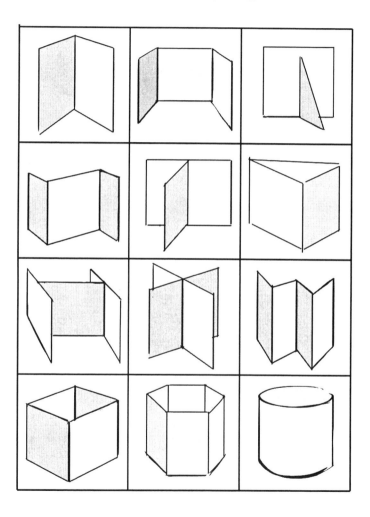

Flag Protocol

Displaying national flags properly is essential. Different countries have different protocols for their flags, making it necessary to research each flag being used in an event. Also, when the American flag is being displayed in a foreign country, the etiquette of that country may apply.

Flag tips:

🖊 Gold fringe can be found on ceremonial flags used indoors and in outdoor ceremonies. The fringe is considered completely within the guidelines of proper flag etiquette.

🖊 Streamers may be affixed to spearheads or flagstaffs in a parade only by order of the president of the United States.

🖊 On flying the flag at night, section 6a of the Flag Code reads: "When a patriotic effect is desired, the flag may be displayed twenty-four hours per day if properly illuminated during the hours of darkness."

🖊 On carrying the flag horizontally, section 8c of the Flag Code reads: "The flag should never be carried flat or horizontally, but always aloft and free."

🖊 **When printing the flag:**

The Pantone system colors are:

Blue PMS 281
Red PMS 193
White #FFFFF

The RGB colors are:

Dark Red #BF0A30
Navy #002868

🖊 **Music for flag ceremonies:**

Raising the flag—"Reveille"

Lowering the flag—The military uses either "Taps," "To the Colors," "Tattoo," or "Retreat." All are appropriate.

🛍 See *flag protocol* on page 107.

PARTS OF A FLAG

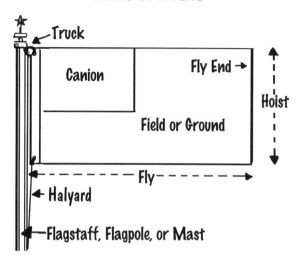

🖉 On the U.S. flag, the fly is 1.9 times the hoist. On British and Canadian flags, the fly is twice the hoist. Other country flags vary.

FLAGPOLE HEIGHT TO FLAG SIZE RATIO

Flagpole Height	Flag Size
15' (4.6 m)	3' x 5' (0.91 x 1.5 m)
20' (6.1 m)	4' x 6' (1.2 x 1.8 m)
25' (7.6 m)	5' x 8' (1.5 x 2.4 m)
30'–35' (9.1–10.7 m)	6' x 10' (1.8 x 3 m)
40'–45' (12.2–13.7 m)	6' x 10'–8' x 12' (1.8 x 3 m–2.4 x 3.6 m)
50' (15 m)	10' x 19' (3 x 5.8 m)
60'–65' (18.3–19.8 m)	10' x 19' (3 x 5.8 m)
70'–80' (21.3–24.4 m)	12' x 18' (3.6 x 5.5 m)

A flag to cover a casket is 5' x 9.5'.

How to Display the U.S. Flag

Displayed over the middle of the street, the flag should be suspended vertically with the union to the north on an east/west street, or to the east on a north/south street.

No flag or pennant may be flown above or to the viewer's right of the U.S. flag. When flags of states, cities, or localities or pennants of societies are flown on the same halyard with the flag of the United States, the American flag should always be at the peak.

When suspended over a sidewalk from a rope extending from a house to a pole at the edge of the sidewalk, the flag should be hoisted out, union first, from the building.

When the flag is displayed from a staff projecting horizontally, or at an angle from a windowsill, balcony, or front of a building, the union should be placed at the peak of that staff unless the flag is at half-staff.

When hung in a window where it is viewed from the street, place the union at the head and over the left shoulder of the viewer.

Displayed in a manner other than by being flown from a staff, it must be displayed flat, whether indoors or out. When displayed either horizontally or vertically against a wall, the union should be uppermost and to the viewer's left.

When the flags of two or more nations are displayed, they are to be flown from separate staffs of the same height. The flags are to be of approximately equal size. International usage forbids the display of one nation's flag above another. An alternative is to fly the U.S. flag higher on a different pole between the other two.

While standing holding the flag, it must be either straight up against the right shoulder or leaning out in the center of the person.

 The U.S. flag must be at the center and at the highest point when a number of flags, such as for a state or organization, are grouped and displayed from staffs.

 When carried in a procession with another flag or flags, the U.S. flag must be on the marching right. Or if there is a line of other flags, it must be in front of the center of that line.

 When flying the U.S. flag, state flag, and company (city, organization, religion, etc.) flag on side-by-side poles, the U.S. flag is on the viewer's left, the state flag is in the center, and the other is on the right.

 When displayed from a staff in a church or public auditorium or on or off a podium, the U.S. flag must hold the position of superior prominence: in front of the audience and in a position of honor at the speaker's right (audience left). Another flag displayed is placed on the speaker's left.

 When displayed on a car, the staff shall be fixed firmly to the chassis or clamped to the right front fender.

 When used to cover a casket, the flag should be so placed that the union is at the head and over the left shoulder. The flag should not be lowered into the grave or allowed to touch the ground. The size of the flag to cover a casket is 5' x 9'.

Flag images and information courtesy Independence Hall Association.

DAYS TO FLY THE U.S. FLAG (IN THE UNITED STATES)

January 1st	New Year's Day
January 10th	Inauguration Day (Every 4th Year)
3rd Monday in January	Martin Luther King Jr.'s Birthday
February 12th	Lincoln's Birthday
February 22nd	Washington's Birthday
3rd Monday in February	President's Day
1st Thursday in May	National Day of Prayer
Last Monday in May	Memorial Day (half-staff until noon)
June 14th	Flag Day
July 4th	Independence Day
1st Monday in September	Labor Day
2nd Monday in October	Columbus Day
November 11th	Veterans Day
4th Thursday in November	Thanksgiving Day
(Variable)	Election Days

WHEN TO FLY THE U.S. FLAG AT HALF-STAFF

Date	Occasion	Duration
May 11	Peace Officers Memorial Day	Sunrise to sunset
Last Monday in May	Memorial Day	Sunrise to noon
Sept. 11	Patriot's Day	Sunrise to sunset
Dec. 11	National Pearl Harbor Remembrance Day	Sunrise to sunset
To be announced	Upon proclamation of the president or state governor	

Half-staff is lowering the flag to one-half the distance between the top and bottom of the staff. To fly a flag at half-staff, first hoist the flag to the peak for an instant, then lower it to the half-staff position. The flag should again be raised to the peak before being lowered for the day. When it is displayed with another flag, both are half-staff, with the U.S. flag at the midpoint and the other flag below.

STAFF ORNAMENTS

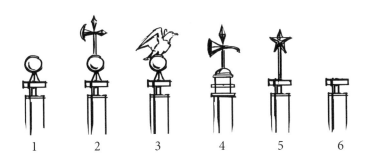

These traditional ornaments on flagstaffs include (left to right):
1. Ball, 2. Halberd, 3. Spread Eagle, 4. Colors or Guidon, 5. Star, and
6. Flat Truck.

Bunting and Rosettes

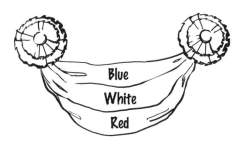

Patriotic decorations are accomplished using the national colors in
buntings of different styles, including the swag with rosettes above.
Protocol dictates that the blue be the top color.

See *bunting* on page 33.

Food Planning

TRADITIONAL EVENT AND MEAL TIMES (AMERICAN)

Type of Event	Starting Time
Breakfast	8 a.m.–10 a.m.
Brunch	11 a.m.–2 p.m.
Lunch	12 noon–3:30 p.m.
Afternoon Tea	2 p.m.–4 p.m.
Cocktail Receptions with Hors d'oeuvre	5 p.m.–8 p.m.
Cocktail Parties with Buffet	6 p.m.–8 p.m.
Complete Dinners	8 p.m. and later
Dessert Events	9 p.m.–10:30 p.m.

 Meal times differ widely in different cultures, regions, and countries.

FOOD AND WINE COMBINATIONS

Dinner Item or Course	Wine Preferred
Cocktail Snacks (nuts, cheeses, etc.)	Dry Sherry, Dry Madeira, Vermouth, Aperitif Wines, Champagne, Sparkling Wines
Appetizers (including hors d'oeuvre)	Dry Sherry, Aperitif Wines, Dry Vermouth
First Courses (clear, creamed, vegetable, or chicken soups; mushrooms on toast)	Dry White Wines, Rosé Wines
Fish and Seafood Dishes	
Typical	Dry to Medium-dry White Wines, Rosé Wines, Champagne, Sparkling Wines
Highly Flavored Fish Dishes (creole, shrimp, lobster)	Full-bodied White Wines, Medium Red or Rosé Wines

Food and Wine Combinations (*continued*)

Dinner Item or Course	Wine Preferred
Fowl	
White meat	Dry and Semisweet White Wines, Rosé Wines, Champagne, Sparkling Wines
Dark meat	Full-bodied Dry White Wines, Medium Red or Rosé Wines
Pork	Dry to Medium-dry White Wines, Rosé Wines
Baked Ham and Dishes with Sweet Vegetable or Fruit Side Dishes	Medium-dry White Wines, Rosé Wines
Lamb	Medium Red Wines
Veal	Medium-dry White Wines, Medium Red Wines, Rosé Wines
Game	Full-bodied Red Wines (if not too rich), Medium Red Wines, Rosé Wines
Hearty Dishes	
Roast Beef, Spaghetti, Barbecued Meat, Steaks, and Strongly Seasoned Dishes	Full-bodied Red Wines
Desserts (cheeses, fruits, sweets, cakes)	Dessert Wines, Sweet Table Wines, Kosher Wines, Extra-dry and Dry Champagne, Sparkling Wines
Party Refreshments	Sherry, Port, Madeira, Marsala, Kosher Wines, Malaga, Muscatel, Aperitif Wines, Flavored Wines
All Festive Occasions and Celebrations	Champagne and Sparkling Wines

HOW FOOD IS SERVED

Food	Serving Dish	Type of Plate	Implements Used
Hors d'oeuvre			
Standard	Platters or Dishes	Dessert Plate	Dessert Knife and Fork or Fork Only
Unusual	Varies	Special, i.e., Champagne Flute	Varies
Oysters	(Individual Servings Only)	Oyster Plate or Dinner Plate	Oyster Fork or Dessert Fork
Soups	Tureen on Plate with Dish Paper	Soup Plates, Soup Cups, Rimmed Soup Bowls, Marmites, or Lugs	Soup Spoon or Tablespoon
Baked Soup	(Individual Servings Only)	Ramekin or Lugs	Soup Spoon or Tablespoon
Salad			
As Main Dish	Bowl—Glass, Wood, or Enameled Metal	Salad Plate or Dinner Plate	Table Knife and Fork
Salad with Hot Meat	(Individual Servings Only)	Crescent-shaped Salad Plate Coupe Bowl or Side Plate	Table Knife and Fork
Fish			
Fried	Platter (with Dish Paper)	Dessert Plate—If part of meal Dinner Plate—If main course	Fish Knife and Fork
Boiled or Steamed with Sauce	Gratin Dish or Casserole	Same	Same
Baked	Platter	Same	Same

How Food is Served (*continued*)

Food	Serving Dish	Type of Plate	Implements Used
Meat			
Roast or Boiled	Platter	Dinner Plate	Table Knife and Fork
Stew, Blanquette, etc.	Gratin Dish, Casserole, or Decorative Kettle	Soup Plate, Nappy, Soup Bowl, or Individual Casserole	Table Knife and Fork
Fried Cutlets	Platter with Dish Paper or Chop Platter	Dinner Plate	Table Knife and Fork
Roulade, Fried Rissoles, etc.	Same	Dinner Plate	Table Fork
Grilled	Platter or Chop Platter	Dinner Plate	Table Knife and Fork
Other			
Curry	(Individual Servings Preferred)	Lugged or Rimmed Soup Bowl, Covered Soup Bowl, Curry Bowl, or Creamed Soup Cup and Stand	Dessert Spoon and Fork or Table Fork
Cooked Vegetables	Covered Vegetable Dish, Oval Vegetable, or Divided Vegetable Dish	Shared on Dinner Plate	Table Fork
Pastas	Large Bowl or Casserole	Soup Plate or Pasta Plate	Table Fork and Tablespoon
Cheese	Board or Flat, Oval Dish	Tea Plate or Side Plate	Dessert Knife
Biscuits	Basket or Oval Dish with Muffin Cover	Tea Plate or Side Plate	Fingers

How Food is Served (*continued*)

Food	Serving Dish	Type of Plate	Implements Used
Bread and Bread Rolls	Basket with Table Napkin or Flat Plate with Dish Paper or Doily	Bread and Butter Plate	Fingers
Cut Fresh Fruit	Oval Vegetable Bowl or Plate with Dish Paper	Dessert Plate or Fruit Plate	Fruit Knife and Fork or Dessert Knife and Fork
Dessert			
Ices or Sundaes	(Individual Servings Only)	Glass Plate or Sundae Glass	Teaspoons
Hot Puddings	Deep Plate or Bowl	Fruit Plate, Dessert Plate, or Lugged Soup Bowl	Dessert Fork if firm, otherwise Spoon and Fork
Milk or Juicy Puddings	Bowl	Fruit Plate or Dessert Plate	Dessert Spoon and Fork
Pastries and Creams	Bowl, Glass Dish, or Plate	Fruit Plate, Dessert Plate	Dessert Fork or Pastry Fork

✎ To serve food to persons at a table, serve from the person's left side. Remove plates from the person's right side. Serve the eldest lady first and then the other ladies, moving counterclockwise. Then serve the men counterclockwise, starting with the man next to the last lady served.

CALCULATING FOOD CONSUMPTION

Cocktail Functions—Suggested Serving Portions

Type of Event	Servings Per Person
Light Afternoon Tea	5 Pieces
Drinks and Nibbles after a Meeting	5 Pieces
Lunchtime Cocktail Reception	8 Pieces
Evening Cocktail Reception (before a dinner)	2–4 Pieces
Evening Cocktail Party (at dinnertime)— No Dinner Served	12 Pieces
Evening Cocktail Party (at dinnertime; mainly men)—No Dinner Served	15 Pieces

🖉 In addition to the above, add nibbles, such as nuts and chips or vegetable sticks.

🖉 People will consume more of anything made of shrimp. If boiled whole shrimp is one of the hors d'oeuvre, plan at least twice as many shrimp per person.

🖉 A cocktail reception at dinnertime, without dinner being served later, suggests that there will be a lot of hors d'oeuvre, and many will come expecting to make a dinner of what is served.

🖉 The best hors d'oeuvre for a cocktail reception are those that can be easily picked up by hand and eaten without a fork. Forcing guests to load a plate and hold it along with their drink glass is a common mistake that is awkward, messy, and forces the guests to search for a place to set one or the other down. The same with hors d'oeuvre that are too large or too juicy.

📖 See *cocktail party* on page 48.

Dinner Meal Portions per Person

Food	Amount
Poultry, Meat, or Fish	6 oz (170 g) of 1 main dish / 8 oz (227 g) if two or more main courses
Rice, Grains	1.5 oz (43 g) as side dish / 2 oz (57 g) if main dish such as risotto
Potatoes	5 oz (142 g)
Vegetable	4 oz (113 g)
Beans	2 oz (57 g) as side dish
Pasta (side dish)	2 oz (57 g) as side dish / 3 oz (85 g) if served as first course
Pasta (main dish)	4 oz (113 g)
Green Salad	1 oz (28 g) undressed weight
Soup	4 oz (113 g) when not main dish
Desserts	
Cake, Tart, or Pastry	1 slice
Creamy Dessert such as Pudding or Mousse	4 oz (113 g)
Ice Cream	5 oz (142 g)
When serving two of above	Reduce each by almost half

✎ Plan one plate of food per person, plus 30 percent extra of each course.

✎ Teens and those in their early twenties eat 1½ to 2 times as much as an adult group.

✎ The more dishes on the menu, the less of each is needed.

✎ Plan at least one entrée suitable for vegetarians or other special diets.

USDA Recommended Portions per Person

Food	Amount
Bread	1 slice
Cereal—Ready-to-Eat	1 oz (28 g)
Cereal—Cooked	½ cup (118 ml)
Rice or Pasta—Cooked	½ cup (118 ml)
Raw or Leafy Vegetables	1 cup (237 ml)
Vegetable Juice	¾ cup (178 ml)
Medium Apple, Banana, Orange	1
Fruit—Chopped, Cooked, or Canned	½ cup (118 ml)
Fruit—Dried	¼ cup (59 ml)
Fruit Juice	¾ cup (178 ml)
Milk or Yogurt	1 cup (237 ml)
Natural Cheese	1½ oz (42.5 g)
Processed Cheese	2 oz (57 g)
Lean Meat, Poultry, Fish—Cooked	2–3 oz (57–85 g)
Dry Beans—Cooked	½ cup (118 ml)
Egg	1
Peanut Butter	2 tablespoons (10 ml)
Nuts	1/3 cup (79 ml)
Fats, Oils, Sweets	None

Buffet Dinner Menu—Food Quantities

Course	Item	100 Persons	50 Persons
Salads	Potato Salad	25 lbs / 11.4 kg of potatoes	10 lbs / 5.3 kg of potatoes
	or Caesar Salad	15 heads of Romaine	8 heads of Romaine
	Caesar Salad Dressing	1 gal / 3.8 liters	2 qts / 1.9 liters
	or Green Salad (Lettuce Heads)	10 chopped heads	5 chopped heads
	Vinegar and Oil	1 gal / 3.8 liters	2 qts / 1.9 liters
	or 3–4 Smaller Specialty Salads	7–10 lbs / 3.2–5.3 kg each	3–5 lbs / 1.4–2.3 kg each
	Appropriate Salad Dressing	Depends on salad	Depends on salad
Side Dishes	Soup (1 cup / 250 ml) servings	6 gal / 22.7 liters	3 gal / 11.4 liters
	Rice (½ cup / 125 ml) servings	6.5 lbs / 2.9 kg raw	3.3 lbs / 1.5 kg raw
	Vegetable 1 (⅓ cup / 83 ml) servings	23 lbs / 10.4 kg frozen	12 lbs / 5.4 kg frozen
		36 lbs / 16.3 kg fresh	18 lbs / 8.2 kg fresh
	Vegetable 2 (⅓ cup / 83 ml) servings	22 lbs / 10 kg frozen	10 lbs / 4.5 kg frozen
		30 lbs / 13.6 kg fresh	15 lbs / 6.8 kg fresh
Meat Entrée	Roast Beef (boneless)	50 lbs / 22.7 kg raw	30 lbs / 13.6 kg raw
	or Carved Roast Beef (bone-in)	70 lbs / 31.8 kg raw	35 lbs / 15.9 kg raw
	or Boneless Ham (4 oz / 0.11 kg) servings	25 lbs / 11.4 kg	13 lbs / 5.9 kg
	or Turkey Breast (4 oz / 0.11 kg) servings	25 lbs / 11.4 kg cooked	13 lbs / 5.9 kg cooked
	or Carved Lamb (3 oz / 0.09 kg) servings	20 lbs / 9 kg raw	10 lbs / 4.5 kg raw
	or Chicken (1⅓ pieces per serving)	135 pieces	75 pieces
	or Hamburger (4 oz / 0.11 kg) servings	32 lbs / 14.5 kg raw	16 lbs / 7.3 kg raw
	or Casseroles (9" / 22.9 cm x 13" / 33 cm) dish	10–12 dishes	5–6 dishes

Buffet Dinner Menu (*continued*)

Course	Item	100 Persons	50 Persons
Optional/Misc.	Potato Chips	20 lbs / 9 kg	10 lbs / 4.5 kg
	Pasta (¾ cup / 187 ml) servings	10 lbs / 4.5 kg uncooked	5 lbs / 2.3 kg uncooked
	Noodles (¾ cup / 187 ml) servings	10 lbs / 4.5 kg uncooked	5 lbs / 2.3 kg uncooked
	Coffee (1 cup / 250 ml) servings	2 lbs / 0.9 kg	1 lb / 0.5 kg
	Sheet Cake (10.5" / 26.7cm x 15.5" / 39cm)	4 sheets	2 sheets

The above menu suggests basic food consumption for average eaters with some second servings. The more dishes added, the less of each is required.

Controlling the Buffet Line

🖊 Have enough lines for the number of guests. Lines too long are uncomfortable and can ruin an otherwise good event. Calling up one table after the other is also highly unrecommended because of the time it takes. Multiple lines cost a little more for service ware and staff, but are well worth it.

🖊 Set up the buffet table with a starting point. Place the dinner plates here. This will keep it from becoming a free-for-all.

🖊 After the plates, place the rolls, butter, salads, and buffet side dishes. These items fill the plate.

🖊 Consider the size of the serving utensil for each item. Use smaller utensils for items for which you want less served.

🖊 Leave some room between serving bowls so that guests can rest their plates as they move through the line.

🖊 Buffet plates are larger (11–14 inches or 28–33.5 centimeters) than typical dinner plates.

🖊 Place the featured entrée last and have a server serve each guest the appropriate portion.

🖊 If not already on the tables, have the flatware wrapped in a napkin as the final item on the buffet table so that the guests do not have to handle it while filling their plates. Or place them on the tables.

🖊 Beverages are best served at the table. If not, place on an adjoining table. Desserts are also on another table, or the main buffet can be cleared and reset for dessert.

🖊 At buffets, people tend to take more than they will eat, so plan accordingly.

📖 See *buffet* on page 30.

KEEP FOOD AT A SAFE TEMPERATURE

🖉 Foods cannot be left out on a buffet table at room temperature for long periods of time.

> Cooked, hot foods must be kept at 140° or warmer.
> Cold foods must be kept at 40° or colder.

WARNING! Outdoors, in the sun, extreme care must be taken with the duration that foods are exposed. Use smaller serving dishes that can be replenished frequently. Remove all the food immediately after serving.

🖉 Do not add food to a serving dish already being used. Replace partially empty platters with freshly filled ones.

TEA PARTY MENU

Food	6 Finger Sandwiches
	1 Scone
	4 Sweets
Tea	1 Pint / 3 Cups
	(coffee is acceptable)

Above servings are per person.

🖉 Black tea is traditional. Coffee is often sometimes offered as an alternative to tea, but it is not traditional.

🖉 The finger sandwiches and sweets should be of different types so that there is a selection. In most cases not all will be consumed.

SAFE COOKING TEMPERATURES

Food	Fahrenheit	Celsius
Beef and Veal		
Rare	140	60
Medium	160	71
Well Done	170	77
Ground	160	71
Chicken	175–180	79–82
Ground	165	74
Duck and Goose	175–180	79–82
Egg		
Fried, Coddled, Poached	Firm Yolk and White	
Sauces, Casseroles	160	71
Fish	120–135	49–58
Lamb		
Rare	140	60
Medium	160	71
Well Done	170	77
Pork		
Chops, Roast	160–165	71–74
Cured	140	60
Ground	160	71
Rabbit	180	82
Sausage	160	71
Stuffing (in or out of poultry)	180	82
Turkey		
Bone-In	180	82
Boneless	170	77
Ground	165	74

Grilling Temperature Hand Test

Temperature	Seconds
Hot (for Searing)	2
Medium Hot (for Grilling)	3
Medium (for Grilling)	4
Low (for Covered Cooking)	5
Medium Low (for Covered Cooking)	6

Hold hard 5" (12.5 cm) above cooking grate.

Helpful Charts

TRADITIONAL ANNIVERSARY GIFTS

Year		Year	
1	Paper or Plastic	13	Lace
2	Calico or Cotton	14	Ivory
3	Leather	15	Crystal
4	Silk	20	China
5	Wood	25	Silver
6	Iron	30	Pearl
7	Copper or Wool	35	Coral and Jade
8	Electrical Appliances	40	Ruby
9	Pottery	45	Sapphire
10	Tin or Aluminum	50	Gold
11	Steel	60	Diamond
12	Linen		

ANNIVERSARY NAMES

Year		Year	
1	Annual	75	Semisesquicentennial
2	Biennial	100	Centennial
3	Triennial	125	Quasquicentennial
4	Quadrennial	150	Sesquicentennial
5	Quinquennial	175	Demisemiseptcentennial
6	Sexennial	200	Bicentennial
7	Septennial	250	Semiquincentennial
8	Octennial	300	Tricentennial
9	Novennial	350	Semiseptcentennial
10	Decennial	400	Quadricentennial
11	Undecennial	500	Quincentennial
12	Duodecennial	600	Sexcentennial
13	Tredecennial	700	Septcentennial
14	Quattuordecennial	800	Octocentennial
15	Quindecennial	900	Nonacentennial
20	Vigintennial	1,000	Millennial
50	Semicentennial		

BIRTHSTONES AND FLOWERS

Month	Stone	Flower
January	Garnet	Snowdrop
February	Amethyst	Primrose
March	Aquamarine, Jasper, or Bloodstone	Violet
April	Diamond	Daisy
May	Emerald	Hawthorn
June	Pearl or Moonstone	Rose
July	Ruby	Water Lily
August	Sardonyx, Peridot, or Carnelian	Poppy
September	Sapphire	Morning Glory
October	Opal	Marigold
November	Topaz	Chrysanthemum
December	Turquoise or Lapis Lazuli	Holly

COLOR WHEEL

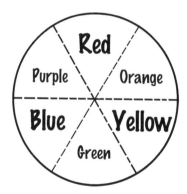

✏ All paint colors, or hues, can be created by mixing various portions of the three primary colors of red, blue, and yellow.

📋 See *color* on page 55 and *color wheel* on page 57.

DECIBEL (dB) LOUDNESS COMPARISONS

Noise	Decibel Level (dB)	OSHA Permissible Duration
Weakest Sound Heard	0	
Quiet Library Whisper	30	
Normal Conversation (@ 3–5'/1–1.5 m)	60–70	
Normal Piano	60–70	8 Hours
Telephone Dial Tone	80	
City Traffic (inside car)	85	8 Hours
Train Whistle (@ 500'/150 m) or Truck Traffic	90	8 Hours
Level at which Sustained Exposure May Result in Hearing Loss	90	
iPod/MP3 (with headsets) set at 50% volume	50–60	4 Hours
Motorcycle/Snowmobile	100	2 Hours
Power Mower (@ 3'/1 m)	107	1½ Hour
Power Saw (@ 3'/1 m)	107	1½ Hour
Rock Concert	115	½ Hour
Symphonic Concert (peak moments)	120–137	¼ Hour
Amplified Band (@ 4–6' /1.2–1.8 m)	120	¼ Hour
Pain Begins	125	
Pneumatic Hammer/Riveter	125	0 Hour
Loudest Recommended Exposure WITH Hearing Protection	140	
Jet Engine (@ 100'/30.5 m) or Gun Blast	140	0 Hour
Rock Concert (peak moments)	150	0 Hour
Death of Hearing Tissue	180	
Loudest Sound Possible	194	

🖉 **OSHA** is the U.S. federal agency, Occupational Safety and Health Administration, responsible for setting and enforcing safety standards.

 See *decibel* on page 74 and *OSHA* on page 189.

PROJECTION AND SCREEN ASPECT RATIOS

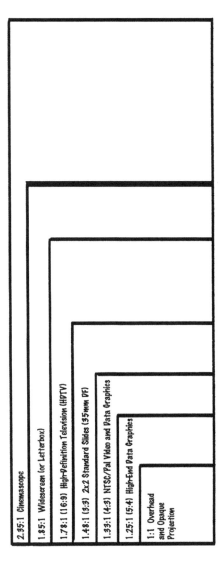

2.35:1 Cinemascope

1.85:1 Widescreen (or Letterbox)

1.78:1 (16:9) High-Definition Television (HDTV)

1.48:1 (3:3) 2x2 Standard Slides (35mm DF)

1.33:1 (4:3) NTSC/Pal Video and Data Graphics

1.25:1 (5:4) High-End Data Graphics

1:1 Overhead and Opaque Projection

✎ Computer screens vary greatly in their aspect ratio. Be aware as you plan visuals to fit the required aspect ratio for how the images will be displayed.

📄 See *aspect ratio* on page 11.

Invitations

FORMAL INVITATIONS

> Mr. and Mrs. Thomas Billings
> Request the pleasure of
> Mr. and Mrs. James North's
> Company at dinner
> On Thursday, July the fourth
> At eight o'clock
> 1824 West Lincoln Avenue
>
> R.S.V.P.

Properly phrased formal invitation (handwritten or printed in script font).

> Mr. and Mrs. James North
> accept with pleasure
> the kind invitation of
> Mr. and Mrs. Thomas Billings
> for dinner
> on Thursday, the fourth of July
> at eight o'clock

Proper acceptance of a formal invitation when R.S.V.P. is required
(handwritten or printed in script font).

Mr. and Mrs. James North
Regret that they are unable to accept
the kind invitation of
Mr. and Mrs. Thomas Billings
for Thursday, the fourth of July

Regrets to a formal invitation (when R.S.V.P. is required).

Mrs. Samuel Louis Simpson
Mrs. Charles James White
Ms. Jayne Semour
request the pleasure of your company
at dinner
Wednesday, the first of December
at half after eight o'clock
1284 Spring Street

R.S.V.P.
Mrs. Samuel Louis Simpson

Multiple host formal invitation (calligraphy).

The Beta Chapter

of

The Liberty Society

requests the pleasure of your company

at a reception

on Monday, the thirteenth of June

at two o'clock

at the Society Hall Ballroom

1855 Franklin Avenue

Formal printed invitation sent by an organization.

🖊 Notice the phrasing of the sentences so that each line is a complete thought, name, or title.

🖊 Formal invitations are always either handwritten in calligraph style (calligraphy) or engraved by a printer. Both techniques are done in black ink only.

📑 **Also see *embossed* on page 88 and *calligraphy* on page 35.**

CORPORATE FORMAL INVITATION

For a Multiple-Function Event

You and a guest are cordially invited to attend

RM CORPORATION'S

Gala Celebration

Commemorating the Opening
of our new store

PRESS PREVIEW
Tuesday, August 22
8:00 PM

GRAND OPENING CEREMONIES
Wednesday, August 23
6:00 PM

COCKTAIL RECEPTION
Immediately following Ceremonies

CELEBRATION DINNER
Grand Hotel Ballroom
8:00 PM

R.S.V.P.   Informal

For a Single-Event Function

The Tripp Company
requests
the pleasure of you company at our

Office Complex Groundbreaking Ceremony

to be held on
Wednesday, March 9, 2011, at one o'clock
1822 Riverside Drive
Burbank, California

Reception immediately following

R.S.V.P. by the first of March

🖉 It is appropriate to include a logo in a business invitation.

WEDDING INVITATIONS

For a Wedding Hosted by the Bride's Parents

Mr. and Mrs. Peter Horne
request the honor of your presence
at the marriage of their daughter
Stephanie Lynn

to

Mr. Ryan Sean Powers
Saturday, the fifth of October
Two thousand and eleven
at six o'clock
Saint Charles Church
Toluca Lake, California
and afterward at the reception
Ledge Hall
4110 Riverside Drive

R.S.V.P.

For a Wedding Hosted by the Bride and Groom

Stephanie Lynn Horne
and
Ryan Sean Powers
would be delighted
to have you share
in the joy of their marriage
Saturday, the fifth of October
at six o'clock
Saint Charles Church
Toluca Lake, California
and afterward at the reception
Ledge Hall
4110 Riverside Drive

R.S.V.P.

All wedding invitations must be composed in either hand calligraphy or a classic engraved typestyle.

For a Wedding with the Ceremony and Reception at the Same Location

Stephanie Lynn Horne
and
Ryan Sean Powers
invite you to witness our vows
and join us afterward for dining and dancing
among the pines
Saturday, the fifth of October
six o'clock in the evening
Tavern Bay Point
Lake Arrowhead, California

R.S.V.P.

Reception Card

Reception immediately following the ceremony
Arrowhead Village Pavilion
200 Lake Road
Lake Arrowhead, California

R.S.V.P.

Should it be preferred to have the reception information on a different card, eliminate the last three lines and the R.S.V.P. and enclose a separate reception card as below.

FORMAL INVITATION SCHEDULE

Time in Advance	Activity
5 Months	Mail a card asking the guest to hold the date. State that an invitation is forthcoming.
4 Weeks	Mail invitations.
10 Days	If an R.S.V.P. is required, call those who have not responded.
5 Days	Call those who expressed uncertainty. Ask for final commitment.

🖉 Basically, give those you are inviting a comfortable amount of time to say yes or no.

🖉 An invitation arriving very late gives recipients the impression that they were invited as an afterthought or replacement.

🖉 Expect up to 10 percent last-minute attrition due to illness and emergencies.

CLASSIC ENGRAVED TYPESTYLES (FONTS)

English Script   Mr. and Mrs. John O'Hagan

Edwardian Script   Miss Anna Aguilar

ENGRAVERS MT   DR. AND MRS. DAVID SCHMITT

Big Caslon   Mr. Robert Singer Esq.

🖉 A tissue over the engraved lettering keeps the ink from smudging.

OTHER INVITATIONS

Multiple-Function / Multiple-Guest List Event Invitation Packet

Individual invitations for each event that nestle into a cover packet allow the packet to be inserted with any one, or all, of the invites intended for the individual invitees. For example, many may be invited to the grand opening ceremony, but only a select few to the dinner.

🖊 This packet can be done in the formal style or any informal style as long as it is the same throughout the entire packet.

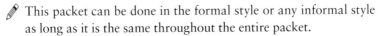

See *invitation—multi-function events* on page 149.

FORM OF ADDRESS

Using the proper manner of address is extremely important when sending an invitation or for any communication with other individuals, particularly with those holding an official or legally recognized title. Many titles have been established by tradition or law.

In the Terms and Tips section, addressing people by age and marriage status is described. The chart on the following pages is a guide to the proper forms of address for those in American government, medicine, academia, and religion. Many of the titles change in other countries and should be researched prior to any communication. The following Table of Titles and Proper Forms of Address excludes monarchies.

See *form of address* on page 116.

TABLE OF TITLES AND PROPER FORMS OF ADDRESS

	The President	The Vice President	The President's Spouse	Former President
Spoken Greeting	First: Mr./Madam President Then: Sir/Ma'am	First: Mr./Madam Vice President; Then: Sir/Mad'am or Mr./Mrs./Ms. [Last Name]	Mr./Mrs./Ms. [Full Name]	First: Mr. President; Then: Mr./Mrs./ Ms. [Last Name]
Formal Letter Salutation	Dear Mr./Madam President:	Dear Mr./Madam Vice President:	Dear Mr./Mrs./Ms. [Full Name]	Dear Mr./Mrs./Ms. [Last Name]:
Envelope Address	The President The White House Washington, D.C.	The Vice President The White House Washington, D.C.	Mr./Mrs./Ms. [Full Name] The White House Washington, D.C.	The Honorable [Full Name] Office Address
Formal Letter Close	I have the honor to remain most respectfully yours,	Very truly yours,	Very truly yours,	Very truly yours,
Informal Letter Close	Very respectfully yours,	Sincerely yours, or Faithfully yours,	Sincerely yours,	Sincerely yours, or Faithfully yours,
Formal Introduction	The President of the United States (when abroad add: "of America") or The President or President [Last Name]	The Vice President of the United States	Varies by preference. If being introduced for a speech, it could be descriptive: the First Lady Martha Washington	The Honorable [Full Name], the former President of the United States
Place Card	The President	The Vice President For Vice President's Spouse: Mr./Mrs./Ms. [Last Name]	Mr./Mrs./Ms. [Last Name]	Mr./Mrs./Ms. [Last Name]

Table of Titles and Proper Forms of Address (*continued*)

	Chief Justice, Supreme Court	Associate Justice, Supreme Court	Cabinet Members	Federal Judge
Spoken Greeting	Mr./Madam Chief Justice or Mr./Mrs./Ms. [Last Name]	Mr./Madam Justice or Justice [Last Name]	Mr./Madam Secretary or Secretary [Last Name] or Mr./Mrs./Ms. [Last Name]	Justice or Judge [Last Name] Madam Justice or Judge [Last Name]
Formal Letter Salutation	Dear Mr./Madam Chief Justice:	Dear Justice [Last Name]:	Dear Mr./Madam Secretary:	Dear Judge [Last Name]:
Envelope Address	The Chief Justice The Supreme Court Washington, D.C.	Justice [Last Name] The Supreme Court Washington, D.C.	The Honorable [Full Name] The Secretary of [Department] Washington, D.C.	The Honorable [Full Name] U.S. Court of [Name] Address
Formal Letter Close	Very truly yours,	Very truly yours,	Very truly yours,	Very truly yours,
Informal Letter Close	Sincerely yours, or Faithfully yours,	Sincerely yours, or Faithfully yours,	Sincerely yours, or Faithfully yours,	Sincerely yours, or Faithfully yours,
Formal Introduction	The Honorable [Full Name], the Chief Justice of the Supreme Court of the United States or The Chief Justice	The Honorable [Full Name], Associate Justice of the Supreme Court of the United States or Justice [Last Name]	The Secretary of [Department] or The Honorable [Full Name] The Secretary of [Department] of the United States	The Honorable [Full Name] or Mr./Madam Justice [Last Name]
Place Card	The Chief Justice	Mr./Mrs./Ms. Justice [Last Name]	The Secretary of [Department]	Mr./Mrs./Ms. [Last Name]

Table of Titles and Proper Forms of Address (*continued*)

	U.S. Senator	U.S. Speaker of the House	Members of the U.S. House	American Ambassador
Spoken Greeting	First: Senator [Last Name] Then: Senator Sir/Madam	Mr./Madam Speaker	Mr./Mrs./Ms. [Last Name]	Mr./Madam Ambassador
Formal Letter Salutation	Dear Senator [Last Name]:	Dear Mr./Madam Speaker:	Dear Mr./Mrs./Ms. [Last Name]:	Dear Mr./Madam Ambassador:
Envelope Address	The Honorable [Full Name] United States Senate Washington, D.C. or District Office	The Honorable [Full Name] The Speaker of the House of Representatives Washington, D.C.	The Honorable [Full Name] United States House of Representatives Washington, D.C.	The Honorable [Full Name] Ambassador of the United States American Embassy, Address
Formal Letter Close	Very truly yours,	Very truly yours, or Sincerely,	Very truly yours,	Very truly yours,
Informal Letter Close	Sincerely yours, or Faithfully yours,	Sincerely yours, or Faithfully yours,	Sincerely yours, or Faithfully yours,	Sincerely yours, or Faithfully yours,
Formal Introduction	The Honorable Senator [Last Name], Senator from [State Name], or Senator [Last Name]	The Speaker of the House of Representatives	The Honorable [Last Name] Representative from [State Name] or Congressman/ Congresswoman [Last Name]	The Honorable [Full Name] Ambassador of the United States of America to [Country Name]
Place Card	Senator [Last Name]	The Speaker	Congressman/ Congresswoman [Last Name]	The Ambassador of the United States [Country Optional]

Table of Titles and Proper Forms of Address (*continued*)

	Ambassador of Foreign Country	State Governor	State Legislator	Mayor
Spoken Greeting	Excellency or Mr./Madam Ambassador	First: Governor [Last Name] Then: Sir/Madam	Mr./Mrs./Ms. [Last Name]	Mayor [Last Name] or Mr./Madam Mayor or Your Honor
Formal Letter Salutation	Excellency: or Dear Mr./Madam Ambassador:	Dear Governor [Last Name]:	Dear Mr./Mrs./Ms. [Last Name]:	Dear Mayor [Last Name]:
Envelope Address	His/Her Excellency [Full Name] / The Ambassador of [Country Name] / The Embassy of [Country Name] / Address	The Honorable [Full Name] / Governor of [State Name] / Address	The Honorable [Full Name] / Address	The Honorable [Full Name] / Mayor of [City] / Address
Formal Letter Close	Very truly yours,	Very truly yours,	Very truly yours,	Very truly yours,
Informal Letter Close	Sincerely yours, or Faithfully yours,	Sincerely yours,	Sincerely yours,	Sincerely yours,
Formal Introduction	His/Her Excellency, the Honorable [Full Name], the Ambassador of [Country Name]	The Honorable [Full Name], Governor of the State of [State Name] or The Governor of [State Name]	The Honorable [Full Name]	The Honorable [Full Name], Mayor of [City] (or "of the City of [City]") or Mayor [Last Name]
Place Card	The Ambassador of [Country Name]	The Governor of [State Name]	[State Name] Senator [Full Name] or Assemblyman/ Assemblywoman [Full Name]	The Honorable [Full Name]

Table of Titles and Proper Forms of Address (*continued*)

	Judge	Episcopal Bishop	Clergyman, Protestant	The Pope
Spoken Greeting	Your Honor	Bishop [Last Name]	Reverend [Last Name]	Your Holiness or Most Holy Father
Formal Letter Salutation	Dear Judge [Last Name]:	Dear Bishop [Last Name]:	Dear Reverend [Last Name]:	Your Holiness: or Most Holy Father:
Envelope Address	The Honorable [Full Name] [Appropriate Court and Division] Address	The Right Reverend [Full Name], [Academic Degrees] Bishop of [Diocese] Address	The Reverend [Full Name] [Name of Church] Address	His Holiness, Pope [Papal Name] Vatican City, Italy
Formal Letter Close	Very truly yours,	Respectfully yours,	Sincerely yours, or Faithfully yours,	Your Holiness's most humble servant,
Informal Letter Close	Sincerely yours,	Sincerely yours, or Faithfully yours,	Sincerely yours,	Faithfully yours,
Formal Introduction	The Honorable Full Name], Judge of the [Appropriate Court and Division]	The Right Reverend [Full Name], The Bishop of [Diocese]	Reverend or Dr. (if degree is held) [Full Name]	His Holiness, Pope [Papal Name] or The Pope or The Holy Father or The Pontiff
Place Card	The Honorable [Full Name]	Bishop [Last Name]	Reverend or Doctor (if degree is held) [Last Name]	His Holiness, The Pope

Table of Titles and Proper Forms of Address (*continued*)

	Cardinal	Bishop, Roman Catholic	Monsignor, Roman Catholic	Priest, Roman Catholic
Spoken Greeting	Your Eminence or Cardinal [Last Name]	Your Excellency or Bishop/Archbishop [Last Name]	Monsignor [Last Name] or Monsignor	Father [Last Name] or Father
Formal Letter Salutation	Your Eminence: or Dear Cardinal [Last Name]:	Your Excellency: or Most Reverend Sir: or Dear Bishop/Archbishop [Last Name]:	Reverend Monsignor: or Dear Monsignor [Last Name]:	Reverend Father: or Father [Last Name]:
Envelope Address	His Eminence, Cardinal [Full Name] Archbishop of [Archdiocese] Address	The Most Reverend [Last Name] Bishop/Archbishop of [Diocese] Address	The Reverend [Full Name] Address	The Reverend [Full Name], [Initials of his Order] Address
Formal Letter Close	I have the honor to remain, your Eminence's humble servant,	I have the honor to remain your obedient servant,	Respectfully yours,	I remain, Reverend Father, yours faithfully,
Informal Letter Close	Faithfully yours,	Faithfully yours,	Respectfully yours,	Faithfully yours,
Formal Introduction	His Eminence, Cardinal [Last Name]	Bishop/Archbishop [Last Name] or His Excellency (with or without [Full Name])	Monsignor [Last Name]	The Reverend [Last Name] or Father [Last Name]
Place Card	His Eminence, Cardinal [Last Name]	Bishop/Archbishop [Last Name]	The Right Reverend Monsignor [Last Name]	Reverend Father [Last Name] or Father [Last Name]

Table of Titles and Proper Forms of Address (*continued*)

	Mormon	Rabbi	Cantor	Imam
Spoken Greeting	Mr. [Last Name]	Rabbi [Last Name] or Dr. (if degree is held) [Last Name] or Rabbi	Cantor [Last Name]	Imam [Name]
Formal Letter Salutation	Dear Mr. [Last Name]:	Dear Rabbi [Last Name]: or Dear Rabbi:	Dear Cantor [Last Name]:	Dear Imam [Name]:
Envelope Address	Mr. [Full Name] President of [Name of Temple] Address	Rabbi [Full Name], (Academic Degrees) Address	Cantor [Full Name] Address	Imam [Full Name] [Masque Name] Address
Formal Letter Close	Respectfully yours,	Sincerely yours,	Sincerely yours,	Sincerely yours, or Inshallah,
Informal Letter Close	Faithfully yours,	Sincerely yours,	Sincerely yours,	Inshallah,
Formal Introduction	Mr. [Last Name], the President of [Name of Temple]	Rabbi [Last Name], of [Name of Temple/ Congregation]	Cantor [Last Name], of [Name of Temple or Congregation]	Imam [Full Name] of the [Name] Masque
Place Card	Mr. [Full Name]	Rabbi [Last Name], Doctor [Last Name]	Cantor [Last Name]	Imam [Name]

Table of Titles and Proper Forms of Address (*continued*)

	University Professor	Physician	Dentist
Spoken Greeting	Professor or Dr. (if degree is held) [Last Name]	Dr. [Last Name]	Dr. [Last Name]
Formal Letter Salutation	Dear Professor: or Dear Professor [Last Name]: or Dr. (if degree is held) [Last Name]:	Dear Dr. [Last Name]:	Dear Dr. [Last Name]:
Envelope Address	Professor [Full Name] or Dr. (if degree is held) [Last Name]: Address	[Full Name], M.D. or Dr. [Full Name] Address	[Full Name], D.D.S. or Dr. [Full Name] Address
Formal Letter Close	Very truly yours,	Very truly yours,	Very truly yours,
Informal Letter Close	Sincerely yours,	Sincerely yours,	Sincerely yours,
Formal Introduction	Professor or Dr. (if degree is held) [Last Name]	Dr. [Last Name]	Dr. [Last Name]
Place Card	Doctor (if degree is held) [Last Name] or Professor [Last Name]	Doctor [Last Name]	Doctor [Last Name]

Linens

STANDARD TABLE LINEN SIZES

Linen Use	Linen Sizes
Round Tables	70" Round (177.8 cm)
	78" Round (198.12 cm)
	90" Round (228.6 cm)
	108" Round (274.32 cm)
	120" Round (304.8 cm)
	128" Round (328.12 cm)
	132" Round (335.28 cm)
Square Tables	54" Square (137.16 cm sq)
	70" Square (177.8 cm sq)
	85" Square (215.9 cm sq)
Rectangular Tables	60" × 102" (152.4 x 259.08 cm)
	60" × 126" (152.4 x 320 cm)
	90" × 132" (228.6 x 335.28 cm)
	90" × 156" (228.6 x 396.24 cm)
Table Runners	39" × 88" (99 x 223.52 cm)
	14" × 108" (35.56 x 274.32 cm)
Napkins	17" Square (43.18 cm sq)
	20" Square (50.8 cm sq)
Table Skirting	
8' table	21' long (6.4 m)
6' table	17' long (5.18 m)
Schoolroom table	14' long (4.27 m)

TABLE LINEN SELECTION CHART

Size/Shape	Linen Options
  24"–30" Cocktail Table (tall) 4–5 Comfortably Stand 24"–30" Cocktail Table (short) Seats 4	132"-round linen covers the entire table and is perfect length when cinched in middle. Ideal for formal events. 120"-round linen covers the entire table and hangs to the floor. Also for formal events. 90"-round or square sheer over 120"-round basecloth adds great look. 60"-square sheer over 120"-round basecloth allows the smaller overlay to hang beautifully over the table sides. 70"-round linen hangs close to the ground. 78"-round linen almost touches the ground.
24" × 24" Square Cocktail Seats 4	70"-square linen hangs nicely with 23" side drop.
30" × 30" Seats 4	85"-square linen hangs nicely with 27" side drop. 70"-square linen is less formal with 20" side drop. 55"-square linen at an angle over either of the above basecloths has a pleasant effect.

Table Linen Selection Chart (*continued*)

Size/Shape   *Linen Options*

30" Round
Seats 4

90"-round linen is the perfect length to hang to floor.
60"-round linen provides a short 15" drop on side. Can
    be used over a 90" round basecloth.
60"-square linen will create a 17" side drop.

36" Round
Seats 4

90"-round linen will create a 27" drop over the side.
108"-round linen is long enough to create a puddle on
    the floor.
60"-square linen will create a 14" side drop.

48" Round
Seats 5–6

90"-round linen will have a 21" drop over the side.
108"-round linen will hang to the floor. Ideal for formal
    event.
60"-square linen will have an 8" drop over the side. Use
    over a 90"-round basecloth.

54" Round
Seats 6–7

108"-round linen will create a 37" drop over the side.
120"-round linen will slightly puddle on the floor.
90"-round linen will have an 18" drop. Ideal with a 120"
    round basecloth.
60"-square linen creates a 6" drop. Should be used with
    120"-round basecloth.

Size/Shape   *Linen Options*

60" Round
Seats 6–8

108"-round linen will have a 27" drop over the side.
132"-round linen is long enough for a slight puddle on floor.
90"-round linen will create a 15" drop over side.
60"-square linen decorative top will reach the table edge.

72" Round
Seats 8–10

120"-round linen will crop 24" over edge.
132"-round linen will hang to the floor.
108"-round linen will create an 18" drop over edge.
90"-round linen will create a 9" drop over edge and is ideal over 132" basecloth.
60"-square linen make decorative frame for centerpiece.

6' Banquet Table
Seats 6

90" × 132"-rectangular linen creates a drop that hangs close to the floor on all sides.
132"-round linen will fully cover with two sides puddled under table.

8' Banquet Table
Seats 8

90" × 156"-rectangular linen will perfectly fit the table hanging to the floor on all sides.
60", 90", 108", 120", and 132" rounds can be used over the 90" × 156" basecloth.

TABLE SKIRTING OR WALL FABRIC PLEATING TECHNIQUES

Simple pleating can be achieved quickly by using a long roll of fabric cut to the required width. By using staples or pins to fasten against a table edge, start at one end and fold the fabric back and forth, fastening each pleat as it is made. The same can be done to cover a wall or frame used as a *backdrop*.

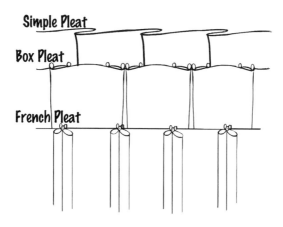

Simple Pleat

Box Pleat

French Pleat

TRADITIONAL TABLECLOTH CORNER FOLD

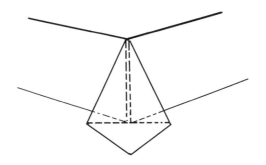

TABLECLOTH SWAGGING

Swagging adds color and interest to the look of the tables and can be achieved quickly and inexpensively.

Under tablecloth

Section off the tablecloth

Top tablecloth

Place the top cloth of contrasting color over the undercloth and section it for the number of swags desired. The larger the table, the more swags necessary. Then follow one of the instructions below.

Rosette Swag

Gather the tablecloth into tight ponytails with a rubberband

Fold the ponytail lengthwise

Roll the ponytail into a rose and secure with a pin

Pull the fabric between the rosettes loose

Bunting Swag

Attach the hem to the lip of the table with a pin so the fabric between gathers hangs. Adorn the spot with a tassel ribbon or flowers

Teadrop Swag

Gather fabric and fix into ponytails with pre-tied bows

CHAIR COVER VARIATIONS

Chair Sash   **Cover with Knot**   **Cover with Sash**   **Bag Style Cover**

STANDARD NAPKIN FOLDS

Formal Dinners

The simple fold of a monogrammed white napkin is most elegant.

Decorative Folds

Table Edge Fold

This is the simplest and quickest of the napkin folds.
  1. Lay the napkin in front of you and fold the top edge to the bottom.

  2. Fold the top right corner and gently fold it to the lower middle. Do not press the fold.

  3. Fold the top left corner and fold it to the lower middle. Do not press the fold.

  4. Pull the sides forward and stand the napkin. It may take a little fluffing of the folds.

For all napkin folds it is helpful to use well-pressed linen with a slight amount of starch.

Bishop's Hat Fold

1. Lay the napkin down square in front of you.

2. Fold the napkin in half with the open end toward you.

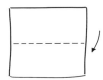

3. Fold the top right corner down to the center and the bottom left corner up to the center.

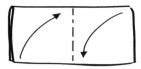

4. Flip the napkin over.

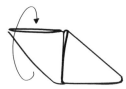

5. Rotate the napkin about 45° counterclockwise so that the folded edges are horizontal.

6. Fold the bottom half of the napkin up so that the top edge lies along the other top edge.

7. Open the triangle on the left side, pointing it down, and then reach underneath the napkin and pull out the flap on the right. You should have two points facing down.

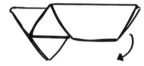

8. Raise the furthest left and gently tuck the point's end underneath the right triangle.

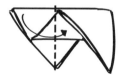

9. Flip the napkin over so the points are away from you.

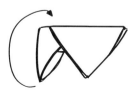

10. Raise the furthermost right point up and gently tuck its end into the other triangle.

11. Open up the hat and press the material inside down to fill it out, making the hat circular.

Water Lily Fold

Unlike the others that stand up, the fold lies nicely on the plate. A small *favor*, flower, company *logo*, or even a small bottle of champagne can be placed in the center.

1. Open the napkin out completely in front of you.

2. Fold all corners into the center.

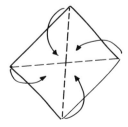

3. Again, fold all corners into the center.

4. Turn the entire napkin over and fold the corners into the center again.

5. Now reach under each corner and fold up and out the triangular point to form a petal.

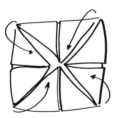 

6. After all corners have been made into petals, additional petals can be created by reaching under the area between the petals and pulling up the remaining points.

Bud Fold

This easy-to-do fold looks great on the plate.

1. Lay the napkin out flat in front of you and fold the opposite corners to meet each other.

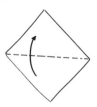

2. Fold the left corner to the top and then repeat with the right corner.

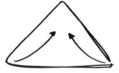

3. Fold the bottom points up to about $1/3$ the distance to the top.

4. Fold the same points back down to the baseline of the napkin.

5. Flip the napkin over.

6. Pick up the left point and roll it over, tucking it into the pocket and the right side so that the cloth forms a circle.

7. Stand it up and pull down the points on each side just a ways to form small flaps on each side.

Silverware Wrap Fold

1. Lay the napkin face down.

2. Fold the napkin from top to bottom in half so that the open end is toward you.

3. Fold the left side to the right so the napkin is in quarters.

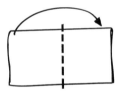

4. Rotate the napkin so that the open corner is facing away and to the right. Then roll the topmost layer of napkin diagonally down so that backside of the roll is in the center and press it flat.

5. Roll the second layer until it meets the first and then the third to the second, and flatten all.

6. Turn the napkin over.

7. Fold the right side toward the left about one-third of the way and press it down.

8. Fold the left side toward the right about halfway.

9. Flip it over and insert silverware.

Other Napkin Treatments

Napkins can add greatly to accenting the theme of the event. The style, color, and pattern of the fabric, how it is secured or decorated, and how it is placed on the table all add visual interest.

Tied with a bow and adorned with dried flowers or berry stems.

A logo or event charm tied to a rolled napkin.

Napkin rings are the simplest treatment. Rings are available in unlimited styles, materials, and prices.

Place Settings and Seating Charts

THE FORMAL DINNER

✏ The bottom edge of the plate and all flatware is placed in a line one inch from the table's edge.

✏ A formal dinner is always served one course at a time.

Progressive Steps of the Meal

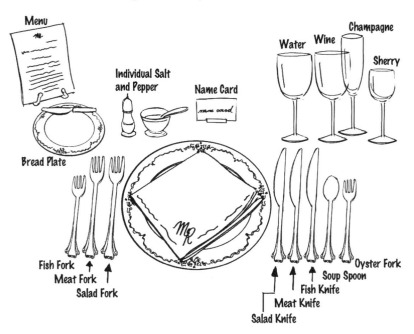

The complete place setting at the start of the dinner.

First Course—Appetizer (or Starter)

A small morsel served first, such as caviar, smoked egg, or as illustrated above, oysters. The appropriate *flatware* for this dish is placed to the right of the soup spoon. The serving is brought in on its own dish and placed on the main dish. When the course is completed the appetizer dish is removed along with the used flatware.

🖋 The flatware is used from the outside in.

🖋 Crystal stemware is to be used. The water goblet is placed above the knife-point of the innermost knife and the wine, champagne, and sherry glasses are placed to the right.

Second Course—Soup

The soup is placed on the main plate in an appropriate bowl or tureen. When the soup is finished, the bowl is removed along with the spoon.

Third Course—Fish

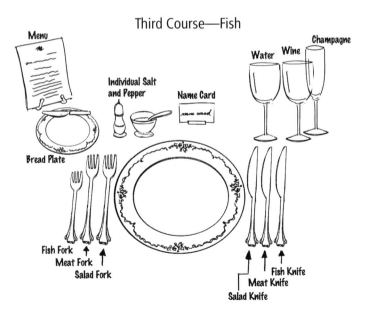

Menu

Individual Salt and Pepper

Name Card

Water Wine Champagne

Bread Plate

Fish Fork
Meat Fork
Salad Fork

Fish Knife
Meat Knife
Salad Knife

After the fish course, a small amount of fruit *sorbet* is often served, intended to clear the palate before the meat course. It is served in a tiny bowl with a small spoon. The bowl and spoon are removed before the main course is served.

Fourth Course—Meat (Main Course)

The meat, or main course, is served on the main dish. The meat is placed on the dish first, followed by a vegetable or other side items.

Sometimes there are two meat courses. For example, one may be beef and a second game.

At the completion of the meat course, the main plate is removed along with the used flatware.

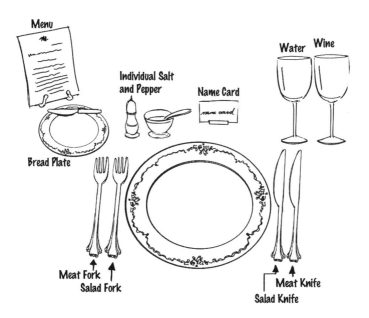

Fifth Course—Salad

The salad is placed on its own plate on top of a second main plate.

 The sequence of serving salad sometimes changes. In very formal dinners it is served after the entrée. Sometimes salad substitutes as the soup serving.

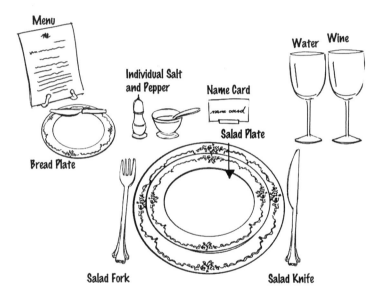

When the salad course is complete, the salad plate, all remaining flatware, and the salt and pepper are removed. The water and wine glasses are replaced with a fresh glass for port or another sweet dessert wine.

A finger bowl on a lace doily and small plate is placed on the main plate to rinse fingers. Shortly, the waiter moves the finger bowl to the side in preparation for the dessert service.

Sixth Course—Dessert

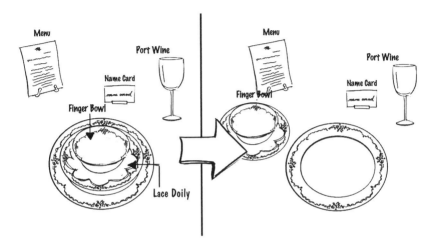

The plate with the dessert is placed on the main dish. Dessert plates vary widely depending on the type of dessert. The appropriate flatware is placed next to the dish. At the completion of the dessert, all dishes and flatware are removed. Only the wine glass remains to be refilled.

🖉 A *liqueur* may be served in an appropriate glass instead of the wine (in which case the wine glass is removed).

🖉 Cups on saucers may be placed on the right side of the dessert and coffee or tea poured, or it can be held until after the cordial serving.

🖉 Often a formal table will also be set with several *compotes* of nuts, candied fruits, or mints. These are passed at this point of the meal. An assortment of cheeses and crackers may also be brought to the table.

POSITIONS AT A FORMAL SOCIAL DINNER BY RANK

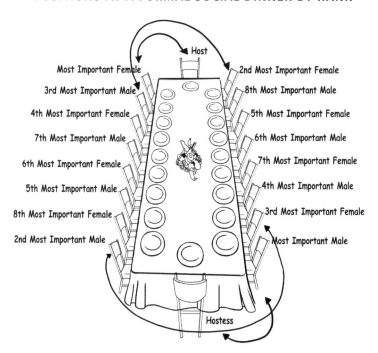

✎ Arrows indicate who walks into dinner together. Typically it is the host with the most important female, the hostess with the most important male, the second-most-important male with the third-most-important female, the third-most-important male with the second-most-important female. Typically it is only the top three or four couples.

✎ The rules change should the dinner be without spouses. The most important guest is on the host's right and the next-most on the host's left. From there they are placed generally in the same sequence as above.

THE INFORMAL DINNER

Rules are meant to be broken. For informal place settings, dress the place setting up or down and mix the styles of wine/water glasses, keeping one larger than the other. Mixing a standard glass with an antique style and adding unique accents such as tiny salt and pepper shakers or colorful place mats all add a personal touch and visual interest.

Place setting for an informal dinner.

Creative casual dinner place setting.

CLASSIC FLATWARE PATTERNS

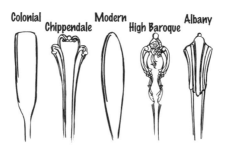

POSITIONS AT A HEAD TABLE

🖉 Prearrange the members of the head table prior to their entering the room so that they move onto the dais at the same time in order.

🖉 For a corporate event, substitute the ranked executive for hosts and the speakers and guests in honored guest positions.

🖉 Technically the dais is the platform under the table, but commonly the reference is to both the platform and the people on it.

📕 See *head table* on page 132.

BANQUET SEATING CHART

Make a chart with the layout of all the tables. Take each guest's name and attach it with tape to a chair position at the appropriate table. Cancellations, or last-minute additional attendees, require constant changes to the place assignments. Using tape permits changing the name's placement right up to the very last minute when no-shows are evident.

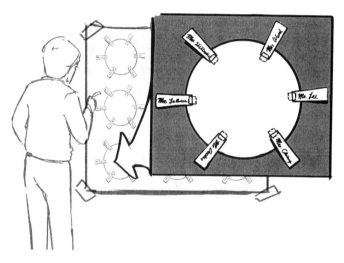

✎ Start with a chart indicating the table placement in the room in relation to the head table, stage, etc. Then affix names printed on small strips of paper to each chair location with a removable adhesive so that they can be moved around with each change. There will be many changes right down to the last minute. This technique enables one to see where each person is and the overall dynamics of everyone in the room.

WEDDINGS

Positions at a Christian Wedding

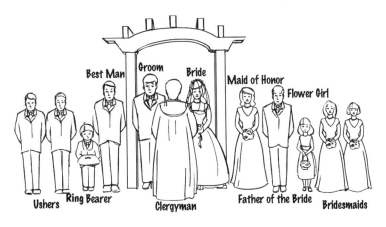

Positions at a Jewish Wedding

Rehearsal Dinner Seating Positions

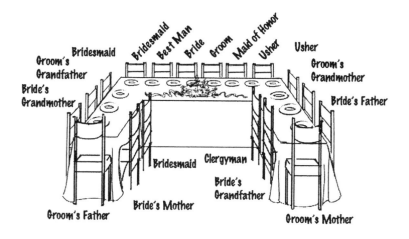

Traditional Seating Positions at the Bride and Groom's Table at the Reception

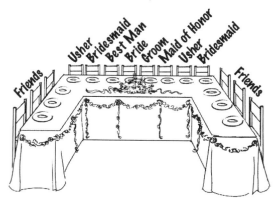

🖉 The table can be either straight or U-shaped, as illustrated.

Positions at the Parents' Table at the Reception

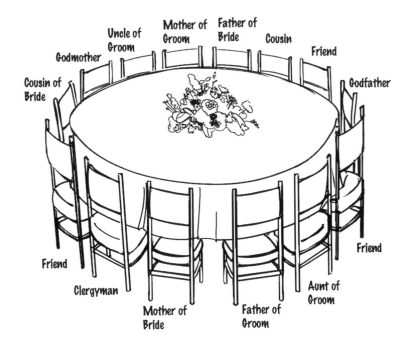

✎ Traditionally the table is round. Sometimes two tables can be used if the families are large, or if the two families are not friendly. In the situation of divorced parents, often each has their own table with selected guests.

✎ Position the cake on its own table for all to see during dinner and so that it can be viewed during the cake cutting by the bride and groom.

📑 **See page 429 for Wedding Party Room Layout.**

Press

A WELL-PLANNED PUBLICITY PHOTO

Organization logo

Eye contact with viewer

Tightly positioned people

Reason for photo

Photo Courtesy of the *Magazine of Sigma Chi.*

This picture tells the viewer a lot. Notice above that the viewer can see the people well, plus the award being given, plus a logo for the organization giving the event, and that it is a black-tie event. Also the subjects are looking directly at the viewer, making strong visual contact. The *photo caption* can be something like, "Mr. Campbell Zane was honored last night with the Notable Award at a banquet held in his honor. Mr. Broderick Case (left), president of the Youth Organization and last year's recipient, presented the award."

PRESS KIT

Includes photos, press release, biographies of key people, etc., all in a folder.

See *press kit* on page 210.

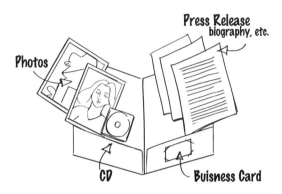

SMALL PRESS CONFERENCE SETUP

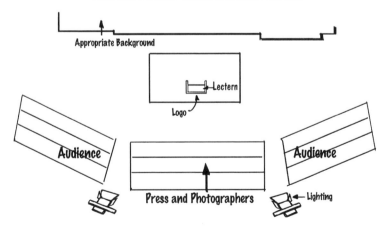

See *press conference* on page 208.

MAJOR PRESS EVENT AND POLITICAL RALLY SETUP

Important press events are staged more for the press, and the very large audience they will reach through the media, than the audience in attendance, so plan the setup to meet press needs.

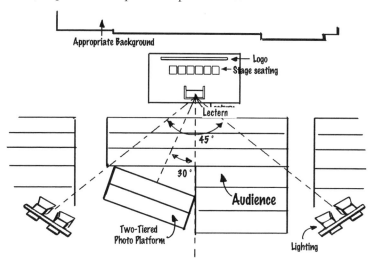

✒ Nothing is more important at a media event then an excellent *loudspeaker* system for both volume and understandability.

✒ The press platform should not be more than 40–50 feet (12–15 meters) from the speaker for excellent video and photos.

I was part of the campaign media team for the Ronald Reagan presidential campaign. We were the first to put bleachers behind the stage, and we filled them with enthusiastic, often hand-selected people behind the candidate. This provided a much more interesting background for press photos than the typical banner or flag. Every candidate for president since has used this technique.

MEDIA ALERT FORM

MEDIA ALERT   Contact:

October 14, 2012   Jenessa Warren (213) 444-5555

PRESS CONFERENCE November 6 at 10:00 a.m.

WILL ANNOUNCE THE LATEST POLLING DATA ON U.S. ATTITUDES TOWARD GRAND EVENTS.

U.S. demonstrates financial commitment to increase spending on outrageous happenings.

WHAT   Conference to announce the results of the national poll on the
                effects of grand events on normal people through lavish spending.

Full polling data and summaries will be made available on paper and disc.

WHEN   10:00–11:00 a.m.
                Wednesday, November 6, 2012

WHERE   White House, Press Briefing Room

WHO   John Jacobs, Senior Vice President, International Special
                Events Society
                Robert Singer, Vice President, Whatsit Society

The survey was conducted by the Whatsit Society, an independent polling organization, for the Spendall Association of America.

Key findings to be announced include:

The astounding increase of attendance at well-planned and financed events and the government's commitment to continue with even higher spending levels to aid events.

 See *media alert* on page 173.

PHOTO RELEASE FORM

AUTHORIZATION TO REPRODUCE PHYSICAL LIKENESS

For good and valuable consideration, the adequacy and receipt of which is hereby acknowledged, I hereby expressly grant to_____, to any third parties it may authorize, and to its and their employees, agents, and assigns, the right to photograph me and the right to use pictures, silhouettes, and other reproductions of my physical likeness (as they may appear in any still camera photograph, video, CD, motion picture film, and/or any other medium) in and in connection with the exhibition and/or broadcast, theatrically or on television, radio, or any motion picture, film, or tape in which my physical likeness may be used or incorporated, and in connection with the publication in magazines, newspapers, or otherwise, of any articles in which my physical likeness may be printed, used, or incorporated, and in the advertising, exploiting, and publicizing of any such live shows, events, motion pictures, television programs, magazines, newspapers, and flyers.

I hereby certify and represent that I have read the foregoing and fully understand the meaning and effect thereof and, intending to be legally bound, I have hereunto set my hand this _____ day of _____ , 20_____.

_____   _____

Signed   Printed

I hereby consent and agree to the above and have signed as the Parent/Guardian of

_____.

Print Child's Name

 Legally every person in a photo released to the press, or used for promotion, or used publicly in any other way, must release their image to the event organizer. If you know who will probably be photographed, this permission is ideally taken care of before the photos are taken.

Room Setup

EVENT SPACE REQUIREMENTS

Event Type	Area Required Per Person*
Cocktail Receptions and other stand-up functions	7–10 sq ft (2.1–3 sq m)
Banquet-Style Seating	
at 60" round tables	10–12.5 sq ft (0.9–1.1 sq m)
at 72" round tables	12–14.5 sq ft (1.1–1.3 sq m)
at 8 ft banquet tables	10 sq ft (0.9 sq m)
If dinner is in a tent add	3–4 sq ft (0.3–0.4 sq m)
Schoolroom-Style Seating	
at 18" tables	7–10 sq ft (0.6–0.9 sq m)
Theater-Style Seating	7–10 sq ft (0.6–0.9 sq m)
Trade Show Exhibit Area	64–200 sq ft (5.9–18.5 sq m)
Dance Floor	
(typically, 50% of guests dance)	3–4 sq ft (0.3–0.4 sq m)

*Based on typical fire codes.

 Areas for presentations, audiovisuals, entertainment, or other activities are not included in the above space allocations.

STANDARD BANQUET AND MEETING ROOM TABLE SIZES

Style	Chairs (Per Table)	Seating Space (Per Person)	Height	Width	Length
Rectangle Tables					
Banquet (Standard)					
4 ft long	4	24" (61 cm)	29" (73.6 cm)	30" (76.2 cm)	48" (1.2 m)
5 ft long	6	20" (50.8 cm)	29" (73.6 cm)	30" (76.2 cm)	60" (1.5 m)
6 ft long	8	18" (45.7 cm)	29" (73.6 cm)	30" (76.2 cm)	72" (1.8 m)
8 ft long	10	19" (48.3 cm)	29" (73.6 cm)	30" (76.2 cm)	96" (2.4 m)
10 ft long	12	20" (50.8 cm)	29" (73.6 cm)	30" (76.2 cm)	120" (3 m)
Banquet (Narrow)					
8 ft long	10	19" (48.3 cm)	29" (73.6 cm)	30" (76.2 cm)	96" (2.4 m)
Luau (Low to Ground)					
6 ft long	8	18" (45.7 cm)	16" (40.6 cm)	30" (76.2 cm)	72" (1.8 m)
8 ft long	10	19" (48.3 cm)	16" (40.6 cm)	30" (76.2 cm)	96" (2.4 m)
10 ft long	12	20" (50.8 cm)	16" (40.6 cm)	30" (76.2 cm)	120" (3 m)
Square Tables					
Cocktail					
Standard	2–4	10"–24" (30.5–61 cm)	29" (73.6 cm)	24" (61 cm)	10"–24" (25.4–61 cm)
Card Table	4	40" (101.4 cm)	29" (73.6 cm)	40" (101.4 cm)	40" (101.4 cm)

Standard Banquet and Meeting Room Table Sizes (*continued*)

Style	Chairs (Per Table)	Seating Space (Per Person)	Height	Width	Length
Round Tables					
Dinner					
4 ft diameter	6–7	21.5–25" (54.6–63.5 cm)	29" (73.6 cm)	48" (1.2 m)	48" (1.2 m)
4.5 ft diameter	8	21" (53.4 cm)	29" (73.6 cm)	54" (1.35 m)	54" (1.35 m)
5 ft diameter	8–10	19"–23.5" (48.3–59.7 cm)	29" (73.6 cm)	60" (1.5 m)	60" (1.5 m)
6 ft diameter	12	19" (48.3 cm)	29" (73.6 cm)	72" (1.8 m)	
Tall Cocktail	Standing				
Small	3	25" (63.5 cm)	40" (101.6 cm)	24" (61 cm)	24" (61 cm)
Large	5	18.5" (47 cm)	40" (101.6 cm)	30" (76.2 cm)	30" (76.2 cm)
Other					
Hexagon	6	27.75" (70.5 cm)	29" (73.6 cm)	48" (1.2 m)	48" (1.2 m)
Octagon	8	23" (58.4 cm)	29" (73.6 cm)	60" (1.5 cm)	60" (1.5 cm)
Trapezoid	5–7	24" (61 cm)	29" (73.6 cm)	27.75" (70.5 cm)	72 & 96" (1.8 & 2.4 m)

TABLE CAPACITIES

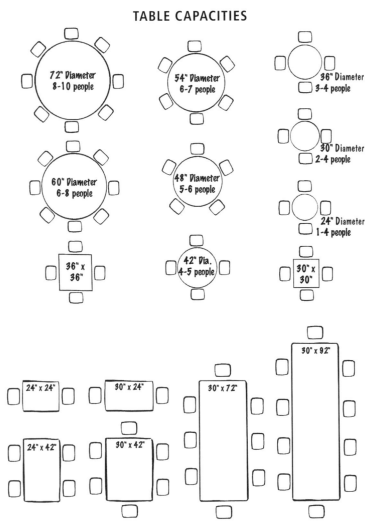

🖉 An 18-inch or 24-inch (46 centimeter or 61 centimeter) round table, ideal for two persons, is often referred to as a deuce.

TABLE POSITIONING

The Classic U

This classic setup requires many guests to turn their chairs or sit sideways to view the speaker's presentation. Eating dinner at the same time as the presentation is difficult. One solution is to place the lectern a bit back of the table line in the open end of the layout rather than centered on the head table.

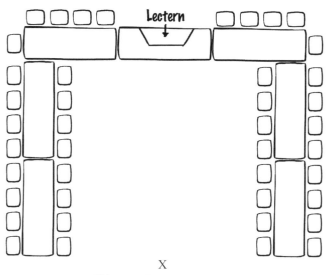

X
(Alternate Lectern Position)

Other Rectangular Table Configurations

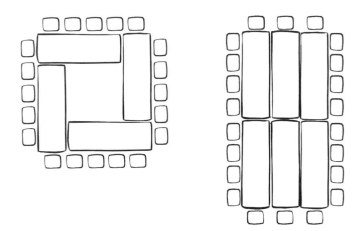

Trapezoidal Table Possibilities

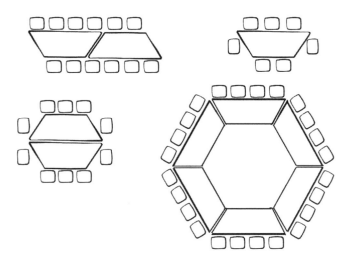

Banquet Rectangular Table Setup

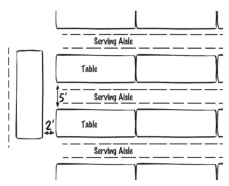

Round Tables Spacing

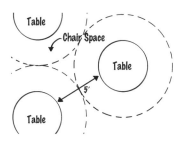

The advantage of banquets with rectangular tables is that more seating is possible within a given space. However, it is considered much less formal and makes it difficult to view presentations.

When planning table layout, include adequate space of 2.5 feet (0.75 meters) around each table or 5 feet (1.5 meters) between tables for when chairs are pulled out from under the table, and for service personnel to be able to move freely. So that servers do not have to go more than two tables deep, plan one aisle for every four rows of tables. Many banquet crews use a 5-foot spacing stick to place tables.

Determining the Number of Tables Possible in Different-Sized Rooms

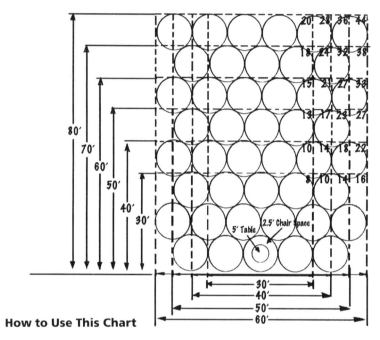

How to Use This Chart

1. Select the length of the room from the distances indicated at the left.
2. Select the width of the room from the widths indicated at the bottom of the chart.
3. The numbers in the right-hand corner of each set of dotted lines indicate the number of 60-inch round tables possible for that size room. For example, a 30-foot (9 meter) wide by 40-foot (12-meter) deep room accommodates 10 tables.
4. Should there be a need to have at one side of the room or another a small stage with a podium, a screen for visuals, a dais, or other accommodation, adjust as necessary.

ROOM LAYOUTS

Cocktail Party Room Layout

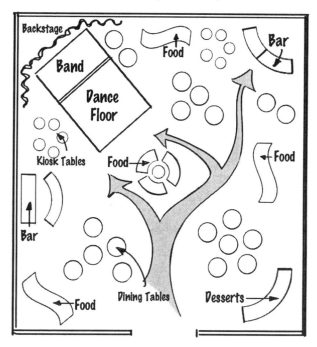

Use the bars to flow people in the room. People like to do different things at a cocktail party. Some like to get lots of food and sit at a regular table and eat. Others like to hang near the bar to interact with others and just snack on food, making use of tall kiosk tables. Since cocktail parties go longer than receptions, guests will move to different parts of the room as the party progresses.

 Break the room into small areas and intermix the different types of seating areas so that everyone has their favorite accommodation yet the room doesn't feel like it is split in two.

Cocktail Reception Room Layout

Proper setup of a room for a cocktail *reception* can greatly enhance the success of the event. The key is to move guests well into the room away from the entry doors, so that others may enter easily, then keep the guests moving around the room mixing with other invitees.

WRONG!

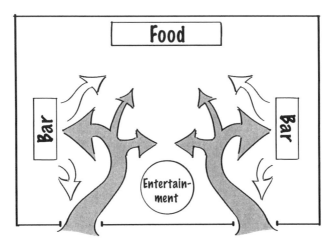

Improper placement of the bars, the target for most guests entering a cocktail party, blocks the flow into the room. The first half of the room will remain crowded, while the rest stays sparse.

CORRECT!

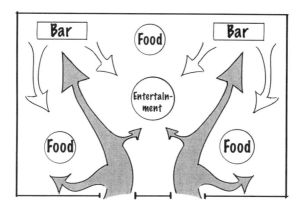

Place entertainment in the center (the ideal location)
and hors d'oeuvre tables for easy access.

CORRECT!

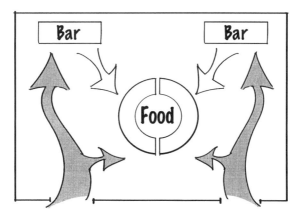

Use hors d'oeuvre tables as a center attraction when there is
no entertainment or the entertainment is strolling.
Bars placed well into the room act as a draw to
pull the guests deep into the room.

Head Tables

When a dinner is served, those on a dais need adequate space for the place setting.

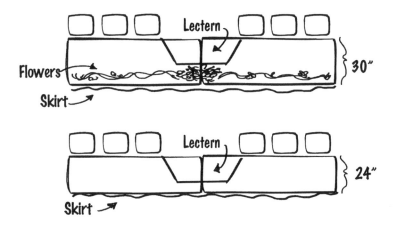

When flowers or other decorations are utilized, a wider table is required.

🖉 The audience side of a head table is always skirted.

📖 See *head table* on page 132 and *dais* on page 72.

Often head tables complicate the room setup when other elements such as a stage for entertainment or dancing or other presentations are included as part of the event. The following diagrams illustrate possible solutions to these common situations:

Head Table Placement

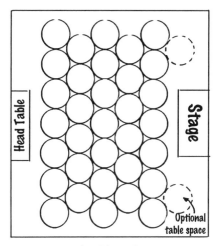

Head Table with Stage

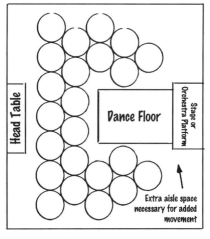

Head Table with Stage and Dancing

Banquet Setup with Round Tables and a Temporary Performance Stage

Consider the *sight lines* to what is presented onstage, be it speakers, visuals, or performance.

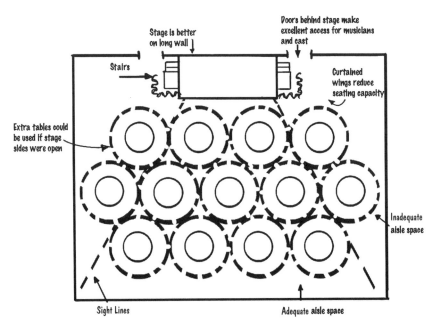

🖉 Room setup is complicated by activities planned for entertainment or presentation. *Sight lines* must always be considered.

Wedding Party Room Layout

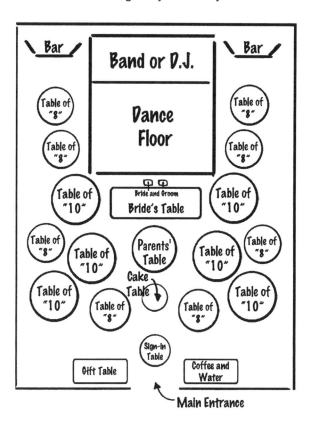

✎ The cake always makes a big impression. Place it effectively, either where all see it as they enter, or in another prominent position.

✎ If seating positions are specified, place a reception table outside the room with the *seating chart* displayed and a host to answer questions and provide *escort cards*.

THE BUSINESS MEETING ROOM

Classic Meeting Room Setup Styles

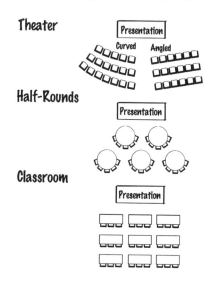

Spacing Requirements

Theater Seating

Schoolroom Seating

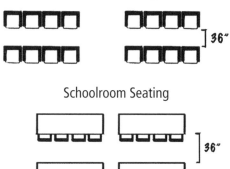

Visual Presentation Space Requirements

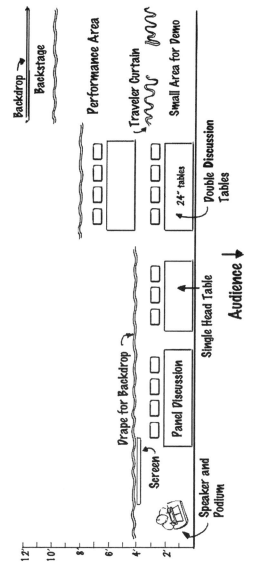

It is better to have platforms extend in front of the screen than to have a deep void between the audience and the screen.

Proper Placement of Speaker and Visuals for Visibility

The bottom of the screen must be above the heads of those in the first row of the audience.

Doubling the number of screens in the room greatly increases viewing possibilities.

✎ Floor to bottom of screen minimum: 54 inches (1.4 meters).

Screen Viewing Height

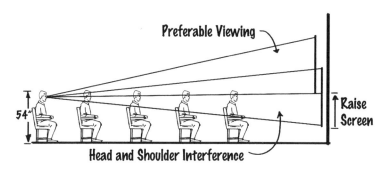

✎ Comfortable viewing is less than 20 percent off horizontal.

✎ The nearest viewer should sit at a distance of twice the width of the selected screen.

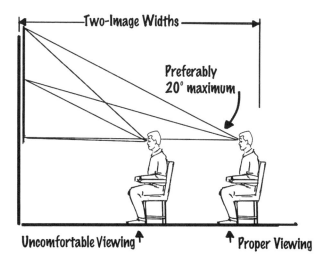

Selecting the Proper Meeting Room

Key to any presentation, particularly if it involves visual materials, is proper room size, including the room's width, length, and ceiling height in relation to the audience size.

For proper viewing of visuals, the ceiling height must be in proportion to the size of the room. Many meeting rooms have a ceiling that is too low, making viewing difficult.

Quick Estimator

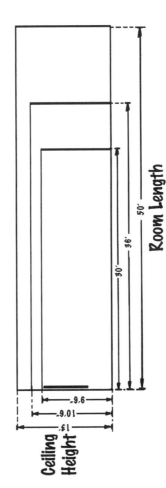

For example, a room 30 feet (9 meters) long requires a ceiling height of 9 feet, 6 inches (3 meters) for proper viewing of a screen 54 inches (1.4 meters) above the floor and large enough to be seen well by all.

✎ The rules outlined are for digital video screens as well as projection screens.

Determining Proper Ceiling and Platform Height in Proportion to Room Size

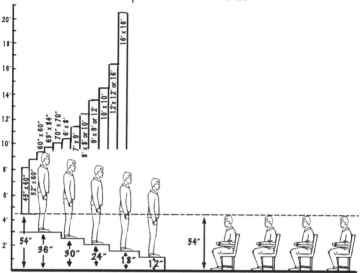

Using This Chart:

1. The dotted line is the unobstructed view limit. Following it to the left, it shows the lowest point for any size screen.

2. Determine the size screen needed for the depth of the room. (See Quick Estimator chart.)

3. The bars above the speaker's head indicate the top height of the different screen sizes. Select the size needed for the depth of the room. Comparing the top of the selected screen to the scale at the left shows the room ceiling height required. For example, if a 6-foot-tall by 8-foot-wide (1.8 meters by 2.5 meters) screen is needed, find that in the numbers above the standing man's head. Then draw a line to the scale on the left. Notice that it indicates a 10.5 foot (3.2 meter) minimum ceiling height is required.

4. Select the appropriate platform height for the speaker in relation to the selected screen size.

Screen (and Font) Size per Audience Size

Distance to Back Row of Audience	Minimum Screen Size for Good Viewing	Minimum Font Size on Screen
96 ft (29.3 m)	16 × 16 ft or 12 × 16 ft (4.9 × 4.9 m or 3.7 × 4.9 m)	3.25" (8.3 cm)
72 ft (22 m)	12 × 12 ft or 9 × 12 ft (3.7 × 3.7 m or 2.7 × 3.7 m)	2.75" (6.7 cm)
60 ft (18.3 m)	10 × 10 ft or 8 × 10 ft (3 × 3 m or 2.4 × 3 m)	2.25" (5.7 cm)
54 ft (16.5 m)	9 × 9 ft or 7 × 9 ft (2.7 × 2.7 m or 2.1 × 2.7 m)	2" (5 cm)
48 ft (14.6 m)	8 × 8 ft or 6 × 8 ft (2.4 × 2.4 m or 1.8 × 2.4 m)	1.75" (4.5 cm)
42 ft (12.8 m)	84 × 84 or 63 × 84 inches (2.1 × 2.1 m or 1.6 × 2.1 m)	1.5" (3.8 cm)
35 ft (10.7 m)	70 × 70 or 52 × 70 inches (1.8 × 1.8 m or 1.3 × 1.8 m)	1.25" (3.2 cm)
30 ft (9.1 m)	60 × 60 or 45 × 60 inches (1.5 × 1.5 m or 1.1 × 1.5 m)	1" (2.5 cm)

Orientation of Visuals within the Room

Properly orient the audience in the room for effective viewing of a presentation.

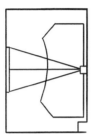

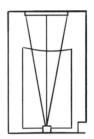

Diagram A: The audience in relation to visual presentation when the room has a lower ceiling.

Diagram B: A higher ceiling permits viewing from further back in the room. Beware of other obstacles in problem rooms, such as columns, air conditioning soffits, or irregular walls.

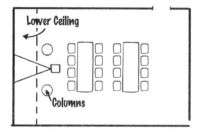

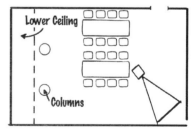

WRONG!

Comfortably place the audience in the most advantageous area of the room to avoid sight-line obstacles.

CORRECT!

Multiple flat-screen monitors can also be used effectively in difficult room situations.

Rear Projection Allowance

Rear projection requires additional space behind the screen that must be accounted for in selecting the room size.

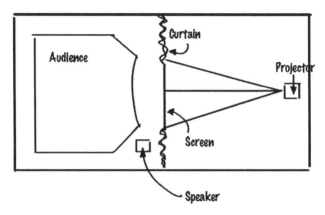

The space required behind the screen varies depending on the screen size and lens on the projector. For many standard large video projectors, the space required is 1:1, one foot for every foot of screen width. Zoom lenses on the projectors change the distance required.

Rooms Too Large

Try not to select a room that is too large. It creates an empty feeling in the audience. Their first reaction is to ask themselves why so few showed up for the meeting.

If the only option is to use a room too large:

1. Properly orienting the viewers in the room for the best viewing of the visual presentations is key.

2. Try filling the extra space with displays, registration tables, a round refreshment table, etc.—anything to keep it from looking empty.

Unimaginative Utilization of Room Space

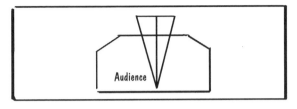

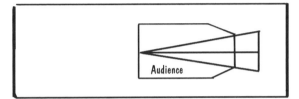

Imaginative Utilization of Room Space

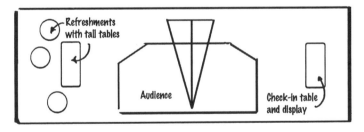

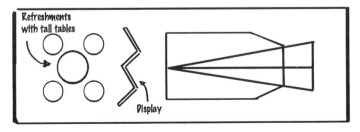

PLATFORMS AND RISERS

Standard Platform Sizes

Measurements	Heights
6' x 8' (1.8 x 2.4 m)	48" (121.9 cm)
4' x 8' (1.2 x 2.4 m)	40" (101.6 cm)
4' x 6' (1.2 x 1.8 m)	32" (81.3 cm)
3' x 8' (0.9 x 2.4 m)	24" (60.9 cm)
	16" (40.6 cm)
	8" (20.3 cm)

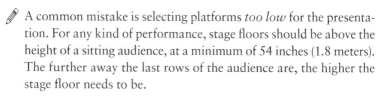

Most platform units come with either hardwood or carpeted tops. Different heights can be achieved by stacking units. A 16-inch-tall (40.6 centimeters) unit stacked on a 40-inch-tall (101.6 centimeters) unit creates a 56-inch-tall (142.2 centimeters) platform.

Some types of portable platforms come with adjustable legs to achieve almost any height.

Many platforms have attachments for skirting.

🖉 A common mistake is selecting platforms *too low* for the presentation. For any kind of performance, stage floors should be above the height of a sitting audience, at a minimum of 54 inches (1.8 meters). The further away the last rows of the audience are, the higher the stage floor needs to be.

🖉 If the presentation is solely by standing speakers, the platform height should be at least 18 inches (0.5 meters). For sitting speakers, or panel discussion, at least 24 inches (0.6 meters).

🖉 Beware of low ceiling height rooms that will force platforms to be too low!

Popular Stage Sizes Created with Platforms

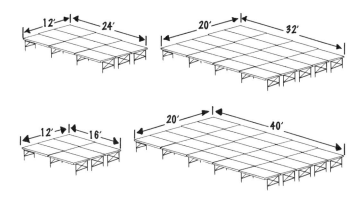

Typical Platform Configurations

Two-Level Dais for Head Tables

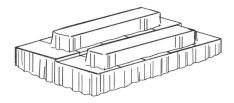

Band, Orchestra, or Choir Riser

Triangular corner pieces are available in different sizes that enable the corners to be angled rather than square.

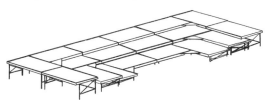

Platforms Forming a Stage

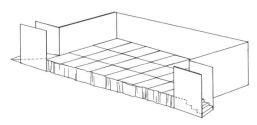

✎ Notice the ramp to the stage. *ADA* requires that all performing platforms be accessible to disabled persons.

Fashion Show or Thrust Configuration

Actual placement of the band onstage, and the size and height of the risers, depends upon the performers' contract *rider*.

Rock Band Stage

View from Side

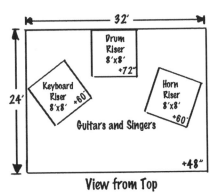

View from Top

Actual size depends on the orchestra's *instrumentation*.

Orchestra Stage

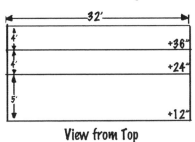

View from Top

View from Side

Folding Platform or Parallel

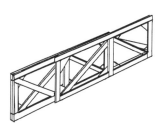

The supporting parallel frame is hinged so it can be folded for storage.

For use, the parallel frame is unfolded and the removable top is put in place. Notice how the guides under the top allow it to fit easily and keep the top from moving.

 The parallel frame is constructed in the same method as a scenic flat.

 See *flat* on page 110.

Theater Presentations

STANDARD THEATER DESCRIPTIONS

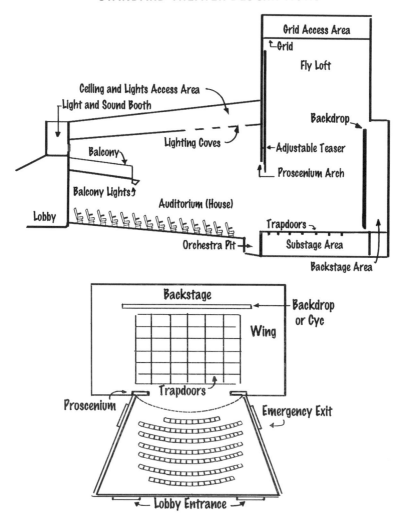

SIGHT LINE CONSIDERATIONS

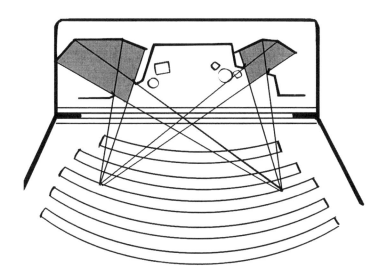

Check the view from extreme seats for *sight lines* and to ensure that *backings* behind the *box set* doors and windows effectively hide the view of *backstage*. In the diagram above, the shaded areas behind the doors could possibly be seen by viewers in side seats. If an open set is used, the placement of the *legs*, *tormentors*, and *tabs* needs to be checked to ensure they block the view *offstage*.

Horizontal Sight Lines and Maskings on a Stage

To mask hanging *drops*, lights on pipes, and other hanging elements above the stage, utilize horizontal *borders*, which are also called *teasers*.

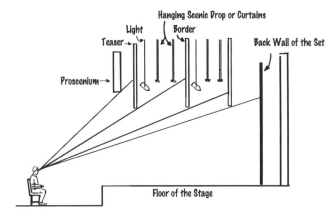

Basic Stage Drapery

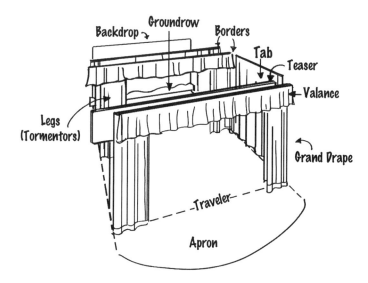

Areas of a Stage

📝 Notice that the *stage area* designations are from the perspective of an actor onstage, not from the audience's point of view.

Stage Areas and Their Respective Mood Values

Stage Area	Tonal or Mood Quality	Type of Scene Suggested
Down Center (DC)	Hard, Intense, Harsh, Strong, Climactic, Great Formality	Quarrels, Fights, Crises, Climaxes
Up Center (UC)	Regal, Aloof, Noble, Superiority, Stability	Formal, Love Scenes, Scenes of Domination and Judiciary, Nature, Royalty, Ideal for Impactful Entrances
Down Right (DR)	Warm, Informal, Close Intimacy	Intimate Love Scenes, Confessions, Long Narratives
Down Left (DL)	Not so warm as DR, Distant Intimacy, Formal, Introspective	Conspiracies, Casual Love, Soliloquies, Formal Business Matters
Up Right (UR)	Soft, Distant, Unreality	Romance
Up Left (UL)	Ghostliness, Infinity, Soft	Supernatural Scenes, Background Scenes

Basic Positions for Stage Lighting

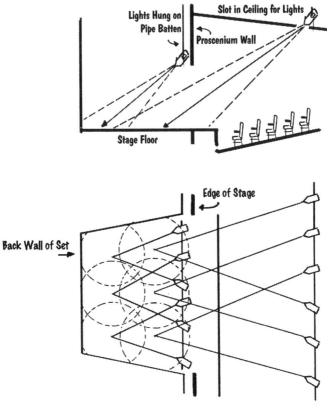

The lower plan view illustrates how two lights, one from the left and one from the right, focus to the same spot onstage. This technique lights both sides of the actor. Typically, one *lighting instrument* has a soft amber *gel* ("bastard amber") and the other a light blue gel ("steel blue"), together creating a natural look on the actor's skin.

See *lighting* on page 164.

Details of a Traditional Scenic Flat

Constructed with 1 × 3-inch (2.5 × 7.6-centimeter) lightweight wood, the frames are covered with canvas, which is tightened with *sizing* and then painted.

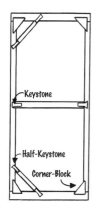 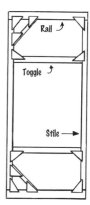

🖉 **Flats are fast, easy, and inexpensive to construct and store.**

✓ Hold corner blocks and keystones in ¾ inch from the edge. This permits right angles with the flats.

✓ *Lash line cleats* and line can be used on the backside of the flats to lash them together.

✓ Bottom and top rails extend completely across the width of the flat, with the stile between.

✓ Stretch the covering fabric as much as possible and stabilize it using the sides of the rails and stiles before sizing.

✓ While canvas is the standard fabric to cover the front side of the flat for painting, a variety of fabrics and other materials can be used for different visual effects. These coverings can be changed inexpensively to meet any new situation with the flats.

Websites for Further Reading

The following websites were consulted in compiling this handbook, and the reader may find them useful for further research and study.

Allrecipes.com—History of the Cocktail Party—Julie Fay

Angelfire.com—Buffet Menu

Apexperformancesystems.com—Schoolroom Setup—Chris Lytle

AudioRx.org—Decibels—Susan Frugone

Blog.ratestogo.com/best-national-drinks-i/—National Drinks—RatesToGo

Drinksmixer.com—Spirits

Ehow.com—Buffet—Wendell Fowler

Ellenskitchen.com—Tea Party

The Emily Post Institute Etipedia—Online Etiquette Encyclopedia

Frommers.com/destinations/Ecuador—Food and Drink

Lineneffects.com—Linen

Napkinfolding.com—Napkins

RoterRochs.de—Napkin Folds

Stanthonyvillagewineandspirits.com—Wine and Spirits

UShistory.org—Flag Protocol—Independence Hall Association

Webtender.com—Drinks and Spirits

Wikipedia.org—All Sorts of Good Things

Wineintro.com—Wine

Zesco.com—Table Skirting and Bartending Equipment

Bibliography

Artwork Size Standards for Projected Visuals. Rochester, NY: Eastman Kodak Company, 1966.

Axtell, Roger E. *Dos and Taboos of Hosting International Visitors*. Hoboken, NJ: John Wiley & Sons, 1990.

Baldrige, Letitia. *New Complete Guide to Executive Manners*. New York: Rawson Associates, 1993.

Barr, Andrew. *Drink: A Social History of America*. New York: Carroll & Graf Publishers, Inc., 1999.

Barrows, Susanna, and Robin Room. *Drinking: Behavior and Belief in Modern History*. Berkeley: University of California Press, 1991.

BizBash Magazine. Bizbash Media Inc.

Blum, Marcy, and Laura Fisher Kaiser. *Weddings for Dummies*. Boston, MA: IDG Books Worldwide, Inc., 1997.

Calloway, Stephen, and Elizabeth Cromley. *The Elements of Style*. New York: Simon & Schuster, 1996.

Carlson, Barbara. *Food Festivals*. Canton, MI: Visible Ink Press, 1997.

Carmel, James H. *Exhibition Techniques—Traveling and Temporary*. Stamford, CT: Reinhold Publishing Corporation, 1962.

Carter, Kelly E. "Cachaça: It is the Essence of Brazil in a Bottle." *USA Today*, February 16, 2007.

Clay, Roberta. *Promotion in Print*. New York: A. S. Barnes and Company, Inc., 1970.

Coon, Horace. *How to Be a Better Member*. Chicago, IL: New American Library, 1956.

Copeland, Lewis Faye, ed. *10,000 Jokes, Toasts and Stories*. New York: Garden City Publishing Company, Inc., 1946.

Corinth, Kay, and Mary Sargent. *All About Entertaining*. Philadelphia, PA: David McKay Company Inc., 1966.

Curtis, Frieda Steinmann. *How to Give a Fashion Show*. New York: Fairchild Publications, Inc., 1950.

Danch, William. *How to Win Sweepstakes Prize Contests*. Hollywood, FL: Frederick Fell Inc., 1966.

Dean, Alexander. *Fundamentals of Play Directing*. Austin, TX: Holt, Rinehart and Winston, 1941.

"Drayage." *Tradeshow Week Magazine*, 1977.

Dresser, Norine. *Multicultural Manners*. Hoboken, NJ: John Wiley & Sons, Inc., 1996.

Duran, Dorothy B., and A. Clement. *The New Encyclopedia of Successful Program Ideas*. New York: Associated Press, 1967.

Fabrican, Florence. "The Cocktail Party." *New York Times*, November 1, 1987.

Fadiman, Clifton, and San Aaron. *The Joys of Wine*. New York: Galahad Books, 1975.

Follet, Barbara Lee. *Check List for a Perfect Wedding*. Worchester: Dolphin Books, 1973.

Ford, Charlotte. *Etiquette: Charlotte Ford's Guide to Modern Manners*. New York: Clarkson N. Potter, Inc., 1982.

Gilbert, Edith. *All About Parties*. New York: Hearthside Press, Inc., 1968.

Gilman, Wilber E., Aly Bower, and Loren D. Reid. *Fundamentals of Speaking*. London: Macmillan, 1969.

Glerum, Jay O. *Stage Rigging Handbook*. Carbondale: Southern Illinois University Press, 1987.

Golden, Hal, and Kitty Hanson. *How to Plan, Produce and Publicize Special Events*. Dobbs Ferry, NY: Oceana Publications, Inc., 1960.

Gourmet Wine Cooking the Easy Way. Sacramento, CA: California Wine Institute for Wine Advisory Board, 2010.

Hayett, William. *Display and Exhibit Handbook*. Stamford, CT: Reinhold Publishing Corporation, 1967.

Herbst, Sharon Tyler. *The Food Lover's Companion*. Hauppauge, NY: Barron's Educational Series, 2001.

Hirst, Arlene. *Every Woman's Guide to China, Glass and Silver*. New York: Arco Publishing Company, Inc., 1970.

Holding, Jocelyn Kerr. *Trompe l'Oeil Stenciling*. New York: Sterling Publishing Co., Inc., 1999.

"Installation Dismantling." *Tradeshow Week Magazine*, 1977.

Krythe, Maymies R. *All About American Holidays*. New York: Harper and Bros., 1962.

Lichine, Alexis. *New Encyclopedia of Wines and Spirits*. New York: Alfred A. Knopf, Inc., 1984.

Mancuso, Jennifer. *Guide to Being an Event Planner*. Avon, MA: Adams Media, 2008.

Martin, Judith. *Miss Manners' Guide for the Turn-of-the-Millennium*. New Delhi: Pharos Books, 1989.

Martin, Judith. *Star-Spangled Manners*. London: W. W. Norton & Company, Inc., 2003.

Meier, Rebekah. *Romantic Weddings*. Cincinnati, OH: North Light Books, 2006.

Milinaire, Caterine. *Celebrations*. New York: Harmony Books, 1981.

Monroe, James C. *Art of the Event*. Hoboken, NJ: John Wiley & Sons, Inc., 2006.

Moran, Jill S. *How to Start a Home-Based Event Planning Business*. Guilford, CT: The Globe Pequot Press, 2004.

Park World Magazine. Datateam Publishing Ltd.

Partridge, Eric. *A Dictionary of Catch Phrases, British and American, from the Sixteenth Century to the Present Day*. New York: Stein and Day Publishers/Scarborough House, 1977.

"Perfection in Planning." *Northstar Meeting & Conventions Magazine*, 2006.

Post, Elizabeth L. *Emily Post's Complete Book of Wedding Etiquette*. New York: Harper Collins Publishers, Inc., 1991.

———. *Emily Post's Etiquette*. New York: Harper Collins Publishers, Inc., 2004.

———. *Emily Post's Etiquette: A Guide to Modern Manners*. New York: Harper & Row, 1984.

Quick, John, and Herbert Wolff. *Small-Studio Video Tape Production*. Boston, MA: Addison-Wesley Publishing Company, 1972.

Reader's Digest Almanac and Yearbook. New York: Reader's Digest, 1968.

Rentals. Los Angeles, CA: Canvas Specialty Company, 1970.

"Scenery Painting." Flyer #21860. Hollywood, CA: Olsen Company.

Special Events Magazine. Penton Media Inc.

Stage Supplies Catalogue. 7th ed. Hollywood, CA: Olsen Company, 1971.

Standards Committee. *Project Development Guidelines*. Burbank, CA: Themed Entertainment Association, 1995.

Stern, Lawrence. *Stage Management: A Guidebook of Practical Techniques*. Needham Heights, MA: Allyn and Bacon, Inc., 1974.

Stewart, Marjabelle Young. *Can My Bridesmaids Wear Black?* New York: St. Martin's Press, 1989.

Stewart, Marjabelle Young, and Elizabeth Lawrence. *Commonsense Etiquette*. New York: St. Martin's Griffin, 1999.

Tarcher, Jeremy, Diane de Nevers, and Geraldine Cook. *West Coast Theatrical Directory*. New York: Times Mirror Company, 1969.

Tompkins, Dorothy, Helen C. Finch, and Ambrose Heath. *Table Layout and Decoration*. London: Ward Lock and Company, 1969.

Tuckerman, Nancy, and Nancy Dunnan. *The Amy Vanderbilt Complete Book of Etiquette*. New York: Doubleday, 1995.

2011 Team. *Creative Handbook*. North Hollywood, CA: Creative Handbook Publications, 2011.

Ways With Wine: The Paul Masson Wine Reader. Saratoga, CA: Paul Masson Vineyards, 1968.

Welch, Scotty Ronnie Welch, and Editors of *Esquire Magazine. Esquire Party Book*. New York: Esquire, Inc., with Harper and Row, 1965.

Welker, David. *Theatrical Set Design: The Basic Techniques.* Needham Heights, MA: Allyn and Bacon, Inc., 1969.

Wise, Herbert H., ed. *Professional Rock and Roll.* New York: Collier Books, 1967.

Your Guide to Gift Giving and Home Entertainment. New York: Beverage Media Ltd., 1969.

About the Author

Ron Miziker
Event Planner, Writer, Director, and Producer

Ron Miziker is a foremost international event planner, showman, and preeminent force in creating major world-class events, spectaculars, and extraordinary entertainment experiences for a mass audience. His events range from gala movie premieres and spectacular grand openings, to corporate meetings and celebrations, to world political events and events viewed globally via television by the world's largest audiences.

A sampling of his projects includes three Super Bowl halftime spectaculars; the grand opening celebration of Walt Disney World; the opening ceremonies of World Cup USA; the XXIII Olympiad in Los Angeles; the Xth Pan American Games; Spain's World Expo; the presidential inauguration of Ronald Reagan; the Sultan of Oman's fifteenth anniversary; the queen of England's dinner gala in Los Angeles; the Emir of Abu Dhabi's son's wedding celebration; the U.S. bicentennial celebration at the Statue of Liberty; We The People national anniversaries; the meeting of Pope John Paul II and President Ronald Reagan; the state funeral of Richard M. Nixon; California's Governor's Gala for the Arts; rock and roll's U.S. Festival; the Very Special Arts International Festival; the California Countryside Festivals; meetings, parties, events, and gala celebrations for leading corporations, including the Walt Disney Company, Intel, Paramount Studios, MGM Studios, PepsiCo, Century 21, Anheuser-Busch, Coca-Cola, Armstrong, Germany's ZDF television network, Lotte of Korea, Sociedad Commercial del Plata of Argentina, and Aldar of Dubai.

Ron is an alumnus of the University of New Mexico and resides in Los Angeles.